The ASSIST Program

Affective/Social Skills: Instructional Strategies and Techniques

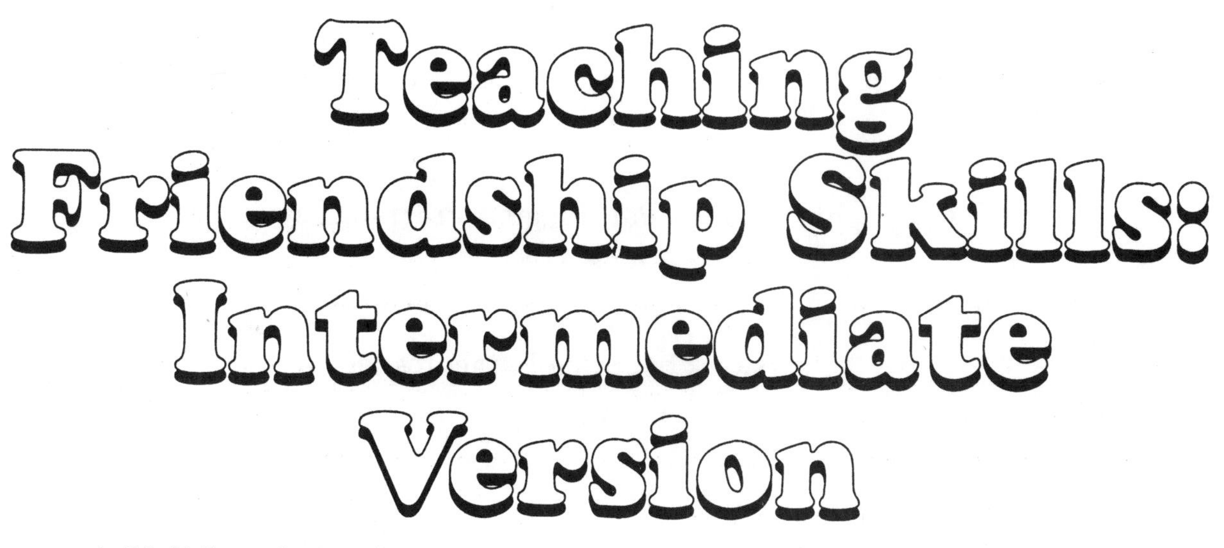

A Validated Washington State Innovative Education Program

This version of *Teaching Friendship Skills* is a product of the joint efforts of

Pat Huggins
Donna Wood Manion
and
Larry Moen

Artwork by: Ernie Hergenroeder

ISBN #0-944584-70-5

Published & Distributed by:

SOPRIS WEST, INC.
1140 Boston Avenue • Longmont, Colorado 80501 • (303) 651-2829

Table of Contents

Overview of the ASSIST Program

Affective/Social Skills: Instructional Strategies and Techniques

ASSIST is an affective education program designed to increase students' growth in the areas of self-concept, self-management, interpersonal relationships, and emotional understanding. ASSIST manuals provide a complete guide for elementary teachers to actively involve students in developing critical personal/social skills. The ASSIST Program can be incorporated into an existing program or it can stand alone as a curriculum for personal growth and interpersonal relations.

The ASSIST curriculum is the result of an extensive review of child development theory and research, a review of existing social/emotional education programs, and the contributions of many teachers and students who participated in the development of the Program. **ASSIST incorporates concepts and procedures from social learning theory, behavioristic and humanistic psychology, and from proven educational practices.** The curriculum involves students in a series of cognitively-oriented lessons and experiential learning activities.

The ASSIST lessons include:

- A "To the Teacher" section which provides a theoretical background for lesson concepts;
- A "scripted" lesson that includes everything necessary to teach lesson concepts and skills;
- A series of transparency masters and handouts (student worksheets); and
- A variety of "Supplementary Activities" designed to integrate the lessons into basic subject areas.

ASSIST was developed with Title IV-C Innovative Education Funds and was evaluated in second through sixth grade classrooms in four school districts. **Statistically significant gains in self-concept and social skills occurred in eight out of nine assessments.** As a result, ASSIST was validated in Washington State and designated cost-effective and exportable. It is now in the State's "Bank of Proven Practices," a clearinghouse for quality programs.

The ASSIST manuals currently in print include the following:

- ***Building Self-Esteem in the Classroom***—This manual includes a series of sequential lessons and activities designed to promote self-awareness. Students learn that they have a unique combination of intelligences, skills, and abilities and learn how to identify their particular strengths. They learn to focus on their strengths and use them as springboards for new successes. They learn to use the techniques of positive inner speech to build self-esteem and to cope effectively with mistakes and put-downs. Also included in the manual are workbooks for both primary and intermediate students and a self-esteem unit for middle school students.

- ***Teaching Cooperation Skills***—This manual includes a series of lessons and experiential activities designed to teach students the skills necessary for cooperative learning to take place. Lessons focus on the skills of self-management, listening, and collaborative problem solving. Students learn to resolve conflicts through negotiation and compromise. A wide variety of cooperative learning activities are included so that these skills can be applied and practiced.
- ***Creating A Caring Classroom***—This manual includes a collection of strategies designed to promote mutual respect, trust, risk-taking, and support in the classroom. Included are: (1) getting acquainted activities; (2) classroom management procedures; (3) an affective behavior scale and behavior improvement strategies for students with special needs; (4) a relaxation training program; and (5) a large collection of activities for building a cohesive and caring classroom community.
- ***Helping Kids Handle Anger***—This manual includes lessons designed to enable students to acknowledge, accept, and constructively express anger. Students learn: (1) to use inner speech to inhibit aggressive behaviors; (2) to use thinking skills for choosing constructive behaviors when angry; (3) appropriate language to express anger; (4) a variety of techniques to release energy after anger arousal; and (5) ways to deal with the anger of others. Role-play and puppets are utilized to encourage active and creative student involvement.
- ***Teaching About Sexual Abuse***—The lessons in this manual are designed to provide students with information about sexual abuse in a low-key, matter-of-fact way. Lessons focus on: (1) children's right to reject inappropriate behavior; (2) assertiveness skills helpful in the prevention of sexual abuse; and (3) establishing family and community support systems.

Introduction

This curriculum provides teachers and school counselors with systematic procedures for enhancing social competence in elementary-age children. The purpose of the lessons and activities in this program is two-fold: (1) to help students learn the key relational skills which will enable them to initiate and maintain friendships, and (2) to improve the social climate within the classroom so that interpersonal problems do not disrupt academic learning. Each lesson introduces specific friendship skills that have been shown to increase peer acceptance and enhance students' ability to interact positively with all their classmates.

The lessons are based on current learning theory and have been field-tested in elementary classrooms. Much of the instructional approach is similar to the teaching of basic academic competencies. In addition to direct cognitive instruction, affective and behavioral components are also used. Each lesson includes a sequence of motivation, practice, and maintenance activities. Students are:

1. Involved in group discussions regarding friendship behaviors, issues and problems;
2. Given opportunities to see friendship skills modeled;
3. Involved in role-play and other structured activities which allow them to practice the skills;
4. Given feedback regarding their practice; and
5. Provided with structures for integrating friendship skills into their daily lives through goal setting and reinforcement (maintenance and transfer of training).

The lessons in this manual bring the fundamental issues of friendship to students' awareness. Students are given opportunities to discover what the ingredients of a relationship are and what makes it a friendship. They engage in activities to discover similarities and positive qualities in their classmates, both of which are prerequisites to friendship. Students determine how they want to be treated by those they consider friends. They then take a close look at their own behavior and set appropriate goals for change. Finally, they learn ways to give authentic praise and help to one another.

Why teach friendship skills in the classroom?

Teachers are well aware of how disruptive interpersonal problems can be in a classroom. Often, considerable time is spent soothing students who are upset because no one will play with them, trying to protect students who are constantly harassed by other class members, encouraging shy students to try to make friends, and dealing with students who are trying to enhance their social status through attention-getting misbehavior. Many teachers have concluded that the time spent trying to cope with students' social deficits could be better spent in teaching students how to get along with others. In so doing they have confirmed the research which shows that friendship skills can be learned. They've also found that direct instruction in friendship-making techniques makes a positive change in classroom climate.

Problems in the classroom related to social immaturity or a lack of friendship skills seem to be on the rise. There are many reasons for this, but the leading cause is that our social institutions are undergoing great changes. Due to the "meltdown" of the nuclear family, more and more students are being raised in high-risk environments where they are not learning basic social skills. Our mobile society also contributes to disruption in socialization. On the average, The American family moves about once every four years. This presents more challenges to students in friendship-making than in the past. Teachers often overestimate how well students know each other or how comfortable they feel with each other. In fact, many students today do not feel a sense of psychological security or safety with their classmates. While teachers cannot take on the responsibility for a child's needs that parenting requires, they can provide some steps to ensure that their classroom is a place where every student feels accepted by at least a few of his or her peers.

Friendship skill deficits do more than lead to class disruptions or to isolated or rejected children. Research evidence over the past several years indicates that there is a direct correlation between friendship patterns and academic performance.

> *Although educators generally have not considered student friendships relevant to individual students' cognitive development, our research evidence and experience indicate that they are related. In fact, friendships classmates have for one another, along with their willingness to help and support one another, represent important ingredients for the enhancement of individual academic achievement . . . . Strong relationships with others are not only valuable in themselves; they also enhance cognitive development in the classroom.*
>
> Richard Schmuck and Pat Schmuck (1974)
> *Group Processes in the Classroom*

Children who feel they do not belong often find it difficult to focus on academic tasks.

> *Positive interpersonal relations among students are necessary both for problem solving in groups and for general classroom enjoyment of instructional activity. The psychological security and safety necessary for open exploration of instructional tasks is based upon feelings of being accepted, liked, and supported by fellow students.*
>
> David Johnson and Roger Johnson (1975)
> *Learning Together and Alone*

Even though some students are able to master academics without experiencing successful peer relationships, academic achievement alone does not prepare a child for a successful life. Friendships are central to the quality of children's lives. Even the presence of nurturing adults cannot alleviate the loneliness children experience when they lack a friend. Children need the confirmation of a peer who is not a family member. Feelings of being accepted socially, of being liked for oneself and for one's own actions and behaviors, are extremely important to the development of emotional security. The inability to make friends erodes a child's self-esteem. Since so many of the problems and joys we experience at each stage in life are interpersonal in nature, teaching friendship skills is a gift we can give to students which will benefit them throughout their lives.

What are the factors that contribute to children's friendship-making?

There are many factors over which a child has little or no control which are likely to affect the way the child is viewed by peers and which influence how easily the child makes friends. Physical appearance, intellectual abilities, family background, and even athletic prowess may influence a child's social status during elementary-school years. Along with these aspects of natural attractiveness, a child's outgoingness toward others is also a strong factor in social attraction.

Sometimes natural endowments present a child with a difficult path to friendship-making. Life events may add to this difficulty. A child may have had poor models and a lack of reinforcement or opportunity for positive social behavior. When these natural forces do not work to help a child find success in peer relationships, a child can benefit from adult help in mastering the skills of friendship. Research over the past ten years has shown that teaching social responses to help improve a child's social interactions can help compensate for limitations which have affected a child's friendship-making abilities.

It should be understood that the objective of social skills instruction is not to create "popular" children, but to help children, whatever their personality styles or life history, to develop positive relationships with at least one or two of their peers.

What are the key skills for friendship-making?

A number of studies have indicated that children tend to like children who have helped them. Additional studies show that to gain acceptance from peers, children must be able to seek out others and be agreeable to them when asked to do something reasonable. Children who give others a large number of positive responses are much more likely to be chosen as friends.

Communication and listening skills are also important. Children who are poor communicators or listeners are more likely to be rejected or ignored. Children skilled in initiating conversations have more friends. Excessive shyness or not knowing how to make positive approaches toward other children will inhibit development of friendship.

The ability to control aggression is also a key skill in social attractiveness. Disrupting the activities of other children or initiating unprovoked physical attacks are major factors in being disliked.

The lessons in this manual are designed to address each of these skill areas. The ASSIST manual *Helping Kids Handle Anger* provides more comprehensive skill training in managing aggression. Conflict resolution, negotiation, and compromise are also key skills. These will be addressed in the forthcoming ASSIST manual, *Solving Friendship Problems*.

How to Use This Curriculum

Lesson Grade Levels

Each lesson in this curriculum presents one or more concepts that are central to social functioning. Because of the timelessness and generality of most of these concepts, the same lessons can be taught to students as they advance through the grades. Each time students are exposed to the concepts in a lesson, they are able to consider them from a new frame of reference and make new and more precise applications. Following each of the lessons, there are specific supplementary activities recommended for 4th, 5th, and 6th graders. Lessons and supplementary activities for 1st, 2nd, and 3rd graders are found in the ASSIST manual *Teaching Friendship Skills: Primary Version.*

Lesson Overview

Each lesson has a clearly stated objective, a list of all the materials needed to teach the lesson, and a "To the Teacher" section. This section outlines the planning necessary for the lesson. It provides theoretical background on the concepts presented. It also includes a summary of the skills taught in the lesson, the methods used, and suggestions for effective teaching.

Lesson Presentation Section

The "Lesson Presentation" section gives step-by-step instructions on how to conduct the lesson. A "scripted" presentation, provided in boldface type, is included to put the "meat on the bones" of the lesson. It provides a model for everything that needs to be said to impart lesson concepts. However, this is simply a model; you will want to rephrase the script, saying things in your own words to accommodate aspects of your particular students' frame of reference. The success of the lesson will depend on your ability to provide examples and illustrations of lesson concepts that your students will relate to. It will also depend on your sense of how to pace the lesson, expanding or shortening sections to fit your students' needs. All this implies that you will need to be very familiar with a lesson before you teach it. One way to gain this familiarity is by taping a lesson and listening to it as you travel to and from school. Or you can order tapes of these lessons from the publisher of this manual. Becoming familiar with the lessons in this way will enable you to "ad lib" the lesson, which frees you to more easily handle the many lesson transparencies.

Lessons conclude with a debriefing section and techniques to facilitate generalization and transfer of training to real life situations.

Transparencies

Each lesson includes a series of transparency masters for students whose learning style says, "Don't just tell me, show me!"

Handouts

Reproducible student handouts/worksheets also accompany each lesson. These worksheets give students an opportunity to process lesson concepts as well as to demonstrate that they were "attending and receiving" during the lesson presentation and discussion.

Supplementary Activities

Following each lesson are a number of "Supplementary Activities" designed to appeal to students of varying abilities. These are designed to help students "process" the ideas presented in the lesson and to provide opportunities for them to practice the personal/ social skills related to the lesson concepts. These activities allow for integration of the lesson concepts and help nudge students into higher levels of social reasoning. Many of these activities relate to basic subject areas in the regular curriculum.

The Appendices: Other Resources for Promoting Friendship Skills

- **A Multiple Intelligences Friendship Center**

  This manual contains a "Multiple Intelligences Friendship Center" which you may wish to incorporate into your classroom "learning center" program. The activities in this center are designed to provide students with a variety of interpersonal skill-building activities in each of the seven intelligences (linguistic, mathematical-logical, musical, kinesthetic, visual-spatial, interpersonal, and intrapersonal).

- **Using Literature to Enhance Students' Understanding of Friendship**

  An extensive list of children's books relating to friendship themes is provided. Reading some of these books to your class or setting up a "Friendship Reading Center" is a wonderful way to promote knowledge and discussion of friendship issues.

- **Friendship Games**

  The games provided in this manual have been tried in many classroom situations and have been found to have high student appeal. They naturally and enjoyably reinforce the concepts presented in the lessons.

- **School-Wide Procedures That Promote Friendship**

  Many schools like to devote a particular week or month to focus on the theme of friendship. This section provides ideas and materials to implement such a plan.

- **Posters**

  The posters included in this section can be hung permanently in the classroom and at other places in the school building to remind students of friendship behaviors.

Scheduling the Lessons

Some teachers integrate these lessons into their health, social studies, and language arts/communication curricula. Others set up a formal "social skills" period and teach lessons once per week, or use a "unit" format, teaching a lesson or doing an activity on a daily basis for a period of time. Some teachers prefer to introduce this material more casually, teaching a lesson from time to time when they see a need for instruction in a specific skill presented in a lesson.

Lessons should last 30 to 45 minutes, depending on students' attention span. Some lessons can be divided and taught in segments.

It is helpful to support the learning and goals generated by the lessons with reminders and suggestions throughout the school day and week. Teaching the lesson early in the school day enables you to capitalize on opportunities during the remainder of the day to use lesson vocabulary and encourage students to apply the skills that were introduced that morning.

Using the Techniques of Role-Play and Group Discussion to Teach Friendship Skills

- **Role-Play**

  Role-play provides students with an opportunity to practice using the friendship skills presented in the lesson. Discussing friendship behaviors helps students learn to talk about friendship skills. Role-play helps students learn to enact these skills. A unique advantage of role-play is the opportunity to practice new ways of behaving. A shy student may practice initiating a conversation through role-playing. As a result of the role-play experience, this student may be able to incorporate a new behavior into his or her daily life.

  By putting themselves in the place of others, students become sensitive to others' feelings. Because role-playing is as close as we can come to actually being another person, it strongly encourages the development of empathy. For example, by playing the role of a scapegoat, a bully may understand how it feels to be picked on. A scapegoat playing a bully may begin to see why his or her behavior attracts a bully. Both can see what some alternative actions are.

  Role-play involves: (1) the discussion and analysis of social situations; (2) an original enactment; (3) discussion of the observers' reaction to the enactment; (4) exploration of alternatives through further role-playing; and (5) drawing conclusions or making generalizations regarding social situations.

  The following are some suggestions on ways to make role-play more effective:

- Wait until the class members are acquainted and at ease with one another before you introduce role-playing.
- Anticipate some self-consciousness on the part of students.
- Set rules to curtail acting silly or aggressive behavior during role-play.
- Help students feel at ease by making clear to them that this is not a performance and that they will not be judged on how well they can act.
- Explain that the purpose of the role-plays is to test ideas to see if certain solutions to problem situations really work.
- Keep a nonjudgmental attitude. Be warm and responsive to what students do and say.
- Choose role-play situations that are relevant to students' lives.
- Make sure both observers and players fully understand the role-play situation before it is enacted.
- Try to create a positive classroom environment by explaining that students should not judge one another and that there is not necessarily one right solution to the role-play situations.
- Invite students to volunteer to role-play only after they have thought of a possible solution to the role-play situation.
- Players should be able to describe their characters, the scene, and the setting in detail before they begin the role-play. Help them by asking questions such as, "Where are you?" and "What are you doing?"
- Ask students to try to feel, act, and talk like the person they are role-playing. They should try to forget that they are being observed.
- Observers should be as quiet and unobtrusive as possible. They should act as if they were hidden cameras watching the action but not interfering with it in any way, especially not through criticizing the players.
- Give observers the task of asking themselves questions like, "What would I do in this situation?" or "Is there another way to solve the problem?" as they watch the role-play.
- Once a role-play begins, address players by their role name, not their real name. This helps them stay in character throughout the scene.
- If students block on what to say, you can either use stage whispers to coach them or stop the action to brainstorm with the audience what could be said or done next. Resume the action as quickly as possible.
- If appropriate to the learning intended from the role, interject questions to the characters as the action unfolds. Questions about what the character might be feeling are particularly helpful.
- Keep each role-play to a maximum of five minutes.

- Debrief the role-play by exploring feelings the student had toward the character he or she played and toward the other characters involved. Make clear by your questions that students and roles are separate. When concluded, thank students by their real names.
- During the discussion of the role-play, emphasize that alternative solutions are possible.
- The same role-play situation can be enacted again with different players who may demonstrate other approaches to the problem.
- Encourage students to generalize the role-play to their own lives by asking them to think about questions such as, "Has a situation like this ever happened to you?" or "Does this situation remind you of something in your own life?"

- **Group Discussion**

Group discussion is a valuable teaching tool, especially when the discussion is structured so that students who are functioning on a high social level can share their knowledge, experience, and opinions with their peers. Studies have shown that, even at the kindergarten level, students are influenced more by the comments of peers than by the comments of their teacher. Thus, when you want students to function on a higher social level it is more productive to expose them to comments of socially mature peers who are discussing appropriate social behavior than for you to talk about this behavior.

The following are some suggestions to make group discussion more effective:

- If possible, use a place in your classroom where students can sit in a circle so they can all see each other.
- Set some basic rules regarding group discussion at the beginning of the first lesson. Some suggested rules are:
  1. Students must raise hands if they want to speak;
  2. When someone is speaking everyone else must look at them and listen quietly; and
  3. Students should not mention names when relating stories. Instead they should say, "Someone I know . . . ."
- At the beginning of each lesson, tell students you will be calling on them frequently during the discussion.
- Ask open-ended questions such as, "What can you tell us about . . . ?" or "Can you tell us more about . . . ?"
- When you call on a student and he or she doesn't answer immediately, be sure to allow sufficient "wait time" (perhaps five seconds) before going on.
- Don't force shy students to participate. Explain that "pass" is an acceptable answer, after they have thought about a question. You can, at times, include

shy students by asking questions that can be answered with one word or a nod.

- If a student who is not attending well is not ready to give a response to a question, say you will come back to him or her shortly for the response.
- If a student is dominating the discussion, say something like, "We have to move on, but I would be interested in hearing more later."
- Use the technique of "thumbs up or down" to get all students' responses to general questions.
- Increase students' opportunity for participation in the discussion by arranging for them to have "Learning Partners" or small groups to discuss topics with.
- Don't ask questions and then answer them yourself.
- Don't rephrase students' responses to make them more acceptable to you.
- Don't repeat a question after calling on a student. This trains students not to listen.
- Don't repeat students' answers. This prevents students from responding directly to each other and encourages students to give less complete answers, since they know you will modify their response in an acceptable manner.
- **Discuss** ideas presented in the lesson with students; avoid giving "sermonettes."
- Whenever possible, structure the discussion to encourage students with high social functioning to suggest examples of the concepts you want to get across.

Suggestions for Enhancing the Teaching of This Curriculum

- Emphasize the fun activities that accompany each lesson.
- Supply students with a "think pad" to write on during lessons.
- Make sure students keep all handouts and materials from the lessons in their "Friendship Folders."
- Let students' interests, responses, needs, and contributions determine the pace of the lessons rather than trying to complete a lesson in a given time.
- Incorporate the vocabulary lists and writing activities in the lessons into your language arts program.
- Use the art ideas as part of your art program.
- Use the "Multiple Intelligences Friendship Center" as part of your learning center program.

- Highlights the parts of the text that are important to you as you read through the lesson, then try to say those parts in your own words.
- Obtain audio tapes of the lessons from Sopris West. Listen to these tapes while you are driving to or from school. This will save you time as you try to become familiar with lesson concepts.

Classroom Procedures That Can Aid in the Development of Friendships Within the Classroom

In addition to the lessons presented in this manual, there are some strategies which can be used throughout the school day to enable students to practice the friendship skills you have taught them and which will establish a more positive social climate in your classroom. The most powerful strategy you can use is cooperative learning. See the ASSIST manual *Teaching Cooperation Skills* for lessons on how to teach your students the prerequisite skills for working cooperatively on academic tasks.

Once you are using a cooperative learning structure, regroup frequently. Frequent regrouping is helpful because: (1) it places students in close personal contact with students they normally do not interact with. This helps initiate new friendships; (2) it provides more opportunities for isolates to interact with other students; (3) it can help prevent the formation of cliques; (4) it can provide opportunities for unpopular students to be "discovered" or to show skills or attractive traits they may have that would otherwise go unnoticed because no one interacts with them; and (5) it provides all students an opportunity to have contact with those socially competent students who can provide models for developing friendship skills.

Both random regrouping and sociometric regrouping are effective ways to make sure all students have maximum opportunity to interact with each other. In sociometric grouping you can identify students who have friendship problems and carefully place them in groups where they have an opportunity to work with potential friends. Random regrouping is beneficial because it: (1) provides a means by which groups accept unpopular classmates (they know groups will be of short existence); (2) avoids student pressure for inclusion of friends; (3) reduces the fear of being chosen last; and (4) allows a group to be formed quickly.

Grouping students randomly or sociometrically creates opportunities for students to make friends because **proximity** is one of the antecedents of friendship. The more often students interact, the more likely they are to become friends.

The Development of Children's Understanding of Friendship

- **Developmental Stages**

  Developmental psychologist Robert Selman of Harvard has found that children go through a series of four stages of friendship development. These stages evolve from an initial preoccupation with self, or viewing friendship in an egocentric way, to the ability to see the perspective of others, or to empathize. The following is a brief description of each of these four stages:

- **Stage 1 (ages four to nine):** At this stage children do not understand that dealing with others involves give and take. A "good" friendship is one in which one person does what the other person wants. If one child says, "Let's ride bikes," and the other says, "I don't want to," a normal response from a Stage 1 child would be, "Then you're not my friend."
- **Stage 2 (ages six to twelve):** The child has the ability to see that friendship doesn't work unless both friends meet each other's needs. "He does things I like, and I do things he likes." This is the stage of two-way "fairweather" friendship. The child still sees the basic purpose of friendship as serving self-interest, rather than mutual interests. "He likes me and I like him. We do things for each other."
- **Stage 3 (ages nine to fifteen):** It is in the transition from Stage 2 to Stage 3, typically in late childhood, that children begin to consider the other person's point of view. They begin thinking about mutual commitment and loyalty in a friendship, rather than "What should I do to get what I want?" The thought often is, "What should I do to make my friend happy?" In this stage, friends share more than secrets, agreements, or plans; they share feelings and personal problems. "She is my best friend. We can tell each other things we can't tell anyone else. We stick with each other through thick and thin." The limitation of this stage is that friendships are often exclusive and possesive, with jealousies being common.
- **Stage 4 (ages twelve and older):** After children finish the stage where friendships are so possessive, they move to a stage where friends can be close, yet grant each other the freedom to develop other relationships. "If you are really close friends you have to trust and support each other. We have to let each other have other friends, too."

These progressions in social understanding are made possible, in part, by parallel progressions from concrete to abstract reasoning in a child's intellectual development. Generally, primary age students are in Stages 1 and 2 of social reasoning. In the intermediate grades, students move into stages 2 and 3. However, this development of social understanding depends on both growing intellectual skills and on specific social experiences. Since these vary widely among individuals, in a given classroom it is possible to have students in many stages of social reasoning.

- **Empathy**

The stages of social awareness which have been outlined by Selman also represent the base for empathy. Young children don't naturally see things from another's point of view. As children reach middle childhood, they become increasingly more facile in cognitive skills and gain in the ability to empathize. Development of empathy, however, depends on experience as well as cognitive capacity.

Elements of empathy are eminently teachable to children of all school ages. The ability to understand what someone else thinks or feels is not an all-or-none phenomenon, but has a gradual and variable development. The younger child will begin by appreciating new perspectives most similar to his or her own. Training in empathy involves providing relevant social experiences and examining them in an educational way. It is thought to occur through exposure to reasoning at one stage above the stage that the student is using. Students will have excellent opportunities to hear the various social reasoning stages of their classmates as they discuss concepts and questions and engage in the role-plays presented in this manual.

Suggested Readings on Children's Friendships

Arrezo, D. & Stocking, H. (1975). *Helping friendless children: A guide for teachers and parents*. Boys Town, NE: Boys Town Center for the Study of Youth Development.

Asher, S. & Gottman, J. (Eds.). (1981). *The development of children's friendships*. Cambridge, MA: Cambridge University Press.

Cottman, J. & Conso, J. (1975). Social interaction, social competence, and friendship in children. *Child Development*, *46*, 709-718.

Damon, W. (1977). *The social world of the child*. San Francisco: Jossey-Bass.

Flavell, J. (1974). The development of inference about others. In T. Mischel (Ed.), *Understanding other persons*. Oxford, England: Blackwell.

Foot, H.C., Chapman, A.J., & Smith, J.R. (Eds.). (in press). *Friendship and childhood relations*. London, England: Wiley.

Fox, C.L. & LaVine Weaver, F. (1983). *Unlocking doors to friendship*. Rolling Hills Estates, CA: B.L. Winch & Assoc.

Hartup, W. (1988). Conflict and the friendship relations of young children. *Child Development*, *9*(6), 1490-1600.

Hayes, D. (1978). Cognitive bases for liking and disliking among school children. *Child Development*, *49*, 906-909.

Oden, S. & Asher, S. (1977). Coaching children in social skills and friendships making. *Child Development*, *48*, 495-506.

Rubin, A. (1980). *Children's friendships*. Cambridge, MA: Harvard University Press.

Selman, R. (1981). The child as a friendship philosopher. In S. Asher & J. Gottman (Eds.), *The development of children's friendships*. Cambridge, MA: Cambridge University Press.

Staub, E. (1971). Use of role-playing and induction in training for pro-social behavior. *Child Development*, *42*, 805-816.

Vorenhorst, B. (1983). *Real friends: Becoming the friend you'd like to have*. New York: Harper & Row.

Youniss, J. & Volpe, J. (1978). A relational analysis of children's friendship. In W. Damon (Ed.), *Social cognition*. San Francisco: Jossey-Bass.

Deciding What's Important in a Friend

Objective

Students will identify their priorities regarding qualities they look for in friends.

Materials

Transparency #1 - "A Friend Is Someone Who . . ."
Handout #1 - "A Friend Is . . ."
Transparency #2 - "Qualities of a Friend"
Transparency #3 - "Want Ad for a Friend"
Handout #2 - "My Want Ad for a Friend"
Handout #3 - "Friendship Word List"
Transparency #4 - "Recipes for Friendship"
Handout #4 - "My Recipe for Friendship"
Transparency #5/Handout #5 - "A Formula for Friendship"
Butcher paper prepared for a "Friendship Graffiti Board"
Colored markers or colored chalk

To the Teacher

This lesson is an orientation to the concept of friendship. Students consider which behaviors they like in their friends and the behaviors they would want most in an ideal friend. They try to agree as a group on what a true friend is like, then write their ideas on a "Friendship Graffiti Board." This can be a part of the chalkboard you've kept open or a long piece of butcher paper you've hung up for this purpose. Block off a space across the top of the Friendship Graffiti Board where you can write the class definition of a friend.

Students are introduced to a list of "friendship words," and from this list they generate a class definition of friendship. Students then write an individualized "want ad for a friend," stating what it is in particular they're looking for.

By having students begin looking at what most people like in a friend and then analyzing what it is in particular that they themselves want in a friend, the way is prepared for them to gain an awareness of what they need to be like themselves in order to have friends. This will be the focus of Lesson 2.

It is important for students to realize that anyone can increase his or her ability to make friends and that this is not a talent we are born with, but something we learn. Students need to know that friendship is within everyone's grasp, provided they are willing to learn friendship skills and use them.

If your school uses a grade-leveled approach to this curriculum, the lesson itself can be taught each year as it contains life skills that need to be emphasized and practiced each year. Use the following Supplementary Activities at these suggested grade levels:

4th "What I Want in a Friend"
(Supplementary Activity #1)
"Friendship Qualities"
(Supplementary Activity #2)

5th "What Makes a Friend?"
(Supplementary Activity #3)
"FRIENDSHIP Spelling and Vocabulary Words"
(Supplementary Activity #4)

6th "Symbol of Friendship"
(Supplementary Activity #5)
"Friendship Cinquains"
(Supplementary Activity #6)

Lesson Presentation

QUALITIES WE WANT IN A FRIEND

For the next few weeks we're going to learn what people need to do in order to make and keep friends. Kids who have a hard time with friendship can learn ways to make friends, and kids who already have friends can learn how to have a better time with them.

For today, let's concentrate on what you want a friend of yours to be like. Stop for a minute and think about someone you know who has a lot of friends. Without using any names, who can tell us what this person does that makes people want him or her for a friend? *Allow for student response.*

Now think of someone you like as a friend. What friendly things does this person do that makes you like him or her? *Allow for student response.*

Transp. #1

Show Transparency #1, "A Friend Is Someone Who . . . ." **Here are some ways other kids have described what they think a true friend is like. For instance: "A friend is someone who will give you an honest answer," or "A friend is someone who**

keeps promises and secrets," or "A friend is someone you have fun with and laugh with." *Read some more of the quotes on the transparency aloud.*

USING GROUPS TO DECIDE WHICH FRIENDSHIP QUALITIES ARE MOST VALUED

Handout #1

Divide students into cooperative learning groups. Give them Handout #1, "A Friend Is . . . ." Say: **I'd like you to work together to try to make some more statements about what a true friend is like. First, I'd like each of you to think about what you value in a friend. See if you can come up with at least two more statements on your own to add to this list. Write these on your handout.** *Allow students time for this.*

Now, share your new statements with the others in your group. Discuss these and the statements that are already on your handout. I'd like you to try to reach agreement on the three statements that you all think are the most important in describing a true friend. After you've had time to pick your top three, I'm going to have one person in each group read to the class the three statements you chose. Another member of your group will write these statements on our "Friendship Graffiti Board." We'll decide who will do these two jobs after your group comes up with your top three statements about what a friend should be like. *Allow students time for group discussion.*

When you feel students have had enough time to reach an agreement on these statements, help them select a Group Reporter and Group Recorder in the following manner: **Now let's pick two people from your group—one who will stand up and read your group's top three statements and another who will write them on our Graffiti Board. Here's how we'll do it. When I count to three, I want you each to point to the person in your group who you think would be the best one to tell the three statements you've picked to the class. Ready? One—Two—Three—POINT!** *(Pause.)* **Are there any ties?** *(Pause.)* **If there's a tie, the shortest person can be the speaker and the**

taller one can be the person who will write your statements on our Graffiti Board.

For the groups without a tie vote, do the same thing again to select the group's Recorder. Say: **When I count to three, point to the person in your group who you think would do the best job at writing your group's top three statements on our Graffiti Board. Be sure not to point to the person who you picked to be your speaker. Ready? One—Two—Three—POINT!**

Have each Group Reporter read the top three selections of the group to the class and have the Recorder write these on the Graffiti Board. In order to speed up the process, call on the next group's speaker while the first group's recorder is writing their choices on the Graffiti Board. When all groups are done, say: **We've got a lot of good ideas from each of your groups on what a good friend is like. As you can see, there are a lot of things you agree on, and there's quite a bit of variety here.**

A CLASS DEFINITION OF FRIENDSHIP

Transp. #2

Let's see if we can find a way to figure out what our class, as a whole, values most in a friend. To do this let's boil these statements down to key words that describe a true friend—words like "fun," or "honest," or "loyal." What are some other key words that sum up some of the statements your group listed on the Graffiti Board? *Allow for student response. Show Transparency #2, "Qualities of a Friend."* **Now let's look at some more single-word descriptions of qualities of a friend. Some of these are words you've just mentioned.**

Here's how we'll use this list. In your groups you reached some agreement on what you want most in a friend. Now let's see if we can reach an agreement as a whole class on what's important in a friend. While I read this list to you, I want you to think about which of these are the things that are <u>most</u> important to you when you choose a friend. In a minute you'll get a chance to vote on your favorite three.

Read the list aloud. Then say: **Did you hear some things you would insist on if you're really going to like somebody? This**

time I'm going to read the list more slowly and give you a chance to vote on the three qualities that are most important to you. I'll write down the number of votes each quality gets so we can see what most kids in this room look for in a friend. Remember, you can only raise your hand three times.

Read through the list again, tallying the number of hands for each word. Write this number beside the word on the transparency. After you've completed the survey, circle the words that received the most votes, making comments like: **"Well, it looks like you should try to be ______, if you want to be liked in this class"; "______ seems to be really important to the kids in this room"; "Most of the people in here like to have a friend who is______"; etc.** *Identify the top three, four, or five words, then say:* **It looks like we've got _____ words here that really stand out in this class as being important in choosing someone for a friend. Let's take these words and call them our class' definition of a friend. A friend is someone who is ______, ______, and ______. So if you want to be liked in this class, it looks like trying to be better at these qualities would be a good place to start.** *Write the class definition of a friend across the top of the Graffiti Board.*

CREATING AN INDIVIDUAL WANT AD FOR A FRIEND

Today we've come up with some group decisions on what's important in a friend and we've also come up with a class definition of what a good friend should be like. This doesn't mean that this is exactly what each of you look for in choosing a friend, though. Everyone is a little different in what they want their friends to be like. This is good, because each of us is different. It means there's a chance for each of us to find at least one person we can "click" with.

Just for fun, I'd like you each to come up with a want ad for the type of friend who would be perfect for you. *Show Transparency #3, "Want Ad for a Friend."* **Here are some examples of want ads other kids have written.** *Read the examples, explaining, as necessary, how they reflect individual preferences in*

friendship. **To make writing your ad even easier, I'm going to give you a list of friendship qualities, including many of the ones we've talked about today.** *Give students Handout #2, "My Want Ad for a Friend," and Handout #3, "Friendship Word List."* **Be sure to put in your want ad qualities that are most important to you.** *Collect the want ads and read some of the more interesting ones to the class. Don't give students' names. Post some on the Friendship Graffiti Board or on another bulletin board if you think it would be appropriate.*

CHOICE OF HOMEWORK ASSIGNMENT

Transp. #4
Handout #4
Transp. #5
Handout #5

You can choose between two activities for homework. You can come up with your own particular "recipe" for the type of friend who would be perfect for you, or you can write a "formula" for friendship. *Show Transparency #4, "Recipes for Friendship."* **Here are some examples of recipes other kids have written.** *Read the examples, explaining, as necessary, how they reflect individual preferences in friendship.* **If you choose this activity, you can use your list of friendship words to help you write your recipe. Be sure to put in your recipe the ingredients that are most important to you. You might want to look at a recipe book at home so you can make your own recipe look like a real one. In our next lesson you'll be sharing your recipe with the class, and we'll add your ingredients for friendship to our Friendship Graffiti Board if they're not already there.** *Give those students interested in this activity Handout #4, "My Recipe for Friendship."*

Show Transparency #5, "A Formula for Friendship," and say: **Your other choice for homework is to create a formula for friendship. Choose what you think would be the best seven "additives," or qualities, to create a formula for a perfect friend. Again, you can use your word list to help you if you like. If you choose this activity, you'll also be sharing your formula with the class during our next lesson.** *Give students interested in this activity Handout #5, "A Formula for Friendship."*

ADDING TO THE FRIENDSHIP GRAFFITI BOARD

Between now and our next lesson I'd like you to be on the watch for times when you see kids doing something friendly. If you see someone doing or saying something you'd like a friend to do for you, write what they did on our Graffiti Board. For instance, you might go over and write, "A friend is someone who sticks up for kids when they get a put-down," or "A friend is someone who takes the time to help others with their spelling words," or "A friend is someone who says just the thing to make you laugh." Let's try to add something to our Friendship Graffiti Board each day. I'll put a different color (marker/chalk) out each morning. When you write a statement on the board, circle it with the color I've put out so we'll know it's a new addition.

LESSON REVIEW AND PREVIEW OF LESSON 2

Summarize the lesson by asking each student to complete the following sentence starters:

- *I learned that . . . .*
- *I was surprised that . . . .*
- *I hadn't thought about it before, but . . . .*
- *I agree that . . . .*
- *I disagree that . . . .*

Use the Supplementary Activities to provide practice for the concepts taught in this lesson. It would also be helpful for you to hang up the posters of the "12 Keys to Making and Keeping Friends," found in Appendix E.

Say: **Today we talked about things we want in a friend—things we like that others do. In our next lesson, we'll be talking about things others do that bug us or keep us from wanting to be their friend.**

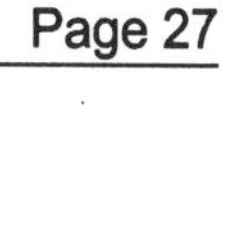

TRANSPARENCY #1

A Friend Is Someone Who . . .

"A friend is someone who will give you an honest answer."

"A friend is someone who keeps promises and secrets."

"A friend is someone who you have fun with and laugh with."

"A friend is someone who listens when you talk."

"A friend is someone who is interested in the same things you are."

"A friend is someone who apologizes if he or she has hurt you."

"A friend is someone who encourages you when you try to do hard things."

HANDOUT #1

A Friend Is . . .

- Someone who will give you an honest answer.
- Someone who listens and understands how you feel.
- Someone who likes to spend time with you.
- Someone who is loyal to you and not two-faced.
- Someone who you have fun with and laugh with.
- Someone who is interested in the same things you are.
- Someone who apologizes if he or she hurts your feelings.
- Someone who encourages you when you try to do hard things.
- Someone who would give up going to a rock concert if you needed him or her to be with you.
- Someone who is really happy when things go well for you.
- Someone who will stand by you when you're down.
- Someone who lets you have other friends, too.
- Someone who won't talk behind your back.
- Someone who sticks up for you.
- Someone who keeps secrets and promises.
- Someone who is willing to make up after a fight.
- Someone who tries to make you feel better when you make a mistake.
- Someone who doesn't put you down.

Now, you make up some:

"A friend is . . . ______________________________

____

"A friend is . . . ______________________________

____

TRANSPARENCY #2

Qualities of a Friend

athletic	generous	outgoing
cheerful	good listener	popular
confident	good looking	sincere
considerate	good sport	smart
dependable	helpful	talented
easy-going	honest	thoughtful
energetic	interesting	trustworthy
fair	kind	understanding
fashionable	loyal	unselfish
fun	outdoorsy	witty

TRANSPARENCY #3

Want Ad for a Friend

Examples

Friend Wanted:

Must be intelligent, honest, and easy-going. Doesn't need to be particularly good looking. Should like to skate-board. A good sense of humor would be greatly appreciated.

— José

Friend wanted who likes sports, especially football. I would like someone who could get together once a week to practice. Someone who plays fair and doesn't make fun of people would be great, too.

— Ted

I'd like a friend who likes horses and likes to read books about them. I also like to read mystery stories and would like to trade books with someone. I'm interested in someone who is outgoing and who would be nice to my other friends.

— Alice

HANDOUT #2

My Want Ad for a Friend

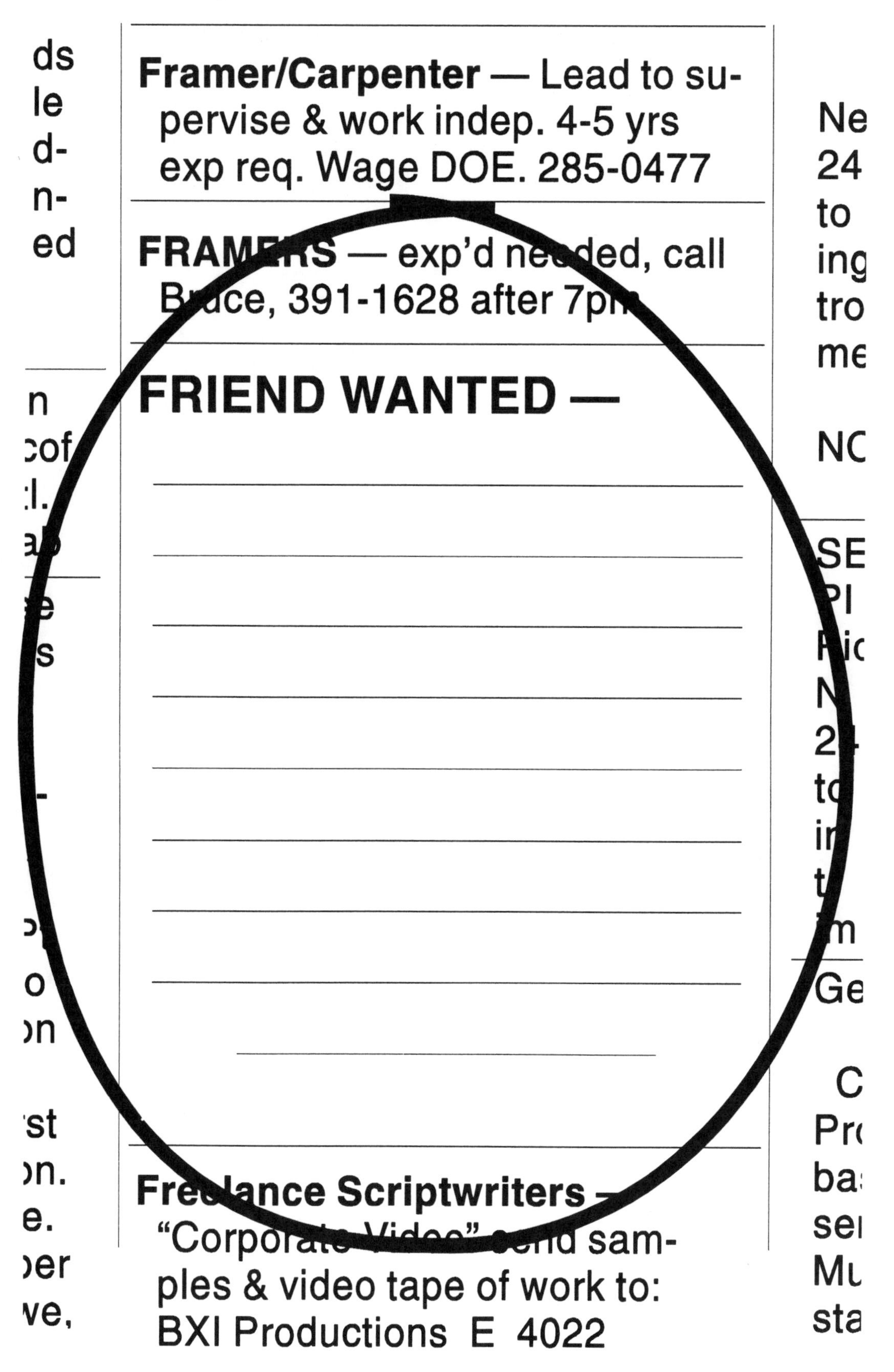

HANDOUT #3

Friendship Word List

accepting	humorous
active	imaginative
caring	intelligent
cheerful	interesting
clever	kind
confident	loyal
considerate	neat
cooperative	nice
creative	outdoorsy
dependable	outgoing
easy-going	patient
energetic	polite
fair	positive
forgiving	reliable
fun	shares
funny	sincere
generous	supportive
genuine	talented
good listener	thoughtful
good-natured	trustworthy
good sport	understanding
helpful	unselfish
honest	witty

TRANSPARENCY #4

Recipes for Friendship

Friendship Feast

Take 2 cups of fun & mix well with 1 cup each of fairness, honesty, and generosity. Stir in 3/4 cup of funny and 5 tablespoons of interesting. Season well with loyalty, helpfulness, & being a good sport.

Friendship Entrée

Start with a heaping measure of unselfishness. Combine with enough sharing and understanding until it's well blended. Throw in a handful of imagination and a pinch of outdoorsiness. Cook together until well done—NO HALF-BAKED FRIENDSHIPS ALLOWED!

HANDOUT #4

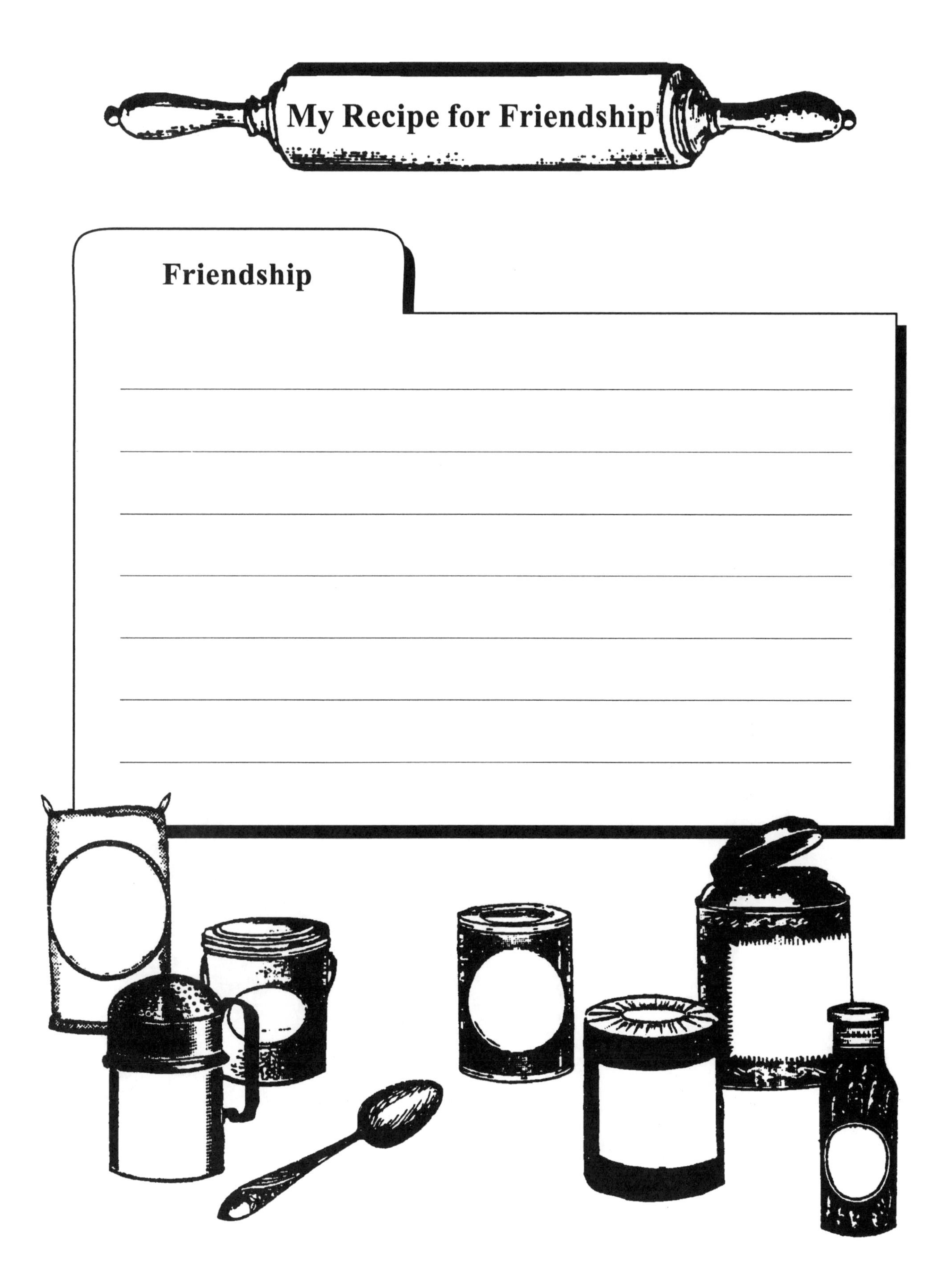

TRANSPARENCY #5/HANDOUT #5

A Formula for Friendship

Directions:

Write the top seven things you want in a friendship onto the beaker, test tubes, and chemical tin to create your own individual formula for friendship.

SUPPLEMENTARY ACTIVITY #1

What I Want in a Friend

Directions:

How important do you think that each quality below would be in a friend? Place an "X" in the boxes at the left, indicating how important each quality is to you. The first item is completed for you as an example.

Not Important	Sort of Important	Very Important	I want a friend who . . .
		✗	Likes to do the same things I do.
			Is funny and jokes a lot.
			Is honest and doesn't lie to me.
			Is a good sport and plays fair.
			Likes me and cares what happens to me.
			Is in the same year in school I'm in.
			Listens when I talk and doesn't interrupt.
			Keeps promises.
			Is good in sports.
			Has lots of money to spend.
			Dresses the same way I do.

SUPPLEMENTARY ACTIVITY #2

Friendship Qualities

accepting	forgiving	loyal
caring	fun	patient
cheerful	generous	sense of humor
considerate	good listener	sincere
cooperative	good sport	supportive
dependable	helpful	thoughtful
easy-going	honest	trustworthy
fair	kind	understanding

List the **six** qualities above that you want most in a friend.

I want a friend who is:

1. ________________ 2. ________________ 3. ________________

4. ________________ 5. ________________ 6. ________________

Of the six you chose, list the **three** that are the most important to you.

Most of all, I want a friend of mine to be:

1.________________ 2.________________ 3.________________

Which of these do **you** most need to work on so you'll be a better friend to others?

I need to work harder on being more________________.

SUPPLEMENTARY ACTIVITY #3

What Makes a Friend?

Directions:

1. **Write the words below into the spaces of this "friend."** If you count the spaces first, you'll know where each word will fit. Some words could fit in more than one place. **Use each word just once.**
2. **Color yellow** the word for the friendship quality you think is your best.
3. **Color orange** the word for the quality you think you need to be more of.

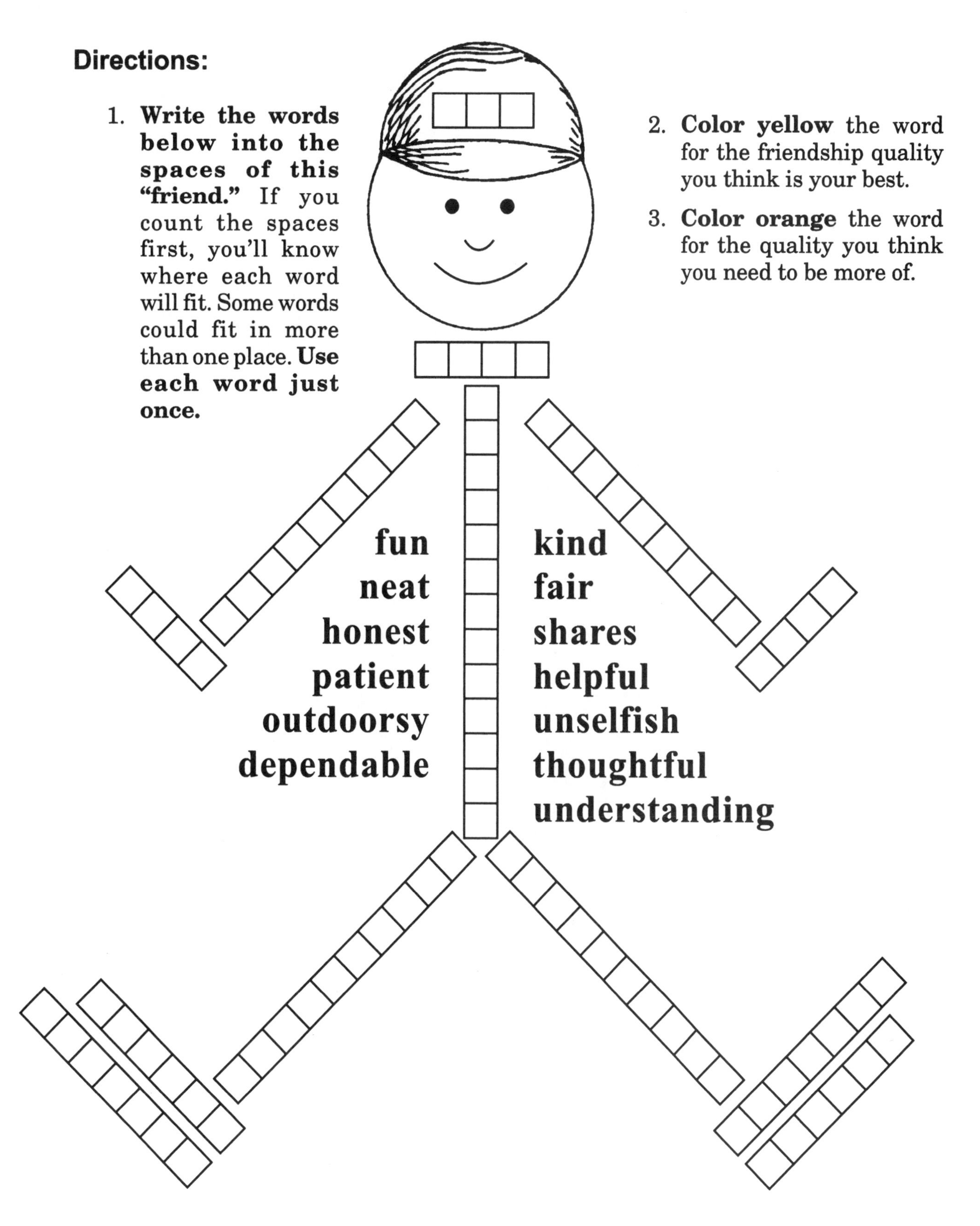

SUPPLEMENTARY ACTIVITY #4

FRIENDSHIP
Spelling and Vocabulary Words

Directions:

Learn the meaning of these words and how to spell them.

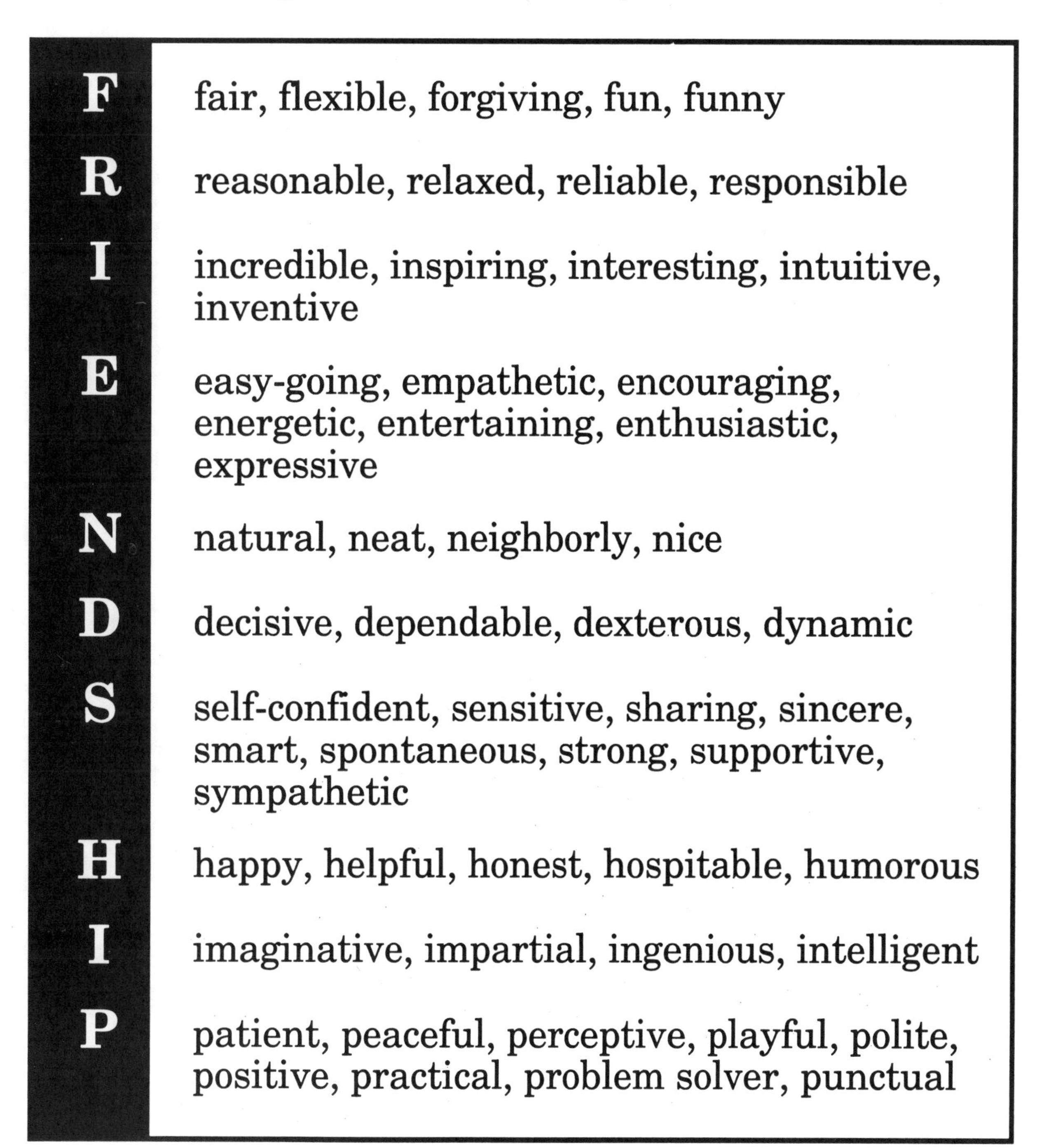

F	fair, flexible, forgiving, fun, funny
R	reasonable, relaxed, reliable, responsible
I	incredible, inspiring, interesting, intuitive, inventive
E	easy-going, empathetic, encouraging, energetic, entertaining, enthusiastic, expressive
N	natural, neat, neighborly, nice
D	decisive, dependable, dexterous, dynamic
S	self-confident, sensitive, sharing, sincere, smart, spontaneous, strong, supportive, sympathetic
H	happy, helpful, honest, hospitable, humorous
I	imaginative, impartial, ingenious, intelligent
P	patient, peaceful, perceptive, playful, polite, positive, practical, problem solver, punctual

SUPPLEMENTARY ACTIVITY #5

Symbol of Friendship

Directions:

Think about the qualities that are most important to you in a friendship, then try to come up with a drawing that would be a symbol of one or more of those qualities. Draw your symbol in the box below.

Example

SUPPLEMENTARY ACTIVITY #6

Friendship Cinquains

Directions:

In this activity you'll create a poem that describes what you think are the qualities of a good friend. To do so, you'll use a type of poem called a "cinquain." A cinquain doesn't use rhyme. Instead you carefully select just the right words to describe what you want to say.

Cinquains are fun and easy to create. Here's how to make up a cinquain about friendship:

FIRST line —	Write "Friend."
SECOND line —	Pick two adjectives that you think best describe what you want in a friend.
THIRD line —	Pick three action words (verbs) that you think describe what a good friend does.
FOURTH line —	Pick another single adjective that describes a good friend.
FIFTH line —	Finally, pick a three-word phrase that you think really describes what being a good friend is all about.

Here are two examples:

Behaviors That Hurt and Help Friendships

Objective

Students will recognize and prioritize behaviors that interfere with friendship.

Students will learn "12 Keys" to making and keeping friends.

Students will evaluate their own friendship behaviors and set appropriate goals for improvement.

Materials

Transparency #1/Handout #1 - "Things Kids Do That Bug Me"

Handout #2 - "Behaviors That Bug Me the Most"

Transparency #2 - "A Little Promise to Myself"

Transparency #3/Handout #3 - "12 Keys to Making and Keeping Friends"

Transparency #4 - "Keys 1#-#4"

Transparency #5 - "Keys 5#-#8"

Transparency #6 - "Keys #9-#12"

Transparency #7/Handout #4 - "The 12 Keys to Friendship Report Card"

Transparency #8/Handout #5 - "My Friendship Goal"

To the Teacher

In this lesson students focus on others' behaviors which annoy them. They vote as a class on what "bugs" them the most and also create an individual list of "bugs." The purpose of this exercise is to subtly raise students' awareness level regarding behaviors they may be doing which keep others from wanting to be their friends.

Next, students are introduced to the "12 Keys" to friendship. These are intended to give the students an overview of the most essential behaviors for making and keeping friends. (Students will be learning skills involving two of these keys—listening and complimenting—in Lessons 3-5. The remainder of the keys are focused on in depth, in the forthcoming ASSIST manual, *Solving Friendship Problems*.)

Students review their friendship behavior and graph their strengths and weaknesses on a "friendship report card." They then formulate a goal for improvement and an action plan. It is helpful if you remind them of their action plan in the days ahead. They will have a progress chart on which they can keep track of their efforts.

Prepare for this lesson by reviewing the homework assignments from Lesson 1—either "My Recipe for Friendship" (Handout #4) or "A Formula for Friendship" (Handout #5). Select samples to read to the class as well as to post on a bulletin board. Be prepared to add any new qualities of a friend students mention to the "Friendship Graffiti Board."

It is also helpful when preparing to teach this lesson to take a piece of paper and cut out a block the size of each of the "12 Keys to Making and Keeping Friends" shown on Transparencies #4, #5, and #6. That way you can mask all but the key you're talking about as you review these transparencies with students during the lesson.

In the Supplementary Activity section you'll find a page called "Taking Time for Friendship," which suggests copying the posters of the "12 Keys" and hanging them around the clock in your room.

If your school uses a grade-leveled approach to this curriculum, the lesson itself can be taught each year as it contains life skills that need to be emphasized and practiced each year. Use the following Supplementary Activities at these suggested grade levels:

4th "Using the 12 Keys to Friendship"
(Supplementary Activity #1)
"Can You Unlock These Friendship Questions?"
(Supplementary Activity #2)

5th "Campmates at Willow Springs"
(Supplementary Activity #3)
"Friendship Word Search"
(Supplementary Activity #4)
"Pick a Friendship Card"
(Supplementary Activity #5)

6th "Friendship Discussion Questions"
(Supplementary Activity #6)
"Quotes About Friendship"
(Supplementary Activity #7)
"Taking Time for Friendship"
(Supplementary Activity #8)

Lesson Presentation

REVIEW OF LESSON 1 HOMEWORK AND PREVIEW OF THIS LESSON

Say or paraphrase: **I'd like to share with you some of the "recipes for friendship" and "friendship formulas" you completed for homework after our last lesson.** *Read selected samples. Ask students to be listening for any new qualities of a friend that are not already written on the Friendship Graffiti Board. When one is noticed, ask a volunteer to add it to the Graffiti Board.*

Say: **We've taken a really close look at the things that people do that make others like them and want them for friends. We've come up with our own class definition of a friend.** *Review this.* **Each of you has had a chance to think about and write down what it is in particular you want in a friend. If someone wanted to know how to make a friend in this room they'd have a pretty good idea if they read our Friendship Graffiti Board or our want ads, recipes, and formulas.**

There is one more thing that might be helpful for someone to know, however, and that's what <u>NOT</u> to do if you want to have a friend. That's what we're going to talk about today. You're going to learn what behaviors bug the kids in this class the most. You'll have a chance to think about your own behaviors to decide if there are some things you want to improve.

TALKING ABOUT THINGS THAT BUG KIDS

Kids who want to have friends do many of the things that are listed on our Graffiti Board, but sometimes they also do certain things that really bug others. Often it's the things they do that bug people that keep them from having as many friends as they'd like. Here are a couple of examples: Let's say a kid is really generous and helpful to others—those are certainly good qualities for friendship—but this kid also has a habit of bragging and trying to be the center of attention; another kid might be fun to be around and have a great sense of humor, but talks behind other people's

backs. In both of these examples, the kids have many good qualities, but they do certain things that really bug others and this keeps them from having very many friends.

Transp. #1
Handout #1

Show Transparency #1, "Things Kids Do That Bug Me." **Here are some of the things that kids say bug them the most. Think about each behavior as we read through the list, because I'm going to ask you to pick out the ones that bug you the most.** *Read through the transparency, stopping now and then to ask students to raise their hands if a certain behavior bugs them. Some students may wish to make comments on some of the items. Remind students not to use names. Then say:* **I'm going to give you each a copy of this page. I'd like you to draw a "mad face" next to the five behaviors that bug you the most.** *Model by drawing on the transparency a mad face beside a few behaviors you particularly dislike, talking through your decision process. Then give students Handout #1 ("Things Kids Do That Bug Me") and allow them a few minutes to mark their five choices.*

"mad face"

Let's take a vote and see which of these behaviors kids in this room dislike the most. I'll read each one again, and this time raise your hand if you put a mad face by that behavior. Remember, you'll only be raising your hand five times. *Read through the list again, tallying the number of hands for each behavior. After the vote, review the list, noting which behaviors received the most votes. Say:* **"It seems as if the kids in our class <u>really</u> hate it when someone . . . "; "Wow! A <u>lot</u> of kids in our room are bugged when someone . . . "; "If you want to have friends in here, you won't want to . . . "; "If you want to <u>lose</u> friends be sure to . . . "; etc.**

STUDENTS IDENTIFY BEHAVIORS THAT BUG THEM THE MOST AND RESOLVE NOT TO DO THEM

Handout #2
Transp. #2

Now that we've looked at the list and seen which "bug" behavior got the most votes, I'd like you to decide on the absolute top three things that bug <u>you</u> the most. They may or may not be on the list we just worked on. *Give students Handout #2, "Behaviors That Bug Me the Most." Allow them time to complete the handout, reminding them to rank their three most disliked behaviors. When most students are done, show Transpar-*

ency #2, "A Little Promise to Myself." Have students write the sentence shown on the transparency in the box at the bottom of their handouts, then sign them and put them in their Friendship Folders.

THE "12 KEYS TO MAKING AND KEEPING FRIENDS"

Transp. #3
Transp. #4

So far you've looked at what bugs others; you've identified what bugs you the most; and you've made a little promise to yourself not to do these things to others. Now I'd like to show you a list of behaviors that people who have studied friendship all agree are important keys to making and keeping friends. *Show Transparency #3, "12 Keys to Making and Keeping Friends," so students can see a quick overview of the 12 Keys. Then show Transparency #4, "Keys #1-#4." Mask out all but the first key.*

Key #1: "Don't put down others."

Say: **I think you'll all agree that this first key, "Don't put down others," is the place you have to start if you want to have friends. You never really get away with giving put-downs. Even if you get a laugh from kids who are listening, deep down they don't trust you. They wonder if you'll turn on them next.**

Key #2: "Tell others what you like about them."

Adjust the mask on the transparency so that only Key #2 shows. **This next key, "Tell others what you like about them," is something we'll have a special lesson on in the weeks ahead. You'll learn how to find just the right words to give a compliment in a sincere way.**

Key #3: "Make others feel special."

Adjust the mask so that only Key #3 shows. Say: **Let's think about this third key now, "Make others feel special." Remember when we looked at friendship behaviors in our last lesson and wrote them on our Graffiti Board? If you think about it, you'll realize that each of these behaviors was really something that made a person feel special. Let's look at our**

Graffiti Board for a moment and make sure this is true. *Read a few of the behaviors on the Graffiti Board to illustrate your point.*

Key #4: "Be honest."

Adjust the mask to show only Key #4. **The fourth key is "Be honest." I bet you can each think of a time when a friend wasn't honest with you. How did you feel after you found out your friend lied to you? Was it hard to make the friendship good again? Does anyone want to give an example of how dishonesty can hurt a friendship? The example can't be about anyone in this class, of course, and don't use any names.** *Allow for student response, then say:* **If you want to have friends, be honest. Real friends don't lie to each other.**

Key #5: "Secrets and promises."

Transp. #5

Show Transparency #5, "Keys #5-#8," masking all but Key #5. **"Keep secrets and promises" is the next key to friendship. If you've ever had a friend tell one of your secrets or break a promise, raise your hand.** *Pause and then say:* **It looks like a lot of you know how much it hurts to have a friend tell one of your secrets or break a promise they've made to you.**

Key #6: "Be a good listener."

Mask out all but Key #6. Say: **The next key, "Be a good listener," is so important that we'll be spending two lessons learning to do it. To listen as a friend is a special kind of listening. It means not thinking about what you want to say while your friend is talking. If you ask any adult what they want most in a friend, one of the first things they will almost always say is "someone who's a good listener!"**

Key #7: "Put yourself in the other person's place."

Adjust the mask to show only Key #7. Say: **Who would like to read the seventh key? Who can give an example of what this means?** *Allow for student response. Elaborate on the concept of empathy, if necessary.*

Key #8: "Encourage others when they try to do hard things."

Adjust the mask and read Key #8 to students. Ask them to stand next to their Learning Partners and to decide who is the shortest. That person will be the speaker. Say: **Pretend your Learning Partner is trying to improve his or her speed in running a mile. Your Learning Partner has been working really hard and doing better, but in the last week his or her speed hasn't improved at all. In fact, it's gotten a little worse. Say something that you think would be encouraging to your Learning Partner and would help him or her keep trying.** *(Pause.)* **One of the keys to friendship is to be there for your friends and encourage them when they need it.**

Transp. #6

Key #9: "Help others feel better if they make a mistake."

Show Transparency #6, "Keys #9-#12," masking all but Key #9 on the transparency. Read Key #9 to students and this time explain that the taller Learning Partner will be the speaker. Say: **This time let's pretend that your Learning Partner is part of a team that was going to do a special science demonstration. The team was really excited about it. On the day of the demonstration, your Learning Partner forgot to bring a piece of equipment from home so the demonstration had to be cancelled! Now the other members of the team are furious. Pretend your Learning Partner feels really terrible. Say something to your Learning Partner that you think would make him or her feel better about this mistake.** *Pause.* **Understanding how a friend feels when they make a mistake and trying to make them feel better is an important key to building a good friendship.**

Key #10: "Apologize if you hurt someone's feelings."

Adjust the mask to show only Key #10. **This key to friendship, "Apologize if your hurt someone's feelings," might seem harder to do than it really is. That's because people often think that apologizing means you're admitting that you were the only one who was wrong about something. Apologizing doesn't have to mean you were wrong—it simply means you're sorry that something happened. If you can remember this, apologizing isn't so hard to do. Can anyone**

share a time when apologizing made a big difference in a friendship? *Allow for student comment.*

Key #11: "Forgive others if they hurt your feelings."

Adjust the mask once more, showing only Key #11. **This key, "Forgive others if they hurt your feelings," means that you don't punish your friends for hurting your feelings by giving them the cold shoulder when they want to make up. It's natural to get mad at a friend once in a while, but good friends don't hold grudges. They let their friends know when they're angry or hurt, but they're also willing to forgive them. Can anyone share a time when being willing to forgive helped a friendship?** *Allow for student response.*

Key #12: "Let your friends have other friends."

Adjust the mask one last time, displaying only Key #12. **This last key, "Let your friends have other friends," is the hardest thing of all to do. This key means that you give your friends the freedom to spend time with other people and to have fun with them without your being jealous. This key means you realize you don't "own" your friends, just as they don't own you.**

STUDENTS EVALUATE THEMSELVES ON THE 12 KEYS

Transp. #3
Handout #3

These 12 Keys are the secrets to making and keeping friends. *Show the complete list of keys (Transparency #3, "12 Keys to Making and Keeping Friends") once again. Give students a copy of this transparency (Handout #3, "12 Keys to Making and Keeping Friends") to keep in their Friendship Folders. Say:* **I see you all doing these friendship behaviors every day. I also have a hunch that a lot of you are interested in being an even better friend. To do this, it won't work just to say "I'm going to do all these twelve things better." It's much easier to improve if you concentrate on one thing at a time. So what I'd like to suggest you do now is to take a look at which behaviors you're already pretty good at, and which ones you think you need to improve.**

Transp. #7

Show Transparency #7, "The 12 Keys to Friendship Report Card." Say or paraphrase: **You can use this "Friendship Report Card" to help make these decisions. Even though we call this a report card, you're the one who will give yourself the grade. No one will see this but you, so be honest with yourself when you fill it out. When you're done, you'll be able to easily see which friendship behaviors are your strong ones and which ones could use a little work. Not one of us is perfect in all these areas. If someone feels they don't need to work on anything, they're just kidding themselves. The wisest people are the ones who see their strengths and also see what they need to work on.**

Handout #4

Model filling out the self-evaluation report card for an imaginary student, circling the appropriate grade for each key. Point out that this student, like everyone else, is a mix of strengths and things that need improving. Distribute copies of Handout #4 ("The 12 Keys to Friendship Report Card"). Allow students time to complete the handout, then say: **The next step is for you to decide on one key—one behavior in particular—to work on. A good way to make this decision is to ask yourself, "Which of the behaviors we have marked would help me <u>the most</u> in my friendships if I improved it? Which one would make the biggest difference in helping other kids like me better?"** *Allow students time to identify this key (behavior).*

STUDENTS IDENTIFY THEIR FRIENDSHIP GOAL

Transp. #8
Handout #5

Show Transparency #8, "My Friendship Goal," and give students Handout #5 ("My Friendship Goal"). Say: **Once you've decided on the friendship key or behavior you're going to work on, write it in the box on this handout in the form of a goal.** *Model doing this for students.*

Now it's time to get a little more detailed. In the spaces below, write down two or three specific actions that you will do this week that will help you improve the behavior you've decided to work on. Write down exactly <u>what</u> you will do, <u>when</u> you'll do it, <u>where</u> you'll do it, and <u>who</u> you'll do it to or with. *Give students time to complete the handout.* **The**

box at the bottom of the page is where you can keep track of how many times you remember to do these actions.

Put your "Friendship Report Card" and your "Friendship Goal" sheets in the front of your Friendship Folders. I'll be reminding you at the beginning and end of each day to read over your goals and to work on the two or three behaviors you've written down.

I'd also like you to put your "Behaviors That Bug Me the Most" handouts with these because I'll also be asking you to read over the things that you said others do that bug you the most. This way you'll be sure to remember not to do them yourself!

LESSON REVIEW

Summarize the lesson by doing a "whip" around the class, asking students to complete one of the following sentence starters:

- *I learned . . . .*
- *I didn't like . . . .*
- *I was surprised . . . .*
- *This can help me because . . . .*
- *The part of this lesson I liked best was . . . .*
- *A way I'm going to use what I learned today is . . . .*

Use the Supplementary Activities to provide further practice of lesson concepts.

In Appendix E there is a poster of each of the "12 Keys to Making and Keeping Friends" that you may wish to hang in your classroom. These can also be used for "Friendship Weeks," as described in Appendix D.

TRANSPARENCY #1/HANDOUT #1

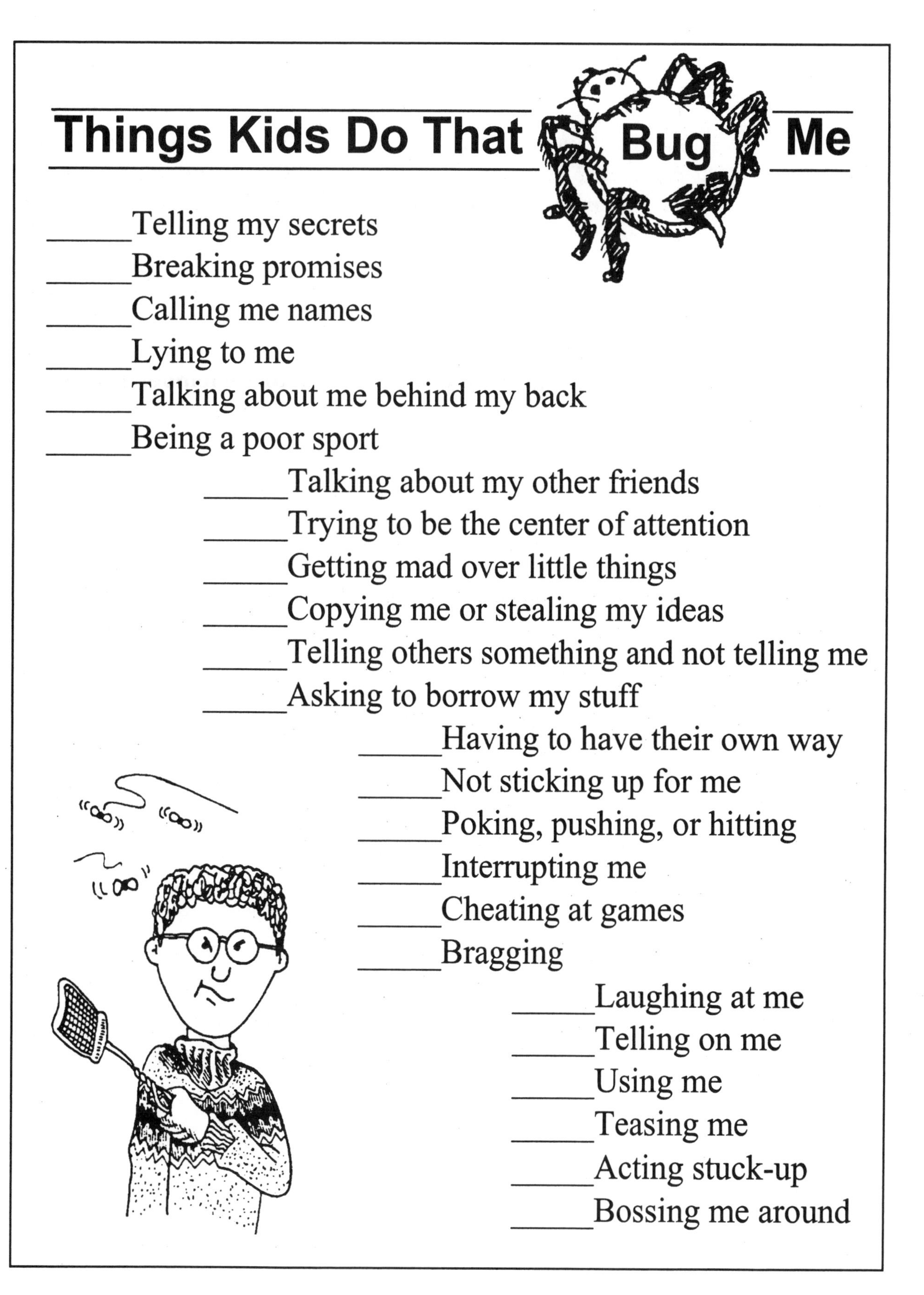

Things Kids Do That Bug Me

_____Telling my secrets
_____Breaking promises
_____Calling me names
_____Lying to me
_____Talking about me behind my back
_____Being a poor sport
_____Talking about my other friends
_____Trying to be the center of attention
_____Getting mad over little things
_____Copying me or stealing my ideas
_____Telling others something and not telling me
_____Asking to borrow my stuff
_____Having to have their own way
_____Not sticking up for me
_____Poking, pushing, or hitting
_____Interrupting me
_____Cheating at games
_____Bragging
_____Laughing at me
_____Telling on me
_____Using me
_____Teasing me
_____Acting stuck-up
_____Bossing me around

HANDOUT #2

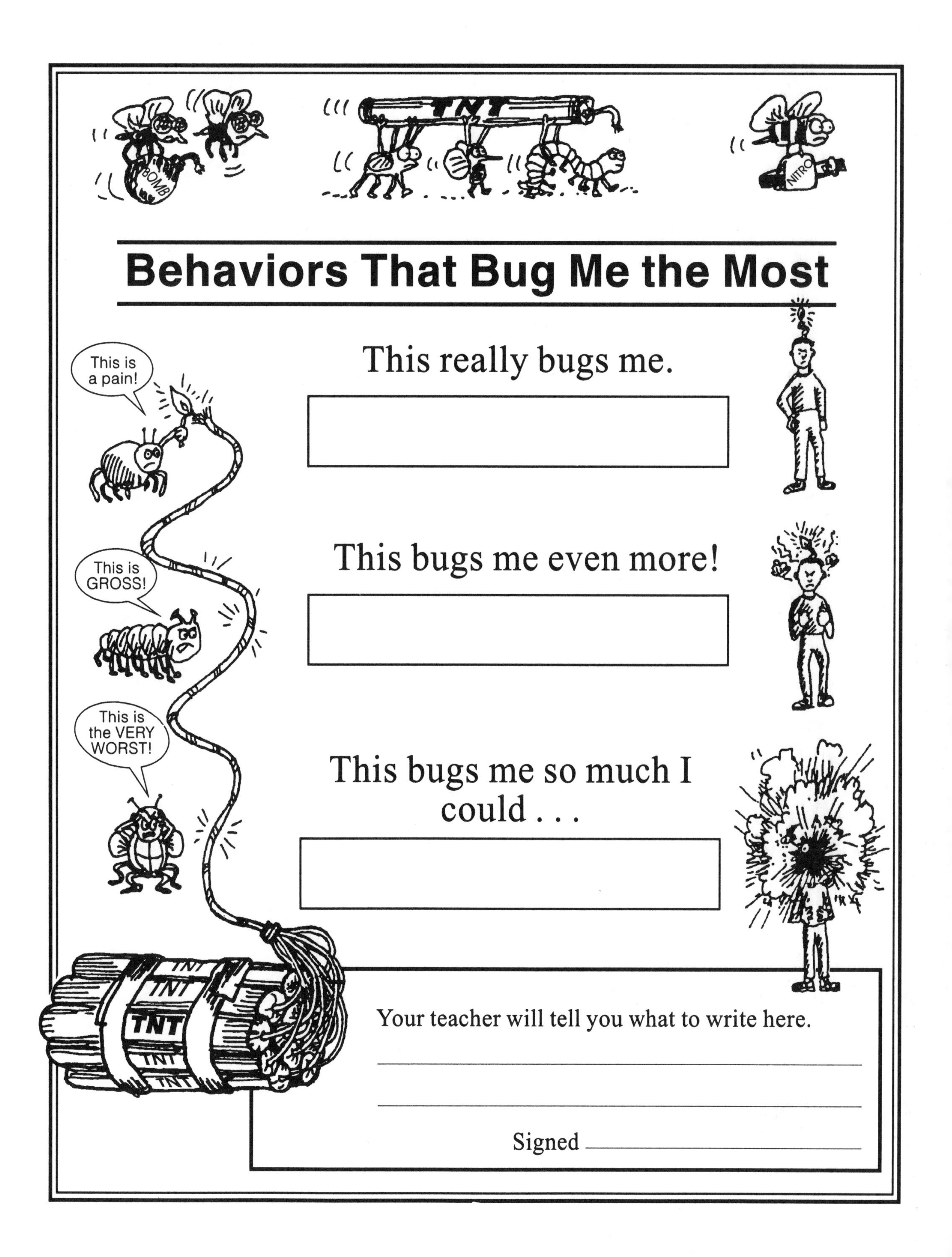
BOMB
TNT
NITRO
Behaviors That Bug Me the Most
This is a pain!
This really bugs me.
This is GROSS!
This bugs me even more!
This is the VERY WORST!
This bugs me so much I could . . .
TNT
Your teacher will tell you what to write here.
Signed

TRANSPARENCY #2

A Little Promise to Myself

Directions:

Fill in the box at the bottom of the "Behaviors That Bug Me the Most" handout like this.

TRANSPARENCY #3/HANDOUT #3

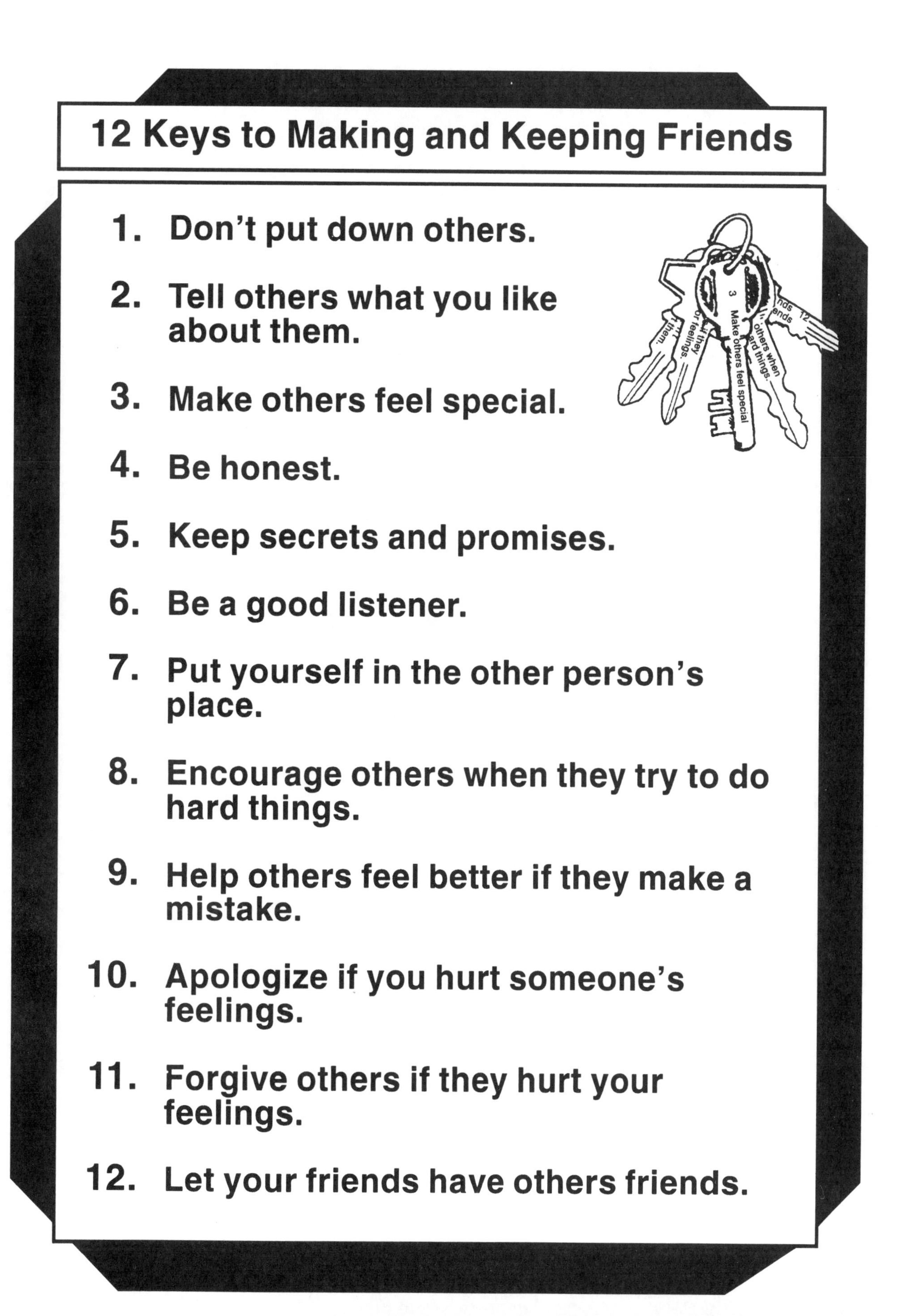

12 Keys to Making and Keeping Friends

1. Don't put down others.
2. Tell others what you like about them.
3. Make others feel special.
4. Be honest.
5. Keep secrets and promises.
6. Be a good listener.
7. Put yourself in the other person's place.
8. Encourage others when they try to do hard things.
9. Help others feel better if they make a mistake.
10. Apologize if you hurt someone's feelings.
11. Forgive others if they hurt your feelings.
12. Let your friends have others friends.

TRANSPARENCY #4

Keys #1-#4

Key #1

Don't put down others.

Key #2

Tell others what you like about them.

Key #3

Make others feel special.

Key #4

Be honest.

TRANSPARENCY #5

Keys #5-#8

Key #5

Keep secrets and promises.

Key #6

Be a good listener.

Key #7

Put yourself in the other person's place.

Key #8

Encourage others when they try to do hard things.

TRANSPARENCY #6

Keys #9-#12

Key #9

Help others feel better if they make a mistake.

Key #10

Apologize if you hurt someone's feelings.

Key #11

Forgive others if they hurt your feelings.

Key #12

Let your friends have other friends.

TRANSPARENCY #7/HANDOUT #4

The 12 Keys to Friendship Report Card

*Your name*____________________

	Keys to Friendship	Excellent	Very Good	O.K.	Could be Better
1.	Don't put down others.	A	B	C	D
2.	Tell others what you like about them.	A	B	C	D
3.	Make others feel special.	A	B	C	D
4.	Be honest.	A	B	C	D
5.	Keep secrets and promises.	A	B	C	D
6.	Be a good listener.	A	B	C	D
7.	Put yourself in the other person's place.	A	B	C	D
8.	Encourage others when they try to do hard things.	A	B	C	D
9.	Help others feel better if they make a mistake.	A	B	C	D
10.	Apologize if you hurt someone's feelings.	A	B	C	D
11.	Forgive others if they hurt your feelings.	A	B	C	D
12.	Let your friends have other friends.	A	B	C	D

TRANSPARENCY #8/HANDOUT #5

My Friendship Goal

My goal is to improve in this "Key to Making and Keeping Friends":

Key # _____: ____
____

The things I will do this week that will help me towards this goal:

1. ____
____
2. ____
____
3. ____
____

Charting will help keep your attention focused on your actions and allow you to see your progress. You will see what you're doing and what else may need to be done. It will help you to know when changes are needed. Charting helps you experience the satisfaction of being successful.

Progress Chart

Directions:

In the square for each day, write down the number of times you remembered to do the actions that will help you reach your goal.

Actions I will do:	M	T	W	TH	F
1.					
2.					
3.					

SUPPLEMENTARY ACTIVITY #1

Using the 12 Keys to Friendship

Objective

Students will gain more practice working with the key behaviors for making and keeping friends.

Materials

Supplementary Activity #1 Handouts #1A and #1B, "My Keys to Friendship" (you may want to run these on stiff paper)

String, yarn, key ring or paper clip, scissors, colored markers, hole-punch (optional)

Procedure

Give students a copy of both handouts. Have them color each key lightly, so that they can still read the words. Then have them cut out the keys and punch a hole where it's marked on the key. They should then connect them using a string, piece of yarn, a key ring, or a paper clip.

Explain to students that at the beginning of each day you will write two numbers from 1 to 12 on the chalkboard. Students will then look through their ring of keys and find the keys with these numbers on them. They will rearrange the ring so that these two keys are visible and set the key ring on the corner of their desk. These will be the two friendship skills the students will work on especially hard that day. At the end of the day, students will have a chance to tell about a time they were able to do something related to the day's keys. If students didn't find an opportunity to work on one of the keys, they can devise a plan detailing when they will do an action relating to one of the keys after school and explain this plan to the class.

VARIATIONS

1. Pick a different key each morning for twelve days and have students write or draw about a time they used that key in a friendship, what happened, and what they learned about using that friendship behavior.

2. The “12 Keys” can be assembled in the form of a mobile and displayed in the classroom.

SUPPLEMENTARY ACTIVITY HANDOUT #1A

My Keys to Friendship

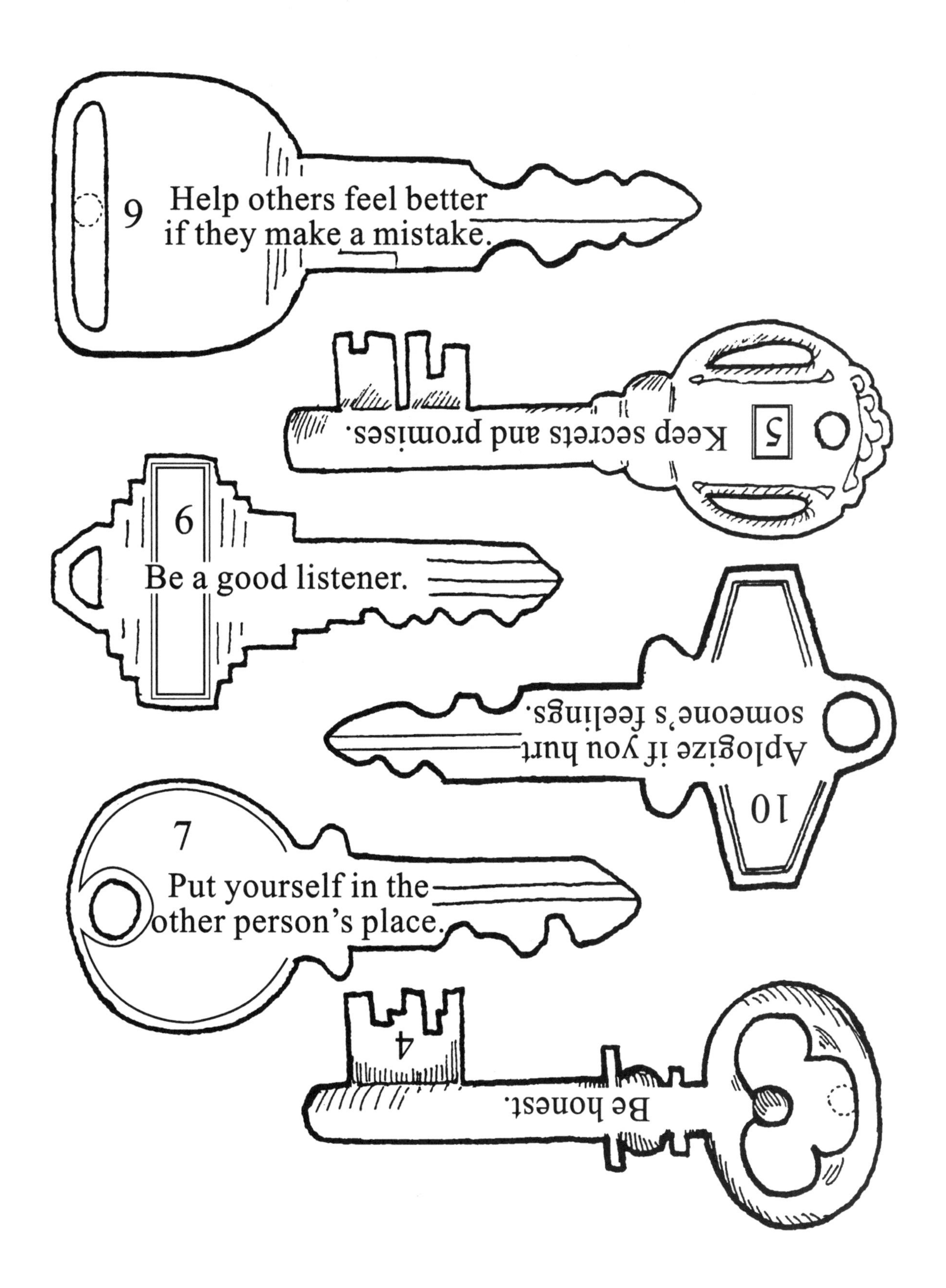

SUPPLEMENTARY ACTIVITY #1 HANDOUT #1B

My Keys to Friendship (continued)

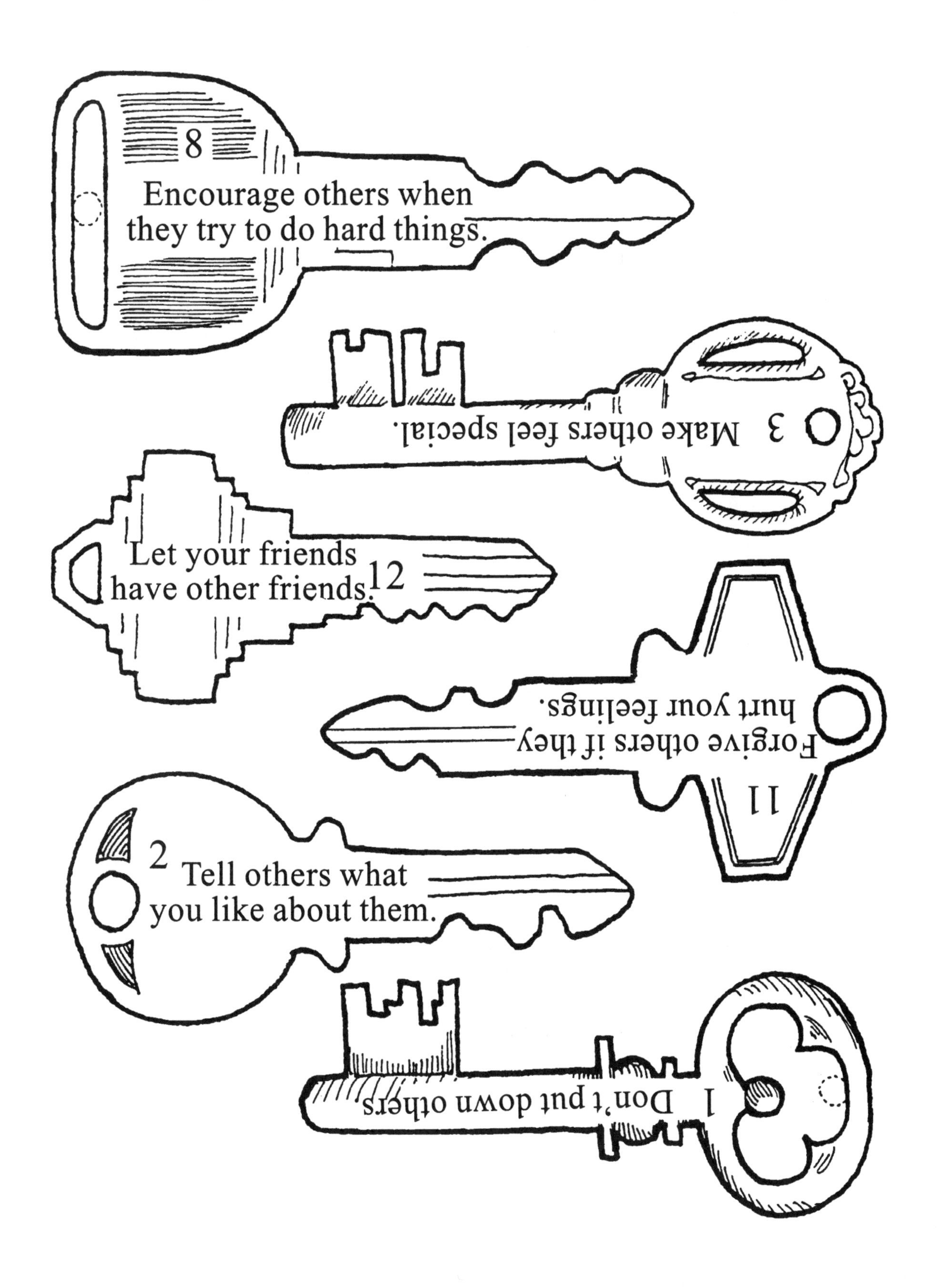

SUPPLEMENTARY ACTIVITY #2

Can You Unlock These Friendship Questions?

Objective

Students will explore friendship problem situations and solutions in small groups.

Materials

Supplementary Activity #1 Handouts #1A and #1B, "My Keys to Friendship"

Supplementary Activity #2 Handout #1, "Unlocking Friendship Questions"

Supplementary Activity #2 Handout #2, "Unlocking Friendship Questions: Answer Key"

Procedure

This activity uses the "Keys to Friendship" theme from Supplementary Activity #1. Divide students into cooperative learning groups. Ask them to find the friendship keys they assembled in the last activity. (If they haven't yet made them, distribute the handouts and have students color the keys lightly, cut them out, and attach them together.) Then distribute the "Unlocking Friendship Questions" and "Unlocking Friendship Questions: Answer Key" handouts, one each to each group.

Each group is to think of two friendship questions that can be "unlocked" by using one of the keys to friendship. Group members should think of situations or problems between kids that could be resolved by using one of the "12 Keys." After discussing one another's ideas, each group should select two of their best problem situations and the Group Recorder should write them down in question format on Handout #6. (The person in their group whose birthday comes the soonest after December 1st will be the Group Recorder.) On Handout #2 they should write down which keys to friendship would help "unlock" these questions. If they feel two keys would be equally helpful for a particular question, they should indicate this on the "Answer Key."

When their pages are prepared, groups will exchange their "Unlocking Friendship Questions" handouts with each other. Groups will then have five minutes to decide which keys will unlock the friendship questions. On the back of the handout, each group's Recorder should write the keys they've decided would solve the problem. They should also give at least two reasons why each key they've selected should work. After five minutes, groups will return the handouts to the groups they got them from, and check their answers. Any questions about several keys working in the same situation or problem situations where no “locks” or keys match should be discussed by the class as a whole.

SUPPLEMENTARY ACTIVITY #2 HANDOUT #1

Unlocking Friendship Questions

SUPPLEMENTARY ACTIVITY #2 HANDOUT #2

Unlocking Friendship Questions: Answer Key

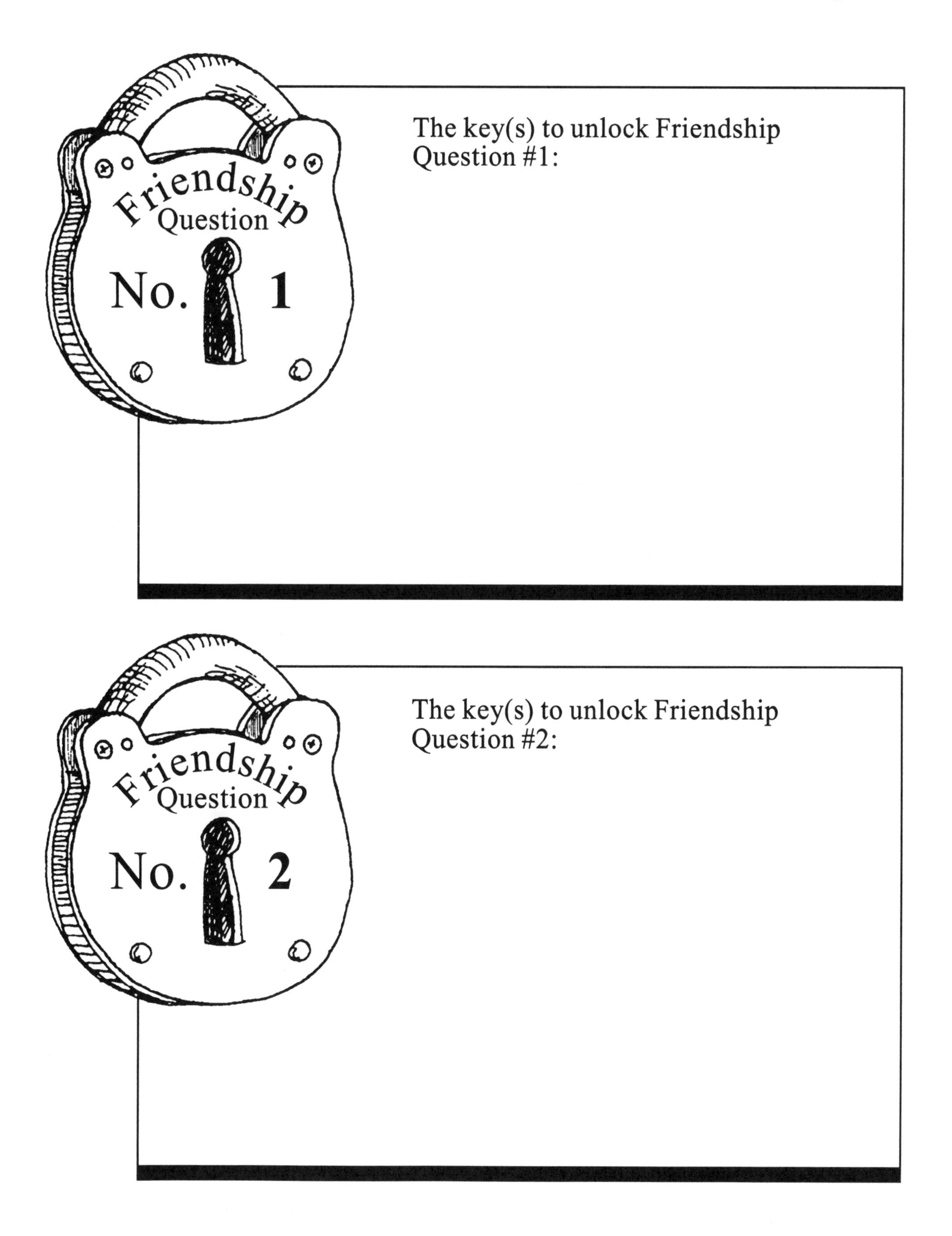

Campmates at Willow Springs

Objective

Students will make choices about what mix of positive and annoying qualities they can accept with a campmate selection simulation.

Materials

Supplementary Activity #3 Handouts #1A and #1B, "Campmates at Willow Springs Camp"

Procedure

Divide students into cooperative learning groups. Explain that this is a simulation activity where you want each group to pretend that they are getting ready to go to Willow Springs Camp for the summer. Each group has to pick six other campers besides themselves to be campmates with. During the summer they will do all their daily activities together. Each of these campers has some good points, but each also does something that really bugs others. Each group's job is to decide which six campers they just could not stand to live with and which six campers would be tolerable.

Give students Handouts #1A and #1B that describe the twelve possible choices of campers. Have them make their own individual decision first regarding which six campers they could and could not tolerate. Then have group members tell their choices to each other. Have them use negotiation and compromise to reach a group decision on six choices. When groups have reached a decision, have them share their choices with the class.

SUPPLEMENTARY ACTIVITY #3 HANDOUT #1A

Campmates at Willow Springs Camp

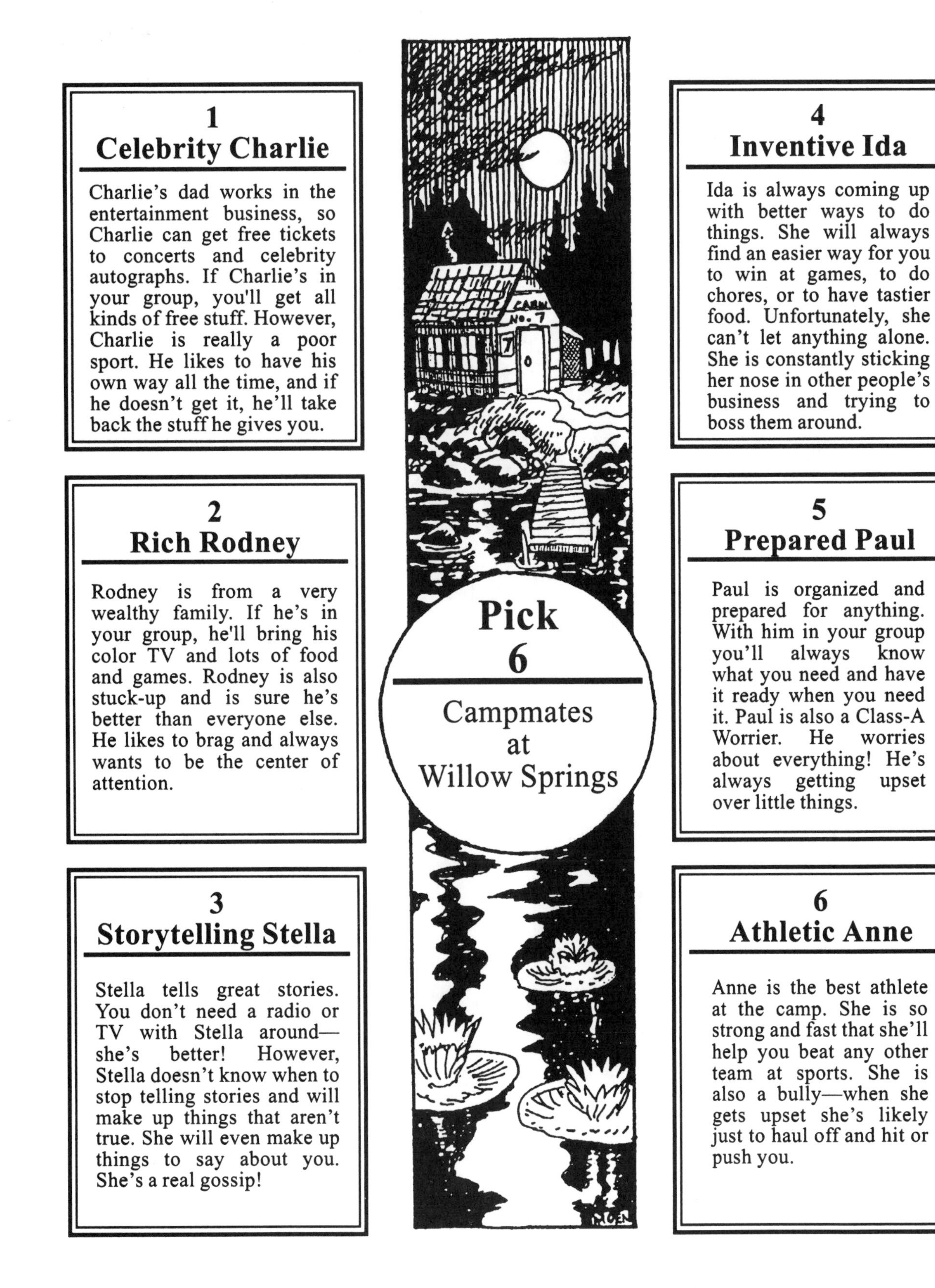

1
Celebrity Charlie

Charlie's dad works in the entertainment business, so Charlie can get free tickets to concerts and celebrity autographs. If Charlie's in your group, you'll get all kinds of free stuff. However, Charlie is really a poor sport. He likes to have his own way all the time, and if he doesn't get it, he'll take back the stuff he gives you.

2
Rich Rodney

Rodney is from a very wealthy family. If he's in your group, he'll bring his color TV and lots of food and games. Rodney is also stuck-up and is sure he's better than everyone else. He likes to brag and always wants to be the center of attention.

3
Storytelling Stella

Stella tells great stories. You don't need a radio or TV with Stella around—she's better! However, Stella doesn't know when to stop telling stories and will make up things that aren't true. She will even make up things to say about you. She's a real gossip!

Pick 6

Campmates at Willow Springs

4
Inventive Ida

Ida is always coming up with better ways to do things. She will always find an easier way for you to win at games, to do chores, or to have tastier food. Unfortunately, she can't let anything alone. She is constantly sticking her nose in other people's business and trying to boss them around.

5
Prepared Paul

Paul is organized and prepared for anything. With him in your group you'll always know what you need and have it ready when you need it. Paul is also a Class-A Worrier. He worries about everything! He's always getting upset over little things.

6
Athletic Anne

Anne is the best athlete at the camp. She is so strong and fast that she'll help you beat any other team at sports. She is also a bully—when she gets upset she's likely just to haul off and hit or push you.

SUPPLEMENTARY ACTIVITY #3 HANDOUT #1B

Campmates at Willow Springs Camp (continued)

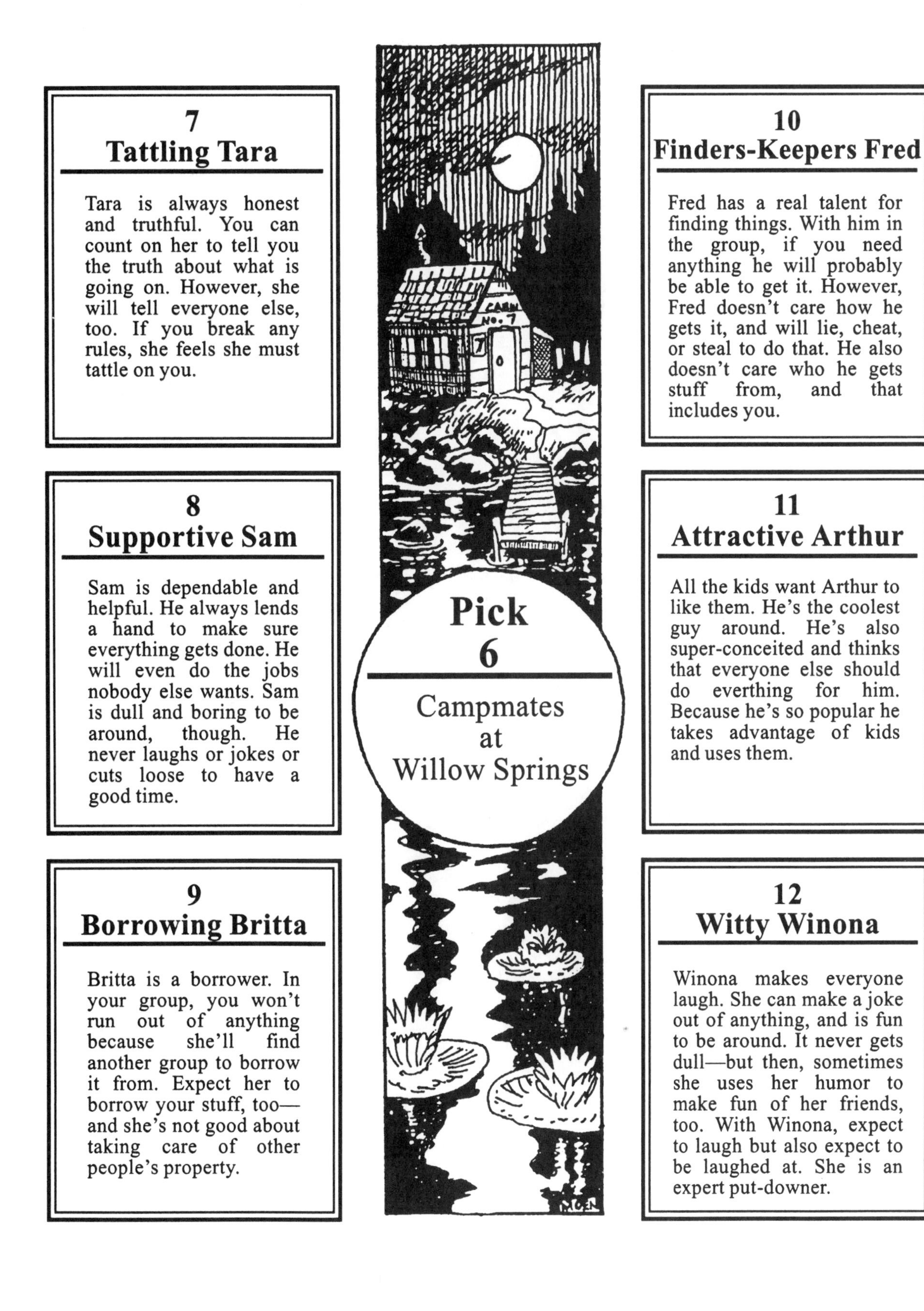

Pick 6

Campmates at Willow Springs

7 Tattling Tara

Tara is always honest and truthful. You can count on her to tell you the truth about what is going on. However, she will tell everyone else, too. If you break any rules, she feels she must tattle on you.

8 Supportive Sam

Sam is dependable and helpful. He always lends a hand to make sure everything gets done. He will even do the jobs nobody else wants. Sam is dull and boring to be around, though. He never laughs or jokes or cuts loose to have a good time.

9 Borrowing Britta

Britta is a borrower. In your group, you won't run out of anything because she'll find another group to borrow it from. Expect her to borrow your stuff, too—and she's not good about taking care of other people's property.

10 Finders-Keepers Fred

Fred has a real talent for finding things. With him in the group, if you need anything he will probably be able to get it. However, Fred doesn't care how he gets it, and will lie, cheat, or steal to do that. He also doesn't care who he gets stuff from, and that includes you.

11 Attractive Arthur

All the kids want Arthur to like them. He's the coolest guy around. He's also super-conceited and thinks that everyone else should do everthing for him. Because he's so popular he takes advantage of kids and uses them.

12 Witty Winona

Winona makes everyone laugh. She can make a joke out of anything, and is fun to be around. It never gets dull—but then, sometimes she uses her humor to make fun of her friends, too. With Winona, expect to laugh but also expect to be laughed at. She is an expert put-downer.

SUPPLEMENTARY ACTIVITY #4

Friendship Word Search

Directions:

Find all the friendship words or short phrases listed at the bottom of the page that are hidden below.

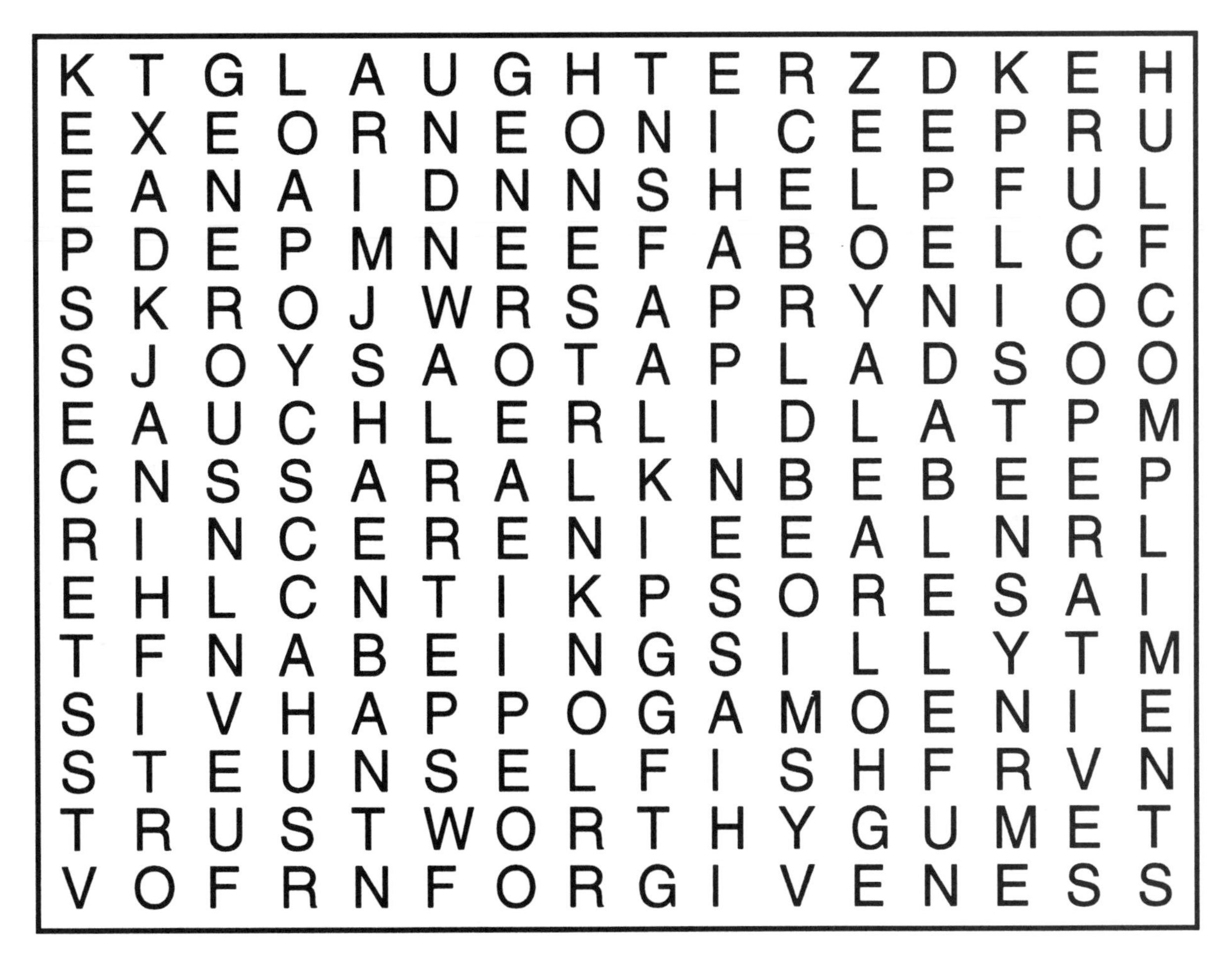

BEING SILLY
CARING
COMPLIMENTS
COOPERATIVE
DEPENDABLE
FAIR
FORGIVENESS
FUN
GENEROUS
HAPPINESS
HELPFUL
HONEST
JOY
KEEPS SECRETS
KIND
LAUGHTER
LISTENS
LOYAL
NICE
SHARES
SINCERE
TEAMWORK
TRUSTWORTHY
UNSELFISH

SUPPLEMENTARY ACTIVITY #4 ANSWER SHEET

Friendship Word Search Answer Key

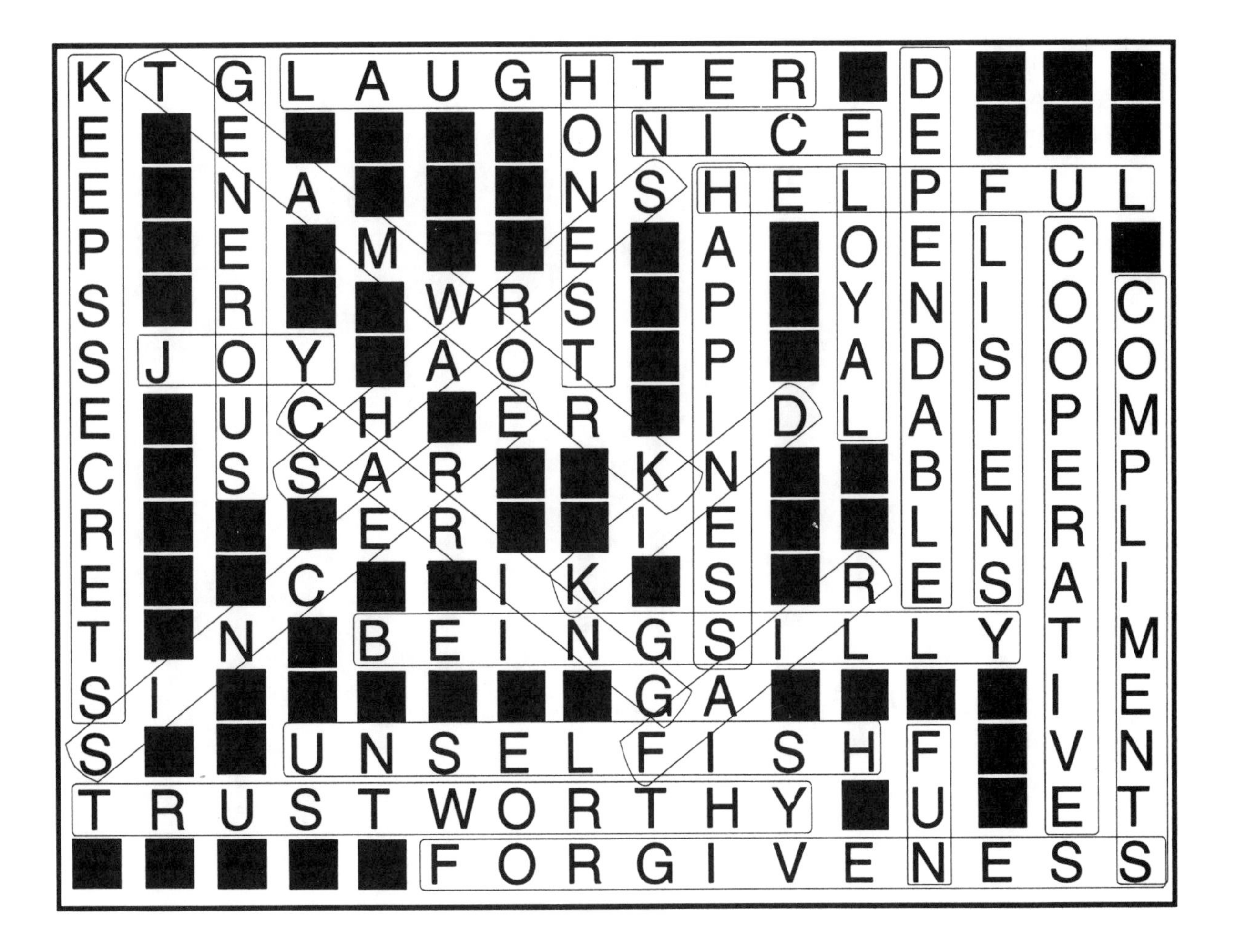

BEING SILLY	GENEROUS	LISTENS
CARING	HAPPINESS	LOYAL
COMPLIMENTS	HELPFUL	NICE
COOPERATIVE	HONEST	SHARES
DEPENDABLE	JOY	SINCERE
FAIR	KEEPS SECRETS	TEAMWORK
FORGIVENESS	KIND	TRUSTWORTHY
FUN	LAUGHTER	UNSELFISH

SUPPLEMENTARY ACTIVITY #5

Objective Students will practice friendship skills.

Materials Friendship Cards (Supplementary Activity #5 Materials Sheet), copied and cut

Procedure Copy and cut up the sheet with the Friendship Cards. Make sure you have made enough for each student to draw a card. Let students pick a card (without looking) and instruct them to try to do what is written on the card during the course of the day or week. When they have successfully completed this "assignment," have students write on the back of the card specifically what they did for their friend, and return the card to you. As students hand the cards back in, place a star by their name on a class list displayed somewhere in the classroom.

SUPPLEMENTARY ACTIVITY #5 MATERIALS SHEET

Friendship Cards

SUPPLEMENTARY ACTIVITY #6

Friendship Discussion Questions

Objective Students will share opinions on a variety of friendship topics.

Materials None

Procedure Students usually welcome an opportunity to discuss friendship issues, even though this may make some students a little uneasy at first. Through classroom discussion, students with friendship problems can learn the mores of the particular groups within which they are attempting to make friends. Additionally, students can give each other practical suggestions regarding the nitty-gritty issues of friendship. Select from the following topics those that you think would be most useful for your students. Ask students to give their reasons for their responses. See which topics students can agree on. On those items where students disagree, be sure to allow all students who wish to share their ideas to do so. Accept all responses in a nonjudgmental manner. Point out that many items are simply a matter of opinion.

VARIATION

If students seem willing, you might invite them to do a standing vote on controversial topics. Those who agree with the statement can bunch up on one side of the room, those who disagree can bunch up on the other side, and those who feel neutral about the statement can stand in the middle of the room. This way students can immediately see how their classmates feel about a friendship issue.

Questions

1. How many good friends does a person need?
2. Can you have more than one best friend?
3. What's the hardest thing about being a friend?
4. Have you ever tried to get someone to make friends with your other friends? How did it work?
5. If a person who trusts you told you that he or she felt they didn't have any friends, what would you say to them?

6. Why are some kids mean to other kids?
7. Would you tell a friend if they were doing something that really bothered you?
8. What's something you would never do if you wanted to be friends with someone?
9. Can you be friends with kids who are really different than you?
10. What kind of people would you rather not waste time with?
11. Which is harder—to make a friend or to be a friend?
12. Have you ever found a way to know someone you wanted to know better? How did you do it?
13. When you first go to a new school, a club, or to a new neighborhood, how do you make friends?
14. What things do you do to keep a friend?
15. Was there ever a time you kept a promise you made to a friend even though it was hard? When?
16. Have you ever had a time you thought you were going to lose a friend but you worked things out? What did you do?
17. What is the best way to make up after a fight?
18. Would you give your lunch money to a friend even if it meant you would go without lunch? If "yes," would you do this only for a best friend or for any friend?
19. Would you let a friend copy your paper and get credit for your idea?
20. Would you loan your allowance if a friend asked to borrow it, even if he or she wouldn't tell you what it was needed for?
21. Would you stop being friends with someone who borrowed a book from you, lost it, and acted like they didn't care?
22. Would you continue to buy presents for a friend who never bought presents for you, even though he or she could afford it?
23. Would you tell a friend if you didn't like a present he or she gave you?
24. Would you remain friends with someone who told a secret of yours after promising not to tell?
25. Would you remain friends with someone who constantly put down your other friends?

SUPPLEMENTARY ACTIVITY #7

Quotes About Friendship

Objective

Students will learn more about friendship by thinking about what others have said about it.

Materials

Pencil and paper

Supplementary Activity #7 Handouts #1A-#1F, "Quotes About Friendship"

Procedure

Since this activity involves high-level thinking skills, you may wish to only use this activity for your advanced or gifted students. Explain to students that friendship is such an important part of life that many famous people have spoken about or written down what friendship has meant to them. By thinking about what they've said, we can sometimes learn new things about friendship for ourselves. That is what this exercise is all about.

Give each student, pair, or small group a copy of the quotation handouts. Ask them to select five of the quotations that interest them, whether they agree or disagree with what was said. Then, ask them to think about and then write down the following four things about each of their five selections:

1. First, they are to put the quote into their own words. Have them find their own way to express the meaning of the quote.
2. Explain why they agree or disagree with the quotation. Why do they think it is true or untrue?
3. Next have them give examples from their own experiences that support the quote or seem to contradict it.
4. Finally, what new way of thinking about friendships has the quote brought up, or what might they do differently because of what the quote says?

When students have finished, ask for volunteers to present their observations on one or more of their selections. If you use small groups, you may choose to have each group make either an oral presentation to the class or a small poster that could be displayed containing one or more of their selections.

VARIATION

Write several of the quotes on separate strips of paper and cut the strips in half in a natural breaking place. For example, "A handful of friends is better than - - - a wagonful of gold." Scramble the pieces and have each student select one. Students then try to find the person who has the other half of their quotation. You might want to use different colors of paper or pens to make the search easier.

SUPPLEMENTARY ACTIVITY #7 HANDOUT #1A

Quotes About Friendship

Directions:

Choose 5 quotations from the list of quotations following. Each quote should be from a different category. You can either agree or disagree with the quote. **Think about the quote, then do the following:**

1. Find your own way to express the meaning of the quote, by putting the quote in your own words.
2. Decide if you agree or disagree with the quote, then explain why you think the quotation is true or untrue.
3. Give examples from your own experience that support the truth of the quote or that seem to contradict it.
4. What new way of thinking about friendship has the quote offered you or what might you do differently now because of what the quote says?

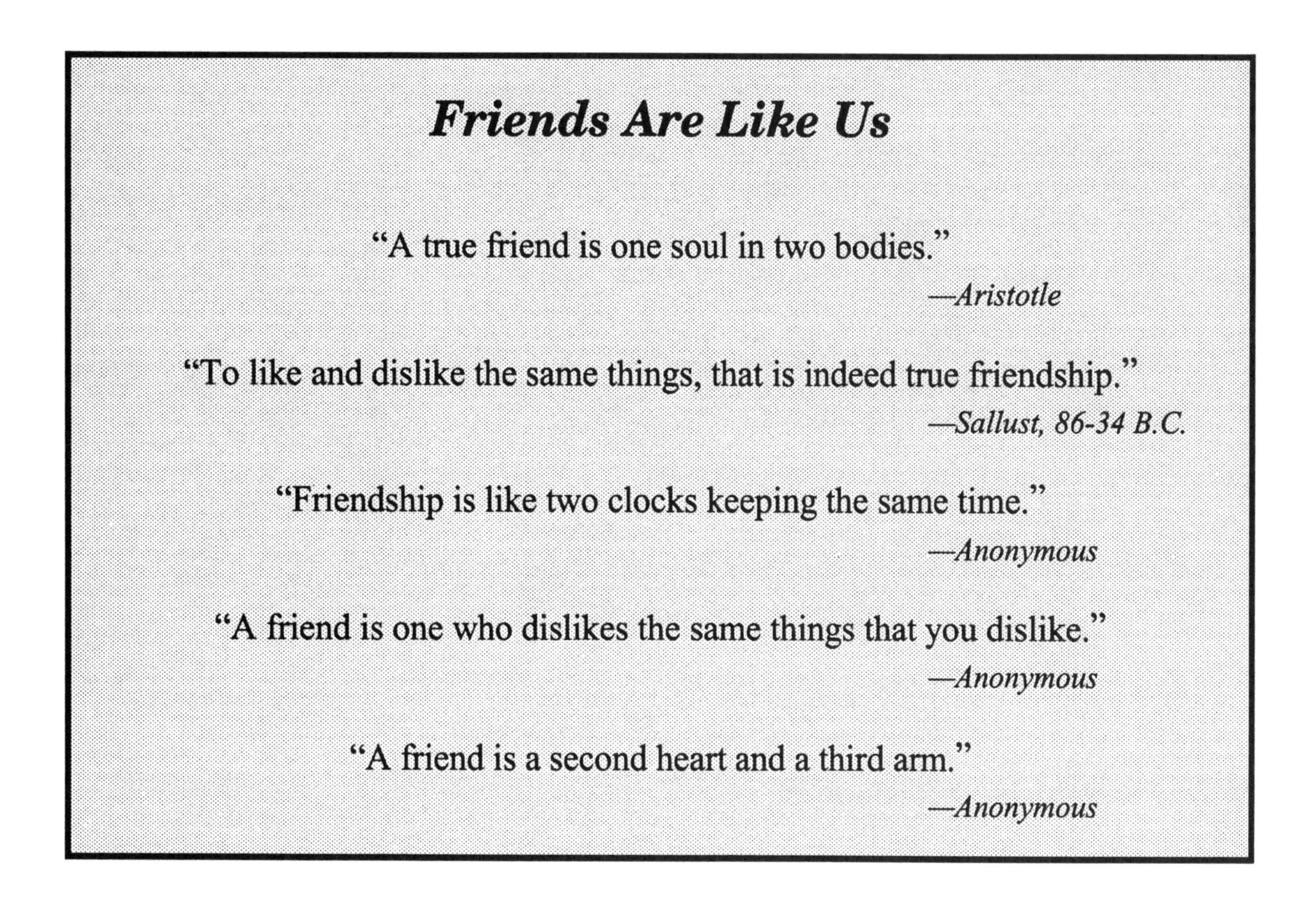

Friends Are Like Us

"A true friend is one soul in two bodies."

—Aristotle

"To like and dislike the same things, that is indeed true friendship."

—Sallust, 86-34 B.C.

"Friendship is like two clocks keeping the same time."

—Anonymous

"A friend is one who dislikes the same things that you dislike."

—Anonymous

"A friend is a second heart and a third arm."

—Anonymous

SUPPLEMENTARY ACTIVITY #7 HANDOUT #1B

Quotes About Friendship (continued)

Friends Accept Us As We Are and Help Us To Be All We Can Be

"A friend is someone who understands your past, believes in your future, and accepts you today just the way you are."

—Anonymous

"A friend is someone who knows all about you and loves you just the same."

—Elbert Hubbard

"A friend is a person with whom I may be sincere. Before him, I may think aloud."

—Ralph Waldo Emerson

"A friend is one to whom one may pour out all the contents of one's heart, chaff and grain together, knowing that the gentlest of hands will take and sift it, keep what is worth keeping and with a breath of kindness blow the rest away."

—Arabian proverb

"A true friend is somebody who can make us do what we can."

—Ralph Waldo Emerson

"My best friend is the one who brings out the best in me."

—Henry Ford

"A friend is someone who knows your needs, shares your joys, and helps you reach your goals."

—Anonymous

"A friend is someone who tells me the truth about me."

—Anonymous

"A friend is someone who likes you just the way you are."

—Anonymous

SUPPLEMENTARY ACTIVITY #7 HANDOUT #1c

Quotes About Friendship (continued)

General Thoughts About Being Friends

"A handful of friends is better than a wagonful of gold."

—*Anonymous*

"A single real friend is a treasure worth more than gold or precious stones. Money can buy many things, good or evil. All the wealth of the world could not buy a friend or pay you for the loss of one."

—*Anonymous*

"The better part of one's life consists of his friendships."

—*Abraham Lincoln*

"The best mirror is an old friend."

—*George Herbert*

"Friends are not luxuries, they're necessities."

—*Anonymous*

"To be able to be by yourself is wonderful and to be able to be with good friends is wonderful, but the most wonderful thing of all is to be able to choose equally between both."

—*Moen*

"Grief can take care of itself, but to get the full value of joy you must have somebody to divide it with."

—*Mark Twain*

"Everything is better when shared with a friend."

—*Anonymous*

"Chance makes our parents, but choice makes our friends."

—*Delille*

SUPPLEMENTARY ACTIVITY #7 HANDOUT #1D

Quotes About Friendship (continued)

General Thoughts About Being Friends (continued)

"Be slow to fall into friendship; but when you are in one, continue firm and constant."

—Socrates

"A friend is a bridge between you and the rest of the world."

—Anonymous

"Friendship is the hardest thing in the world to explain. It's not something you learn in school. But if you haven't learned the meaning of friendship, you really haven't learned anything."

—Mohammad Ali

"What do we live for if not to make life less difficult for each other?"

—George Elliot

Friends Come From Being a Friend

"The only way to have a friend is to be one."

—Emerson

"We keep our friends not by accepting favors, but by doing them."

—Thucydides

"You can make more friends in two months by becoming interested in other people than you can in two years by trying to get other people interested in you."

—Dale Carnegie

"The most I can do for my friend is simply to be his friend."

—Henry David Thoreau

SUPPLEMENTARY ACTIVITY #7 HANDOUT #1E

Quotes About Friendship (continued)

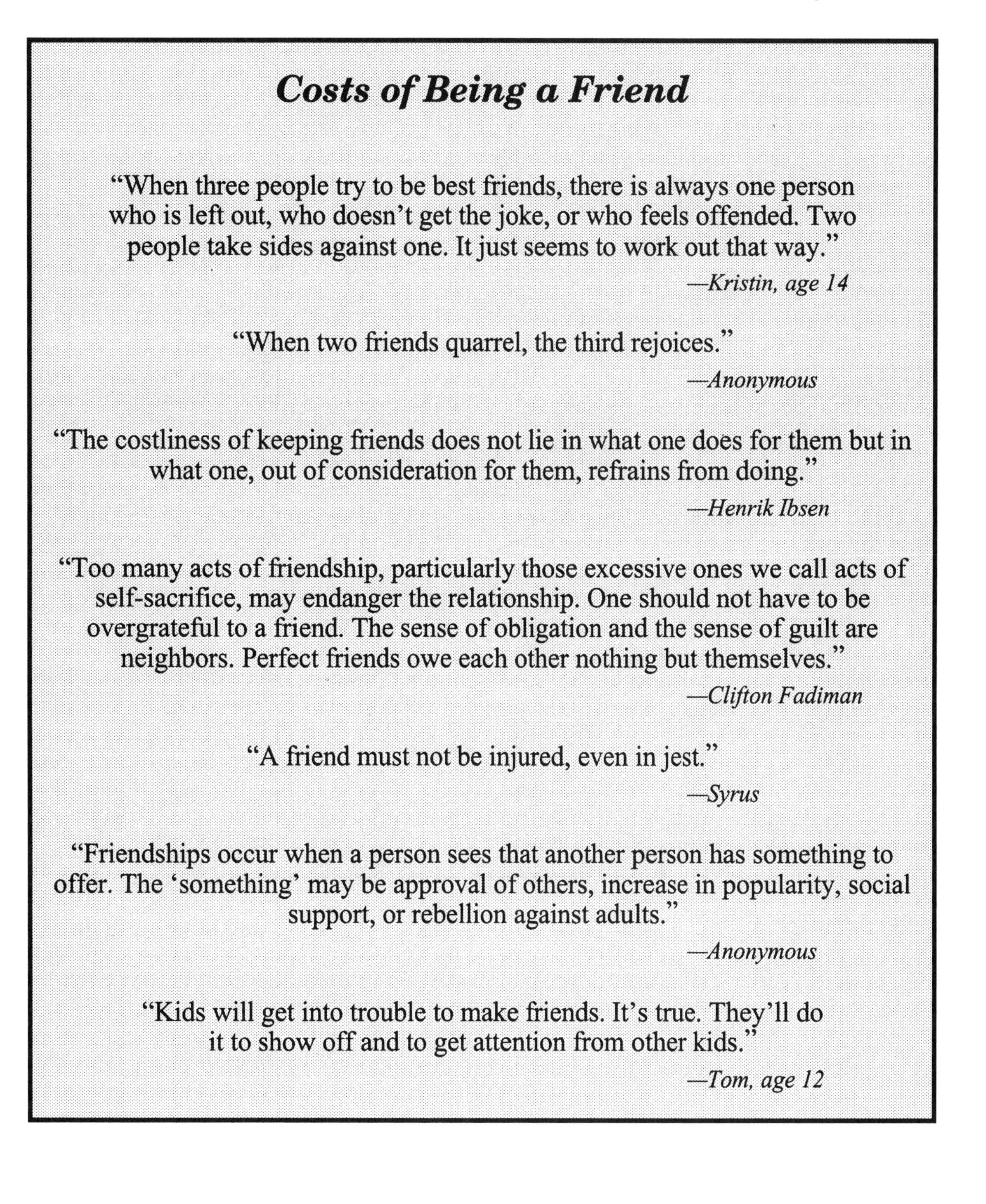

Costs of Being a Friend

"When three people try to be best friends, there is always one person who is left out, who doesn't get the joke, or who feels offended. Two people take sides against one. It just seems to work out that way."

—*Kristin, age 14*

"When two friends quarrel, the third rejoices."

—*Anonymous*

"The costliness of keeping friends does not lie in what one does for them but in what one, out of consideration for them, refrains from doing."

—*Henrik Ibsen*

"Too many acts of friendship, particularly those excessive ones we call acts of self-sacrifice, may endanger the relationship. One should not have to be overgrateful to a friend. The sense of obligation and the sense of guilt are neighbors. Perfect friends owe each other nothing but themselves."

—*Clifton Fadiman*

"A friend must not be injured, even in jest."

—*Syrus*

"Friendships occur when a person sees that another person has something to offer. The 'something' may be approval of others, increase in popularity, social support, or rebellion against adults."

—*Anonymous*

"Kids will get into trouble to make friends. It's true. They'll do it to show off and to get attention from other kids."

—*Tom, age 12*

SUPPLEMENTARY ACTIVITY #7 HANDOUT #1F

Quotes About Friendship (continued)

Costs of Being a Friend (continued)

"Popularity is one of the major concerns of all kids. Most kids would do anything to be popular."

—Jared, age 14

"When your needs change, you grow out of friendships. And there's nothing wrong with not being good friends anymore. Just because you're friends for a long time doesn't mean you have to be friends always."

—Jeff, age 12

SUPPLEMENTARY ACTIVITY #8

Taking Time for Friendship

Objective

This activity reinforces the learning of the "12 Keys to Making and Keeping Friends" handout.

Materials

Transparencies #4-#6 from the lesson, copied onto heavy paper (you may wish to enlarge these on your copy machine for better visibility)

Tape

Procedure

Copy Transparencies #4-#6 and cut out the "Keys." Tape these around the perimeter of your classroom clock, as shown in the illustration below. Now every time students check the clock, they'll also see the keys of friendship.

Listening—The Way to Show You Are a Friend

Objective

Students will learn three Keys to Good Listening: looking at the speaker, allowing the speaker to finish, and saying something to show that they're listening.

Materials

Blank transparency and pen

Transparency #1 - "Nonlistening Behaviors"

Transparency #2 - "Keys to Good Listening—#1"

Transparency #3 - "Keys to Good Listening—#2"

Transparency #4 - "Keys to Good Listening—#3"

Transparency #5 - "Things a Good Listener Can Say"

Handout #1 - "How Well Did You Listen?"

Handout #2 - "How Well Were You Listened To?"

Handouts #3A and #3B - "Encouraging the Speaker to Tell You More"

To the Teacher

This lesson attempts to help students realize that one of the key elements to having friends is listening. Someone once said, "Listening is loving." When we listen to others we show them we think their ideas are important. True listening works wonders in human relations, yet few people have an awareness of the importance of this day-to-day social interaction. Teaching students to truly listen to one another is a gift that will be useful to them throughout their lives.

No one was born knowing how to listen effectively to others; it is an acquired skill and one of the hardest to learn. It demands a high level of concentration and energy. It involves the ability to put oneself in another person's place, to see the world through that person's eyes, and to sense the feelings behind the person's words.

In this lesson students learn the posture for listening. Good listeners move their bodies in response to the speaker. They almost unconsciously use nodding, smiling, frowning, and raising eyebrows to respond to a speaker's message.

Students are encouraged to look at the person talking. Effective eye contact expresses interest and a desire to listen. It involves gently focusing one's eyes on the speaker. Occasionally the gaze will shift from the face to other parts of the body; i.e., to a gesturing hand, then back to the face, and then to eye contact once again.

Poor eye contact occurs when a listener repeatedly looks away from the speaker, stares at him/her constantly or blankly, or looks away as soon as the speaker looks at the listener. However, if looking at a speaker, particularly an adult, is not appropriate in a student's culture, the student's cultural custom should be honored.

Students are also encouraged to make comments to show they're listening, and to ask appropriate questions and rephrase information in a summary statement.

Don't be concerned if when practicing these skills students come across as artificial. Much research has been done regarding the components of authentic listening, and unless students use the behaviors that have been isolated and identified as keys to listening, they will not be perceived as good listeners. Although they may begin using these listening skills in an artificial and deliberate manner, students will gradually internalize these skills. Allen Ivey, a researcher in the area of listening, puts it this way:

> *Once listening has been initiated, the person to whom one is listening tends to become more animated, and this in turn reinforces the listener, who very quickly forgets about listening deliberately and soon listens naturally.*
>
> Allen Ivey (1988)
> *International Interviewing*

Thinking about the importance of good listening brings up the issue of how teachers listen to students. Listening is the best way to teach students that they are valuable. If you tried to really listen to everything your students want to tell you, however, you would be too exhausted to accomplish anything else. What is required is a balance of selected listening and true listening. You can explain to students that there are times when you simply can't listen to them well, and that they should not take this personally. If a student has an urgent need for totally focused listening, he/she should be encouraged to tell you so and then the two of you can try to arrange a time for this.

After teaching this lesson, look for opportunities to compliment those students who listen well. Ask students to tell you when they have used the listening skills they've learned. When you are presenting information in any subject area, stop in the middle of your talk and ask students to turn to a person next to them and share what they have just heard. Now and then ask a student to repeat the last thing you said. This teaching technique aids in retention of material as well as providing practice in the listening skill "summarizing."

If your school uses a grade-leveled approach to this curriculum, the lesson itself can be taught each year as it contains life skills that need to be emphasized and practiced each year. Use the following Supplementary Activities at these suggested grade levels:

4th "The Talk Show Game"
(Supplementary Activity #1)
"Listening Only With Your Ears"
(Supplementary Activity #2)
"Listener of the Day"
(Supplementary Activity #3)

5th "Listening Role-Plays"
(Supplementary Activity #4)
"Active Listening"
(Supplementary Activity #5)
"Mirroring"
(Supplementary Activity #6)

6th "The Listening Game"
(Supplementary Activity #7)
"Good or Poor Listener Role-Play"
(Supplementary Activity #8)

Lesson Presentation

Say or paraphrase: **We've been talking about what a good friend is and behaviors that cause people to like us. Today we're going to talk about one of the most important things to do if you want to be well-liked by others. You may be surprised to hear this, but one of the friendliest things you can do is to LISTEN when people talk to you. Way back in 300 B.C., a wise person said, "The reason we have two ears and only one mouth is so that we may listen more and talk less."**

Listening is a hard thing to do. It takes a lot of self-control to listen to what someone is saying instead of thinking about what you want to say. It's especially hard to listen when you have something important to say.

BEHAVIORS TELL WHETHER OR NOT YOU'RE LISTENING

How many of you have ever tried to tell someone something and felt like they weren't listening to you? Maybe it was another kid you were talking to, or maybe it was an adult. *Hold up your hand and encourage students to indicate if they've had a similar experience.* **It's not much fun to talk to someone who doesn't listen, is it?**

We can usually tell whether someone is listening by the way they act. Let me show you what I mean. Will someone volunteer to help me do a role-play? I need someone to tell me about something they have done or seen, and I'll play the role of a poor listener. I want the rest of you to watch and see if you can find all the things I do that show I'm not listening.

Choose a volunteer and help him / her choose a topic to talk about—a past experience, a sports event, a movie, something he / she is doing at home, etc. While the volunteer speaks, model as many inappropriate listening behaviors as you can—<u>inattention</u> (e.g., by not looking at the speaker, looking out the window, turning your body away, fidgeting with your hair or clothing, or looking for something in your purse or on your desk); <u>acting bored</u> (e.g., by rocking back and forth on your feet, etc.); <u>putting the speaker down</u> (e.g., saying, "So what's so great about that?"); and <u>changing the subject or interrupting</u>, (e.g., saying "You think that's good? Wait until you hear what <u>I</u> did! I . . .").

Blank Transp.
Transp. #1

After a few minutes, stop the role-play and ask the volunteer how it felt to talk to someone who behaved as you did. Ask the class to identify poor listening behaviors they saw modeled; write them on a clean transparency. Then show them Transparency #1, "Nonlistening Behaviors."

No one wants to talk to someone who acts the way I did, do they? If I want to be liked by others I'll need to listen when someone talks. Let's give me another chance, O.K.? Will someone else volunteer to come up and talk to me? This time I'll try to be a good listener; the rest of you watch

carefully and see if you can notice the things I'm doing to show that I'm listening.

Repeat the role-play. While the volunteer is speaking, model the following behaviors in a sincere manner: turn your body toward the speaker and make good eye contact; have an interested expression on your face; nod your head from time to time and make encouraging comments, such as "Oh, no!" "Hmmm," "Really," or "Wow"; and ask questions such as, "And then what happened?" as they are appropriate.

After a few minutes, stop the role-play and ask the volunteer how it was to talk to you—did he or she feel listened to? Why? Ask the class to identify behaviors that showed you were listening. If necessary, coach them with questions such as,"What did I do with my eyes?" "What did I do with my body?" "How did I show I was listening by what I said?" Add any behaviors overlooked by the students.

LOOK AT THE PERSON TO SHOW YOU'RE LISTENING

Transp. #2

All the things I did to show I was listening can be summed up as three "Keys to Good Listening." The first one is probably the easiest. *Put Transparency #2, "Keys to Good Listening—#1, on the overhead.* **That key is to "Look at the person."**

When we look at someone, they know our attention is on them. They know we're interested in what they're saying. If I were to walk over and look out the window while you were talking to me, I could probably still hear what you were saying, but how would that make you feel? Would you feel listened to? *Allow for student response.* **No, you would probably think I didn't care what you were saying. So it's important to keep your attention on the person who's speaking to you so they'll know you're interested.**

There's another reason for looking at someone who's talking to you. Sometimes you can learn a lot about how a person is feeling by the way their face looks or how they move their body. Let me show you what I mean. In a minute I'm going to ask you to close your eyes. I'm going to say "Put

the book on the table." As soon as you think you know how I'm feeling, I want you to open your eyes and see if you're right. Does everyone understand how the game goes? O.K. Now, close your eyes and see if you can guess how I'm feeling.

When students have closed their eyes, assume an angry expression, hands on hips, and say, "Put the book on the table." Use a calm, level voice without inflection.

O.K. How many of you guessed right? Let's try again. Close your eyes. When you think you know how I'm feeling, open your eyes.

Do the exercise two more times, assuming a sad expression and then assuming a cheerful expression. Each time say, "Put the book on the table" in the same calm, even voice. Ask students if they were able to guess your feeling.

So you see—a person's face and body can tell you a lot! You can use your eyes as well as your ears to listen. With practice you can almost "see" what people are thinking and feeling. Really, only a small amount of the meaning of what a person expresses to us comes from the words we hear. More than two-thirds of the meaning (actually 85%) comes from what we call their "body language." This includes the way they stand, their gestures and movements, and their facial expressions. Someone's face can tell you a lot about what is being said. So you can use your eyes, as well as your ears, to listen.

Looking at people who are talking to you is often a way to show them you are listening to them. Looking at a person doesn't mean "staring them down," but it does mean looking at their face most of the time when they are talking.

LET THE OTHER PERSON FINISH SPEAKING

Transp. #3

The second of the Keys to Good Listening is just as important as the first one, and it's a little harder to do. *Put Transparency #3, "Keys to Good Listening—#2," on the overhead.*

If you're going to be a good listener, you will let the other person finish what he or she is saying. That means that, even if you think of something WONDERFUL to tell, you won't interrupt! You won't say something like, "That's nothing! Listen to what happened to me!" Not only are we interrupting when we say something like that—we're giving a put-down. We might as well just come right out and say, "Your story is no good; mine is better!" No one wants to talk to someone who says things like that!

When we think of something we want to tell, it wants to pop right out of us. But if we want to be good listeners, we'll let the other person finish before we tell ours.

If you can look at the person who's talking to you and let them finish what they're saying, then you'll be a good listener. People will be glad to talk to you because they'll know that you pay attention to them when they talk.

SAY SOMETHING TO SHOW YOU'RE LISTENING

Transp. #4

The third of our Keys to Good Listening is kind of a bonus key. You don't have to do it to be a good listener, but it makes you sort of a "Super Listener" if you do. *Put Transparency #4, "Keys to Good Listening—#3," on the overhead.*

The most fun people to talk to are the ones who say things to let you know they're listening. They don't jump in with their own stories before you're finished with yours—instead they say little things to show they're interested in what you're saying.

Transp. #5

Put Transparency #5, "Things a Good Listener Can Say," on the overhead. Cover Items 2 and 3. **A good listener can use what we call "brief encouragers." A brief encourager is just a little sound like "Mmm" or a word like "Wow" that lets the speaker know you're listening.** *Go over the list of brief encouragers and ask students for their favorites to add to the list.*

Uncover Item 2 on the transparency. **Another thing the Super Listener can do is to ask questions to show that you're interested in knowing more. These are questions that help**

the speaker tell their story and make it more fun for both of you. These are "what/where/when/how" kinds of questions. *Go over the list of questions and ask students for their favorites to add to the list.*

When we ask a speaker questions, we need to ask them at a good time. If we ask too many questions, it can be just like interrupting. When we <u>do</u> ask a question, it's important to listen to the answer. We don't want to make the speaker think we're asking questions just because we want to <u>seem</u> like good listeners!

Uncover Item 3 on the transparency. **Another great way to show that you're listening is by summing up what the person is saying. It gives you a chance to check out what you think you've heard and it shows the speaker you care enough to be sure you've understood. Here are some ways you can summarize what was said.** *Read the examples on the overhead and write down student suggestions.*

Let's do an easy practice on this. See if you can tell whether I'm using a brief encourager, a question, or summarizing what the speaker said. I'll ask a volunteer to come up and tell me about an experience he or she has had or something they've done. I'll be the listener, and I'll practice saying things to show the volunteer I'm listening. If you hear me use a "brief encourager," you hold up one finger for #1 on the transparency. If you hear me ask a question, hold up two fingers for #2 on the transparency. If I summarize what the volunteer is saying, hold up three fingers for #3 on the transparency.

Choose a volunteer who you think could narrate an experience. Use one of the topics bulleted in the next section of this lesson if necessary. Model listening using the three categories on Transparency #5; have students hold up fingers to indicate which type of response you are modeling. You may wish to choose a second volunteer and repeat the exercise. If you think some students could model these skills well, ask them to take the listener role and model listening using the three categories of responses.

PRACTICING THE THREE KEYS TO GOOD LISTENING

Let's see if anyone can tell us what the three Keys to Good Listening are. *Call on volunteers to recall the three keys and put Transparencies #2, #3, and #4 on the overhead as each is recalled.*

Let's practice the three Keys to Good Listening with our Learning Partners. The taller partner will be the first speaker. *Suggest that students talk about one of the following topics (you may want to list two or three on the board or overhead so they can choose one they can talk a lot about):*

- *Something that doesn't seem fair to you;*
- *The biggest surprise you ever had;*
- *Your favorite movie and the parts you liked best;*
- *A time your brother or sister really made you mad; or*
- *Your favorite pet and some experience you've had with it.*

Say: **Listeners, it will be your job to use the three Keys to Good Listening—you will look at the speaker, you will let him or her finish without interrupting, and you will say things that show you're listening. Afterwards we will fill out some evaluation sheets that tell how good a listening job you did. All right! Speakers, begin your story.**

Handout #1
Handout #2

After two or three minutes, stop the narratives and distribute Handout #1, "How Well Did You Listen?" to the Listeners and Handout #2, "How Well Were You Listened To?" to the Speakers. Have both students write the Listener's name on the line at the top of their handout. After the checklists are completed, have students turn them over on their desks. Have Learning Partners switch roles and repeat the speaking / listening exercise. Distribute Handouts #1 and #2 again, so that all Learning Partners have evaluated both themselves and their partners. Have Learning Partners give each other the sheets that have their own names on them.

Lead students in discussing their evaluation sheets by asking the following questions: How did your own evaluation compare with your Learning Partner's evaluation of you as a listener? Did you find some ways you could improve? What were you good at? Do you think it would be good if everyone tried to listen as well as you tried to in the exercise? Is listening a good way to get to know someone? How much real listening takes place on the playground or in the lunchroom? Do kids listen better to adults or to each other?

LESSON REVIEW AND NOTICING HOW OTHERS SPEAK AND LISTEN

Say or paraphrase: **So, today you learned to show someone you're listening by looking at them, by not interrupting, by nodding or saying something to show you understand, by asking questions, and by summing up what the person said.**

Now that you're learning to be a good listener, don't be surprised at how much work it is! Some people are just plain boring and take a long time to say things, repeat themselves, or give too many details. When you notice people going on and on when they tell about something, make a promise to yourselves that you won't do that when you tell about things. Promise yourself you won't bore people—that you'll get right to the point. Even if a person does speak quickly and to the point, our brain is still able to think faster than any person can talk. That's why it takes a lot of patience to be a good listener. Both by being a good listener and not boring people when you talk, you'll be the kind of friend everyone wants to have.

Another thing you'll probably notice as you get to be a better listener is that a lot of other people don't listen very well. They haven't been lucky enough to have a lesson on listening. Most don't even realize they're not good listeners. It's not a good idea to criticize the way others listen—just be glad that you're learning how to and that people will respect you for it!

PRACTICING LISTENING SKILLS FOR HOMEWORK

Handout #3A
Handout #3B

Using the Keys to Good Listening may seem a little awkward at first, but with practice, it will become natural for you. There are two things I want you to do to practice. The first is a homework assignment. *Distribute Handouts #3A and #3B, "Encouraging the Speaker to Tell You More."* **I want you to write on the "Listener" blanks something you could say to encourage the Speaker to tell you more. Don't give them any advice; just show them you're interested in what they have to say.**

The second thing I want you to do is to choose one person you're going to practice <u>really</u> listening to between now and the next listening lesson. It can be anybody—even someone at home! I want you to take your pen or marker and write that person's name on your hand in tiny letters. Use the three Keys to Good Listening on that person and see how good a friend you can be! Write down on your think pad what the three keys to being a good listener are, then hold it up and show me.

LESSON REVIEW

Invite students to reflect on and evaluate the lesson by having them respond to one or more of the following sentence stems:

- *The thing about this lesson I'll remember most is . . . .*
- *The main idea seems to be . . . .*
- *I like it when . . . .*
- *It will be hard to . . . .*
- *The thing I will do as a result of this lesson is . . . .*

Use the Supplementary Activities to provide practice of the skills taught in this lesson.

TRANSPARENCY #1

TRANSPARENCY #2

Keys to Good Listening—#1

TRANSPARENCY #3

Keys to Good Listening—#2

TRANSPARENCY #4

Keys to Good Listening—#3

TRANSPARENCY #5

Things a Good Listener Can Say

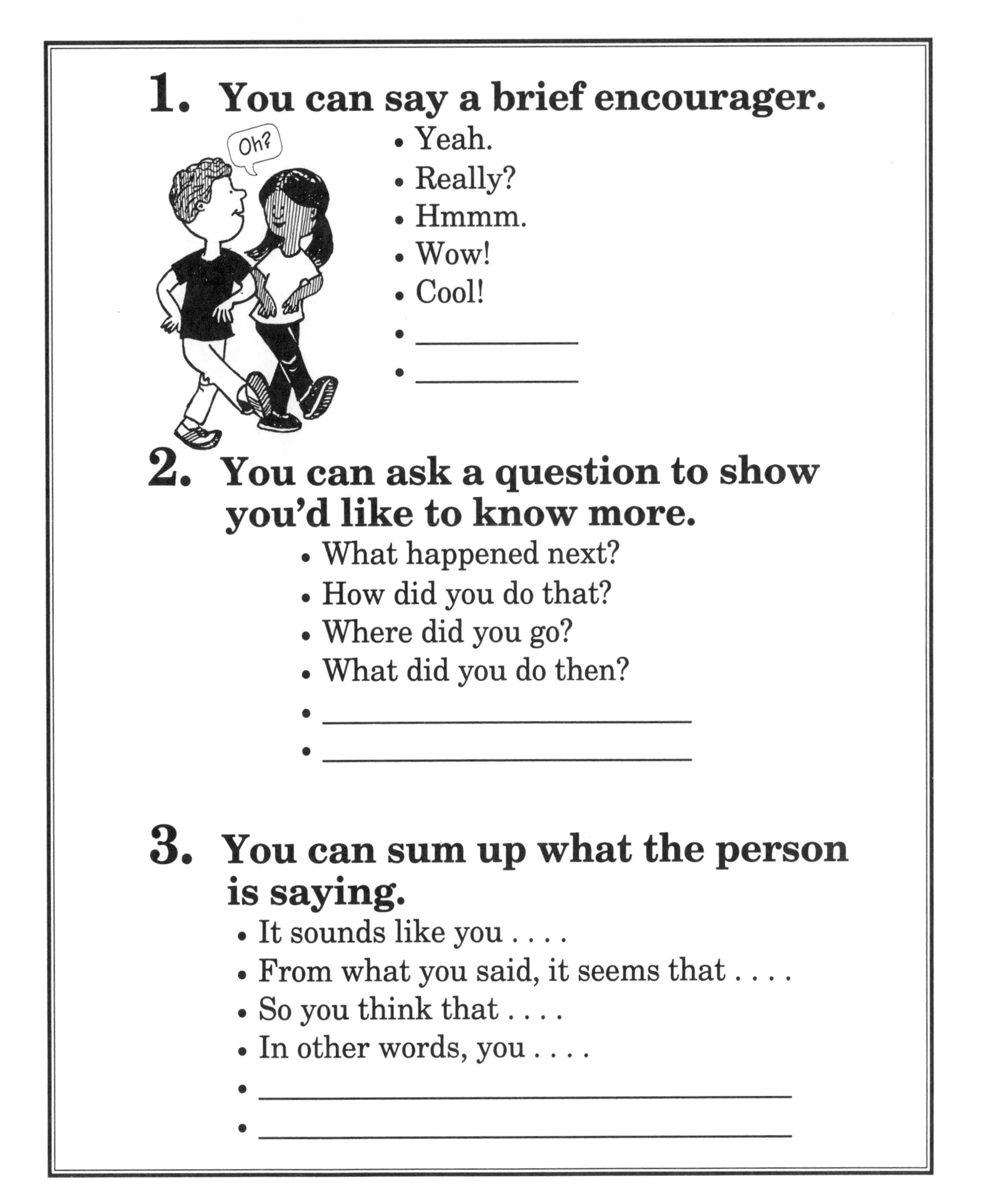

1. You can say a brief encourager.

- Yeah.
- Really?
- Hmmm.
- Wow!
- Cool!
- ____________
- ____________

2. You can ask a question to show you'd like to know more.

- What happened next?
- How did you do that?
- Where did you go?
- What did you do then?
- ____________________________
- ____________________________

3. You can sum up what the person is saying.

- It sounds like you . . . .
- From what you said, it seems that . . . .
- So you think that . . . .
- In other words, you . . . .
- ____
- ____

HANDOUT #1

How Well Did You Listen?

*Listener*_______________________

Put a check next to the things you did while you were listening.

1. _____ I sat quietly while the Speaker was talking.
2. _____ I ignored the distractions around the room.
3. _____ I faced the Speaker.
4. _____ I watched the expression on the Speaker's face.
5. _____ I thought about what the Speaker was saying and not just about what I wanted to say.
6. _____ I nodded my head now and then to show I was interested in what the Speaker was saying.
7. _____ I made little comments to show I was listening.
8. _____ I asked questions to encourage the Speaker to tell me more.
9. _____ I let the Speaker finish talking before I asked a question.
10. _____ I summed up what the Speaker said.

One of the things I could have done a little better is

_______________________________.

HANDOUT #2

How Well Were You Listened To?

*Speaker*______________________

Put a check next to the things the Listener did while you were speaking.

1. _____ Did the Listener sit quietly while you were talking?
2. _____ Did the Listener ignore any distractions around the room?
3. _____ Did the Listener face you?
4. _____ Did the Listener notice your facial expressions while you spoke?
5. _____ Did the Listener nod his or her head to show interest in what you were saying?
6. _____ Did the Listener make comments to show he or she was listening?
7. _____ Did the Listener ask questions to encourage you to tell him or her more?
8. _____ Did the Listener allow you to finish talking before asking questions?
9. _____ Did the Listener sum up what you said?
10. _____ Did the Listener give you his or her complete attention?

HANDOUT #3A

Encouraging the Speaker to Tell You More

Directions:

Write something in the Listener's space to show you are listening and to encourage the speaker to tell you more. Don't feel you have to solve any problems for the Speaker or give advice. Just say something to show you are interested in what the Speaker is talking about.

Speaker: Did we ever have a close call this morning! A car pulled out in front of the school bus and we had to swerve off the road to miss it. Everybody was pretty shaken up by the time we got to school.

Listener: ______________________________

Speaker: I just found out today. I didn't make the team.

Listener: ______________________________

Speaker: There is room at both of the camps I wanted to go to. Now I really have a problem trying to decide which one to attend.

Listener: ______________________________

Speaker: We had so much fun at Waterworks Park.

Listener: ______________________________

HANDOUT #3B

Encouraging the Speaker to Tell You More (continued)

Speaker: You know, I think I'm old enough now to have a little privacy, but my parents are nosing around my room all the time, and I get the feeling that they don't trust me.

Listener: ______________________________

Speaker: Just because I had one good game, the coach expects all my games to be great.

Listener: ______________________________

Speaker: If I could just do as well in baseball as I do in basketball, things would be O.K.

Listener: ______________________________

Speaker: I built this thing myself.

Listener: ______________________________

Speaker: Every time I try to get reasons from my parents, they just say, "because I say so."

Listener: ______________________________

Speaker: It's a hassle trying to keep my parents happy and do what my friends want me to do.

Listener: ______________________________

SUPPLEMENTARY ACTIVITY #1

The Talk Show Game

Objective

Students will practice showing they listened by repeating or summarizing what the speaker said.

Materials

Real microphone or makeshift "microphone" made from a wad of paper or rubber ball taped to the end of a pencil

Show-and-tell objects from students' homes

Procedure

The day before the game is played, instruct students to bring something from home that they would like to show to the class. (Plan to bring a few objects yourself for any students who forget.)

Choose four or five students to act as a performance group and play the game in front of the class (alternately, divide the class into small groups so that all can play simultaneously). Designate one student in the group to be the Talk Show Host and give that student the "microphone." The remaining students in the group are to be the "guests" who are there to tell about the object they brought from home.

The Talk Show Host holds the microphone and asks one of the guests his or her name and what he or she brought to share with the TV audience (the rest of the class). The Guest answers. The Host repeats the Guest's name and asks him or her to tell the audience two or three things about the object. The Guest responds. The Host repeats the information and thanks the Guest. The Guest then becomes the Talk Show Host and interviews the next Guest in the same way.

VARIATIONS

1. **For a simultaneous groups format:** After each student has been interviewed, everyone in the group writes several sentences about each of the objects shown in their group.
2. **For a performance group format:** After each student has been interviewed, ask each student in the class to tell what he or she remembers about one of the objects shown by the group.

3. **For a performance group format:** After several groups have performed, place all the objects from those groups at the front of the room and have everyone in the class write all they can remember about 5-10 of the objects they heard described.

SUPPLEMENTARY ACTIVITY #2

Listening Only With Your Ears

Objective

Students will experience the value of "eye contact" when listening to others.

Materials

Blindfolds (for each student)

Procedure

Explain to students that you would like them to try an activity that will help them understand why looking at someone is one of the Keys to Good Listening. Have students divide into groups of three or four. Blindfold everyone. Have groups have a short discussion on one of the topics below.

- What is a fair bed time for kids our age?
- How many recesses should students in grades 1-3 have? How many should students in grades 4-6 have?
- How many minutes of homework should each grade level have?
- Should schools have pop and candy vending machines? Why or why not?

After the discussion, ask students to share their reactions to this activity.

SUPPLEMENTARY ACTIVITY #3

Listener of the Day

Objective

Students will practice the good listening skills which were taught in the lesson in a daily classroom setting.

Materials

Supplementary Activity #3 Materials Sheet, "Listener of the Day Badges" decorated with glitter, stars, etc. if you like

Five 4" x 3" pin style name badges (convention size)

Procedure

At the beginning of the day, tell the class that you are going to designate several students to be official "Listeners of the Day." Tell them that the class can count on these official Listeners to model the three Keys to Good Listening—"Look at the person."; "Let the person finish."; and "Say something to show you're listening." Encourage students to give these Listeners plenty of opportunity to practice their listening skills. The Listeners of the Day will report to the class at the end of the day.

Choose five students to be Listeners of the Day and give them their badges. Talk to them about the importance of their job for that day and the role they can play in making their classroom a friendlier place.

At the end of the day, have the Listeners of the Day sit in front of the class. Ask for a show of hands of all the students who "helped" the five Listeners practice their listening skills. Call on two or three students to "evaluate" each of the five Listeners by saying something positive about the way the Listener listened when they talked to one of them. Ask the Listeners if they have any comments.

The next morning, designate five new Listeners of the Day. After the "evaluation" of the new Listeners at the end of that day, ask one or more of the previous day's Listeners if they can give an example of a time on that day when they continued to listen well. Continue designating five new Listeners each day until all students have had a turn.

In order to further reinforce good listening habits, in the following days or weeks be sure to ask any of the previous Listeners to give you recent examples of times they listened well.

SUPPLEMENTARY ACTIVITY #3 MATERIALS SHEET

Listener of the Day Badges

SUPPLEMENTARY ACTIVITY #4

Listening Role-Plays

Objective

Students will practice the three Keys to Good Listening using a role-play format. Students will observe and evaluate the skills of their peers.

Materials

Supplementary Activity #4 Handout, "Observation Sheet" for each Observer

Optional Supplementary Activity #4 Transparency, "Observation Sheet"

Procedure

Review the three Keys to Good Listening from the lesson. Divide the class into triads and assign each student a role within their triad—Speaker, Listener, or Observer.

Tell the students you will read a topic (following) and the Speaker will speak about that topic for 20-30 seconds. (You may wish to read two topics and let the Listener choose one to discuss.) The Listener will practice looking at the person, letting the other person finish, and saying something to show they are listening. Read over the "Observation Sheet" or show it on the overhead and explain to the Observers that they are to watch for the three Keys to Good Listening, marking them on the Observation Sheet when the Listener uses them. Stress that all students will have an opportunity to play each of the three roles and that each student will be observed.

Observers may give their Observation Sheets to the Listeners as soon as each role play is over or keep them until the end of the activity. When all students have had their turn to be observed as a Listener, discuss the Observation Sheet results with the class. Ask for volunteers to answer such questions as, "What were your strong points?" "How could you improve as a listener?" "What was something you said to show you were listening?"

Possible Discussion Topics

1. Something that doesn't seem fair to me.
2. The funniest thing I ever saw.
3. If I ran the school.
4. A time I really had fun.
5. What I would do if I won $1,000.
6. My favorite place to go.
7. Something my brother/sister does that bugs me.
8. What I see as the biggest waste there is.

SUPPLEMENTARY ACTIVITY #4 HANDOUT/OPTIONAL TRANSPARENCY

Observation Sheet

Your Name ____________________

The Listener's Name____________________

The Listener . . .

- **Looked at the person.** yes ❑ no ❑
- **Let the other person finish.** yes ❑ no ❑
- **Nodded or said something to show they were listening.** yes ❑ no ❑

An example of what the Listener said was:

____

____

Observation Sheet

Your Name ____________________

The Listener's Name____________________

The Listener . . .

- **Looked at the person.** yes ❑ no ❑
- **Let the other person finish.** yes ❑ no ❑
- **Nodded or said something to show they were listening.** yes ❑ no ❑

An example of what the Listener said was:

____

____

SUPPLEMENTARY ACTIVITY #5

Active Listening

Objective

Students will practice showing they're listening by making an appropriate comment when given cue statements.

Materials

Handout #1A and #1B, "Say Something to Show You're Listening"

Procedure

This activity can be done in either of the two variations listed below.

VARIATIONS

1. Read the statements from the "Say Something to Show You're Listening" handout one at a time, calling on two or three students to practice the skill of saying something to show they're listening by: (1) using an "encourager," (2) asking a question, or (3) summing up what the speaker said. After each student's response, discuss whether it showed the speaker that they were listening and which of the three kinds of responses it was.

2. Distribute copies of the "Say Something to Show You're Listening" handout to students. Do the first two examples together, then ask them to complete the exercise individually. After the students have completed the exercise, read each statement and call on volunteers to read the statement they wrote on their papers. Discuss whether their response showed that they were listening and which of the three kinds of responses it was.

SUPPLEMENTARY ACTIVITY #5 HANDOUT #1A

Say Something to Show You're Listening

1. I'm going to run my first 5K on Saturday. 3.1 miles is a long way!

   ____

2. My mom and I had a really long talk last night. I think she really listened to what I had to say.

   ____

3. Mr. Rodriguez asked me to leave class this morning. I can't seem to do anything right in there anymore!

   ____

4. I can't believe it! I got an "A" on my math test for a change!

   ____

5. I've got a book report due on Friday, a science test tomorrow, a baseball game tomorrow after school, and my folks expect me to go to my brother's graduation tonight!

   ____

6. Mrs. Gustafson caught me daydreaming again today. I can't seem to keep my mind on schoolwork.

   ____

7. Jason and I have been friends a long time, but lately he seems to be mad at me about something.

   ____

SUPPLEMENTARY ACTIVITY #5 HANDOUT #1B

Say Something to Show You're Listening (continued)

8. Wow! After three months I finally saved enough money for a new skateboard. I'm going to get it this weekend!

____

9. I saw a really great movie on TV last night!

____

10. I can't believe it! Just because I left off a little decimal point, I failed the math test! The teacher is too picky!

____

11. I won't be able to go to the video game shop with you this afternoon. I'm grounded for the next two weeks.

____

12. My dad and my sister had a major argument last night. They yelled and carried on for a long time. Then my sister stormed out of the house and we haven't heard a word from her since.

____

SUPPLEMENTARY ACTIVITY #6

Mirroring

Objective

The students will practice listening skills with paired activity and group discussion

Materials

None

Procedure

Divide the students into pairs. Each student should give his or her partner a verbal autobiography, including things like interests, hobbies, likes, dislikes, and wishes. Have students brainstorm the specific personal topics they will talk about and list these on the board. After topics are decided upon, explain these rules:

1. Each person is to talk for three minutes about themselves, telling their partner as much as they can. After the first person finishes, the second member of the pair begins the same thing.
2. When the Speaker is talking, the Listener should not speak, interrupt, or ask questions. They should simply listen.
3. The conversation should be kept in a low tone so as not to disturb the other pairs.

When they understand what they are to do, have them begin. After one minute is up, have the Speaker become the Listener.

When both partners have had their turns, explain that now you are going to test how well they listened. Form a circle and have the partners pretend they are each other. For example, if John and Mary are partners, John will say, "I am Mary and I . . . ." As much as possible, John should use the exact words and mirror the feelings and expressions Mary used in describing herself. Mary will then respond by stating the degree to which John accurately represented her and how she feels hearing someone speak and act as if they were her. When done, she will then represent John and he will respond as she did previously.

SUPPLEMENTARY ACTIVITY #7

The Listening Game

Objective

Students will identify positive and negative listening behaviors as they are modeled by other students using a role-play format.

Materials

Stack of Scenario Cards (Supplementary Activity #7 Cards Pages #1-#3), cut up prior to the activity

Stack of Action Cards (Supplementary Activity #7 Cards Pages #4-#5), cut up prior to the activity

Two chairs at the front of the room

Procedure

Divide the class into two teams. Tell the teams they'll be watching role-plays and trying to identify the listening behavior the actor is modeling. When they think they know what is being modeled, they are to raise their hands. You will call on someone first from one team and then from the other until someone gives the correct answer. Whoever can correctly describe the listening behavior and tell whether it is a positive or negative behavior will win a point for their team.

Choose a pair of volunteers. One will be the Speaker and the other the Listener. Seat them at the front of the room where everyone can see them. The Speaker draws two Scenario Cards from the stack, and the Listener draws one Action Card from the stack. The Speaker reads the two cards silently, chooses one, and talks to the Listener for 20-30 seconds about the topic on the card. The Listener models in a realistic manner the behavior written on the Action Card. (You may wish to make a rule that a gross exaggeration of the behavior by the Listener can cause his or her team to lose a point or a turn.) After they have done the role-play and the point has been awarded, choose two new volunteers and continue with the next role-play.

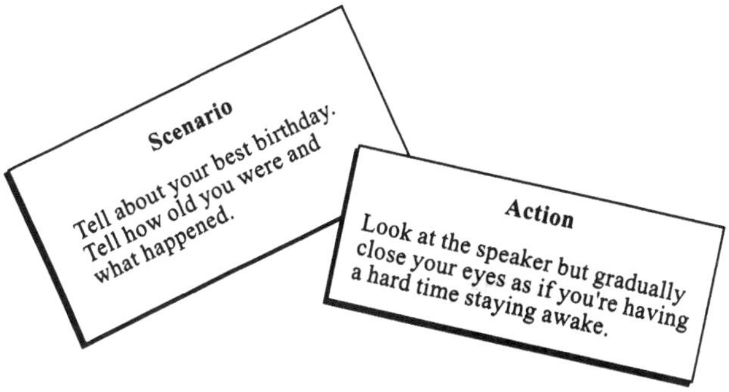

SUPPLEMENTARY ACTIVITY #7 CARDS PAGE #1

Scenario Cards

Scenario Talk about something you like at school. Describe it and tell why you like it.	Scenario Tell about your best birthday. Tell how old you were and what happened.
Scenario Talk about something you don't like about school. Describe it and tell why you dislike it so much.	Scenario Tell all about a time your brother or sister made you really mad.
Scenario Talk about your favorite sport. Tell about a player you especially look up to and about experiences you may have had playing or watching the sport.	Scenario Tell about one of the funniest things that ever happened to you.
Scenario Talk about your favorite animal and any experiences you may have had with that animal.	Scenario Tell what you would do if you won $10,000.

SUPPLEMENTARY ACTIVITY #7 CARDS PAGE #2

Scenario Cards (continued)

Scenario Describe how to do something you know how to do. Tell all the steps of doing it well.	**Scenario** Tell about the biggest surprise you ever had.
Scenario If you could take a trip anywhere, where would it be? Describe your dream trip.	**Scenario** Tell about a movie you really liked. What were your favorite parts?
Scenario Tell about a time you were injured and had to go to the doctor.	**Scenario** Describe your very best vacation.
Scenario Describe your favorite place.	**Scenario** What would your ideal Saturday be like? Describe it.

SUPPLEMENTARY ACTIVITY #7 CARDS PAGE #3

Scenario Cards (continued)

Scenario	Scenario
What is the hardest thing you've ever done? Describe it and tell how you did it.	Give your opinion of homework. Do you think teachers should give it? Why or why not? Give reasons for your opinion.
Scenario	**Scenario**
What are some things you think could be done to make school a better place? Why?	What do you think your life will be like when you grow up? Will you get married or have children? What kind of work will you do? Where will you live? What kinds of things will you do?
Scenario	**Scenario**
What are some things you would do if you were President of our country?	If you could be any person in history, who would you be and what would you do?
Scenario	**Scenario**
What is your idea of a perfect bedroom?	What are the clearest memories you have of when you were small?

SUPPLEMENTARY ACTIVITY #7 CARDS PAGE #4

Action Cards

Action	Action
Lean forward and look at the Speaker.	Pick at your fingernails and look down.
Action Look at the Speaker but fidget in your chair as if you can't get comfortable.	**Action** Look at the Speaker and nod your head now and then to show you're listening.
Action Retie your shoestrings or adjust your socks.	**Action** Smile at the Speaker, but look at the clock several times.
Action Look at the Speaker and nod every once in a while.	**Action** Look at the Speaker and smile, but yawn several times, covering your mouth when you yawn.
Action Look at the Speaker with an interested expression on your face.	**Action** Glance out the window while the Speaker is talking.
Action Look at the Speaker but adjust your clothing while the speaker talks—for instance, tuck in your shirt, roll up your sleeves, straighten your collar.	**Action** Play with your hair or comb it.

SUPPLEMENTARY ACTIVITY #7 CARDS PAGE #5

Action Cards (continued)

Action Look at the Speaker and smile, but sigh several times as if bored.	**Action** Get up and walk away right in the middle of the Speaker's story.
Action Look at the Speaker but tap your feet.	**Action** Look at the Speaker and smile or frown at appropriate times in the story.
Action Look at the Speaker and use your eyes to show you're listening—raising your eyebrows, smiling, frowning when it fits what is being said.	**Action** Look at the Speaker but tap your fingers against your leg.
Action Look at the Speaker but gradually close your eyes as if you're having a hard time staying awake.	**Action** If you have pockets, start going through them as if you're looking for something while the Speaker is talking.
Action Put an elbow on your knee and lean slightly forward toward the Speaker while the Speaker is talking to you to show you're interested.	**Action** Look at the Speaker with an interested expression on your face. Nod your head occasionally.

SUPPLEMENTARY ACTIVITY #8

Good or Poor Listener Role-Play

Objective Students will observe appropriate and inappropriate listening.

Materials Supplementary Activity #8 Handout, "Script for Good or Poor Listener Role-Play"

Procedure Have a pair of students (or several pairs) practice modeling both listening and nonlistening behaviors. Select student volunteers to role-play the conversation on the handout; choose students who can read with good expression for this demonstration. Have one student take the part of the Speaker and the other of the Poor Listener who interrupts.

After they have modeled the nonlistening behavior, ask them to do the role-play again and this time have the Poor Listener be a Good Listener who uses the Keys to Good Listening taught in the lesson.

Give copies of the script to students and have them redo this procedure themselves with their Learning Partners. Have each student practice playing all three parts: the Speaker, Poor Listener, and Good Listener.

SUPPLEMENTARY ACTIVITY #8 HANDOUT

Script for Good or Poor Listener Role-Play

Speaker: Hi! Guess what I did last night?

Poor Listener: What?

Speaker: I went to the big football game and we . . . .

Poor Listener: (Not looking at the Speaker) I went to the game they played last week. I went with one friend and then we saw some of my other friends there. We sat together. We cheered louder than anybody there.

Speaker: I cheered too, but the team lost the game. It all came down to the last play of the game—we almost won, but the receiver dropped that last pass.

Poor Listener: Yeah, I heard about it. Last week the team won.

Speaker: Even if we lost, it was still a good game. I . . . .

Poor Listener: (Not looking at the Speaker) Yeah, but not as good as the one I saw. Last week the team was really hot. We started off with two touchdowns in the first quarter. The best play was made when they intercepted that pass and ran it back for a touchdown. Everybody just went wild.

Speaker: (Looking at the Poor Listener) I know. From what you've said, it seems that it was a good game.

Poor Listener: (Not looking at the Speaker) Best game I ever saw. I liked the way it ended, too. They just held those guys back for the entire last quarter. Those guys just couldn't move the ball at all because our defense was so good. They kept calling for time out and trying different plays, but nothing worked. Well, have to go now. See ya!

Listening for Feelings

Objective

Students will learn to listen for feelings behind words by watching facial expressions and body language, and also by listening to tone of voice.

Materials

Transparencies #2, #3, and #4 from Lesson 3

Transparency #1 - "You got a 'C' on the math test."

Transparency #2 - "Same Words—Different Meanings"

Transparency #3/Handout #1 - "Feeling Words"

Transparency #4 - "How Is This Person Feeling?"

Transparency #5/Handout #2 - "Sentence Starters for Letting Another Person Know You Understand"

Handout #3 - "Guessing the Speaker's Feelings"

Sheet of stiff paper for covering face

Paper bag with eye-holes (optional)

To the Teacher

In this lesson students are taught to listen for the feelings behind a speaker's words and to reflect those feelings back to the speaker when doing so would enhance friendship. Listeners frequently miss many of the emotional dimensions of a conversation. Often, even the questions they ask elicit only factual answers. In this lesson students learn to look for clues regarding how a person is feeling so that they can utilize their friendship skills with greater awareness.

The most helpful clues in determining how people are feeling are found in their body language and tone of voice. Since so much of interpersonal communication is nonverbal, being able to read body language is one of the most important skills of effective listening. Body language is usually very clear, although at times it can be difficult to decipher. Even if people are aware of their body language and try to hide their feelings by controlling it, usually enough of their true feelings "leak through" so that students can still observe them. In this lesson students are encouraged to focus on those more obvious nonverbal clues to how a person is feeling—facial expression, posture, gestures, and voice tone.

In conjunction with learning to develop their skill at reading body language, students are also taught the skill of reflection of feelings. This is accomplished in the following way. Students are given a review of feeling words, then they are encouraged to use nonverbal cues and verbal context to make inferences about the feelings of others. They also learn to ask themselves, "How would I feel if I were doing or saying that?" which helps them in developing empathy. Finally, they learn how to share their observations with the speaker at those times when it would help make the speaker feel understood or cared about.

Everyone has at least a partially developed capacity to understand the feelings of others. However, living in a society where feelings are not often talked about or are trivialized tends to block some of our natural sensitivity. This makes it likely that students will feel awkward at first when reflecting feelings in a conversation. Through practice, students can become more comfortable with this valuable listening skill.

The focus of the listening skills taught in lesson 3 and this lesson is on using listening to deepen friendships. If you would like to carry over the listening skills you have been teaching the students into their group work and class discussions, three lessons in the companion ASSIST manual *Teaching Cooperation Skills* may prove helpful. These are Lesson 3, "Learning How to Listen to Others," Lesson 4, "Encouraging Others to Share Their Ideas," and Lesson 5, "Responding to Others in Group Discussion."

If your school uses a grade-leveled approach to this curriculum, the lesson itself can be taught each year as the concepts bear repeating and students each year will bring a new awareness level, new abilities to process, and new examples to each repeated lesson. The Supplementary Activities that follow the lesson can be used to extend the learning and provide more practice with lesson concepts. You may even prefer some of these activities to those used in the lesson. If so, substitute them or add them to the lesson.

Use the following Supplementary Activities at these suggested grade levels:

4th "This Is How They Might Look"
(Supplementary Activity #1)
"How Do They Feel—What Do They Say?"
(Supplementary Activity #2)

5th "Match the Faces With the Feeling Words"
(Supplementary Activity #3)
"Getting the Meaning Without the Words"
(Supplementary Activity #4)

6th "Can You Hear Feelings?"
(Supplementary Activity #5)
"Find Words to Describe Their Facial Expression"
(Supplementary Activity #6)
"Letting Friends Know You Understand How They Feel"
(Supplementary Activity #7)

Lesson Presentation

Lesson 3, Transp. #2, #3, and #4

Say or paraphrase: **We've been talking about listening and how important listening is to being a good friend and being liked by others. In our last lesson we talked about the three "Keys to Good Listening." Can anyone tell me what these were?** *Lead students through a review of the three listening skills taught in the previous lesson: (1) look at the person; (2) let the other person finish; and (3) say something to show you're listening. As students recall each of the three keys, put the corresponding transparency on the overhead.*

Great! I'm glad to see you remember! At the end of the lesson we decided we would practice those listening skills on a special person—we wrote their name in tiny letters in our hand—remember? Does anyone want to tell us about a time you used these three keys to listen to your special person? *Allow several students to respond. If necessary model with a "listening story" of your own. Point out the following:* **Listening is like focusing a spotlight on a person. The spotlight keeps wanting to veer off to the left or to the right to shine on someone else or your own ideas. You have to continually be bringing the spotlight back to the person you're listening to.**

LISTENING AND WATCHING FOR FEELINGS BEHIND WORDS

Today we're going to talk about another way to listen. It's a little trickier than the three keys—it's sort of like being a detective. I'll bet some of you are already good at it. Let me show you what I mean. How many of you have ever asked someone, "What's wrong?" And they said, *(in an angry voice)* **"Nothing!" How many of you knew something was the matter**

even though they said it wasn't? *Ask for a show of hands.* **Or, what about this? How many of you have ever walked into the house and your mom looked like this?** *(Assume an angry stance.)* **Even though she didn't say anything, what did you know about your mom?** *Allow for student response.*

LISTENING BY WATCHING A PERSON'S FACE

Transp. #1

It's amazing how much you can find out about a person's feelings by listening and watching. One of the best ways to do this is by looking at their face. The face has so many muscles it can make hundreds of expressions! Sometimes you can't tell how a person feels by the words he or she says, so you have to depend on the facial expression. *Put Transparency #1, "You got a 'C' on the math test." on the overhead, covering all but the teacher and first frame of the girl's face.* **Here you see the teacher has just told the girl, "You got a 'C' on the math test." And she says, "I did?" Look at her face; how do you think she feels about it?** *Allow for student response. Uncover each of the other three frames and discuss with students how the girl must be feeling and why she might be feeling that way. (Perhaps she usually gets "A"s, had studied the night before, or was afraid she might fail.) Draw attention to the fact that in each frame the words, "I did?" didn't offer any clues about how the girl was feeling.*

We can often learn a lot by watching a person's face. Even when people try to cover up their feelings, their face can give us clues.

LISTENING TO A PERSON'S TONE OF VOICE

You can also tell how a person is feeling by listening to how he or she says something. How something is said can be just as important as what is being said. How something is said includes the person's tone of voice and how loudly or softly he or she is speaking. How it is said also has to do with how quickly the person is speaking and which words are said the loudest. Listen to my voice and see if you can guess how

I'm feeling. *Hold a sheet of paper in front of your face and say the sentence, "I don't care." Each time, change the way you say it. By changing how you say the sentence you might show frustration, anger, nervousness, sadness, or happiness. Emphasize different words in each sentence. Change the tone of your voice. Make changes also in the speed and loudness with which you say the sentence. Have students call out how they think you're feeling before you lower the sheet of paper revealing your expression.*

Transp. #2

Let's see if you can do it. Place Transparency #2, "Same Words—Different Meanings," on the overhead. Point to any one of the sentences on the transparency and say: **Who will volunteer to read this sentence? You can use any tone of voice you want—happy, angry, scared, sad. Then we'll try to guess how you're feeling by listening to your tone of voice.** *(You may wish to suggest that the volunteers hold their notebooks in front of their faces.) Call on another volunteer to read the same sentence using a different tone. Continue to skip around on the transparency having volunteers read the sentences in different tones of voice while the class guesses the feeling behind their words.* **Sometimes we can learn more about how a person is feeling by listening to their tone of voice than by listening to the words they're saying, can't we?**

LISTENING BY WATCHING A PERSON'S BODY LANGUAGE

There's a third way you can tell how a person is feeling. Who can guess what it might be? *Allow for student response. If no one mentions it, say:* **By watching a person's body language—how they're standing or how they're moving—we can also get clues to how they're feeling. Let's see if you can guess how I'm feeling. Watch my body language and be ready to tell me what my body did that gave you a clue.** *If you desire, put a paper bag over your head with holes cut for the eyes in order to emphasize attention to body language, rather than facial expression. Model the following postures for students. Have them guess your feeling tone, as well as identify the body language clue they used in making their guess.*

- *Sad—shoulders slumped, head hanging*
- *Impatient—one hand on hip, glancing at watch, tapping foot*
- *Nervous or scared—pacing back and forth, biting fingernails or wringing hands*
- *Angry—fists clenched or hitting one fist into the palm of other hand; folding arms across chest with shoulders hunched*
- *Shy or embarrassed—looking down at feet, fidgeting with hands; turning toes inward*

People's bodies give a lot of clues about how they are feeling, don't they? Have you ever asked someone who looked sad what was wrong and they said "Nothing," yet you could tell that something was wrong? It's easier to understand a person if their body language matches what they say. It's also easier to understand them if the way they say something matches what they say. Even if they don't do either of these, you can still understand the feelings of someone by looking closely, listening closely, and thinking what you would feel if you were looking, talking, and acting that way.

Your mind is able to receive information at least three times faster than your ears are able to pick up the spoken word. A person speaks at a rate of about 120 words per minute. The mind, however, is able to understand at the rate of over 400 words per minute. So, when you're listening, you have time to do more than just hear words. You can watch the person's face and body and notice their tone of voice. You can think about how you would feel if you were saying what the person is saying.

GUIDED PRACTICE IN LISTENING AND WATCHING FOR FEELINGS

Transp. #3
Handout #1

There are basically four different kinds of feelings—happy feelings, sad feelings, angry feelings, and scared feelings. But there are a lot of different words for those feelings. Here's a list of feeling words. Let's see how many of them you know. *Put Transparency #3, "Feeling Words," on the over-*

head. Give students a copy of Handout #1 (same title) as they will need it for the next part of the lesson. Go over the list, adding any student suggestions to the bottom of the list.

I'm going to read some statements to you and I want you to pretend that I'm a friend talking to you. Listen carefully to my tone of voice and see if you can find feeling words on this list that tell how I must be feeling. Don't just listen with your ears and eyes, but also with your heart.

Read the following statements, adding feeling tone to your voice. Call on students to choose words from the list that describe your feeling tone. Accept any responses they can justify.

- **"I got an 'A' on that test! Can you believe it? I thought I'd flunked!"**
- **"Everyone else is having fun after class, but I always go home by myself!"**
- **"It's no use to try—I'll just mess up again."**
- **"Since I made a new best friend, everything has been great!"**
- **"I wanted to go out for baseball, but I'm not sure I'll be able to because of my paper route."**
- **"It seems like every time my older sister talks to me, she tells me I'm doing something wrong."**
- **"If my mom finds out I lost my new jacket, I'm really going to be in trouble."**

Transp. #4

Good job! You did listen with your heart! You're getting really good at listening for feelings. Now let's practice watching body language. *Put Transparency #4, "How Is This Person Feeling?" on the overhead. Cover all but the first frame.* **Here all you can see is the outline of a person. Look at the words next to him. Which ones might describe how he's feeling?** *Highlight the words which students identify. (You may wish to go down the list one word at a time, either circling or marking out each word.) Use the remaining frames in the same way.*

RESPONDING TO FEELING TONE

When someone is talking to you and you can sense that they want you to know how they're feeling, it's important as a friend for you to let them know you understand. Let me give you an example—pretend you said to me, "Last night someone backed over my bike. It's so broken up I don't think it can be fixed." I would be a good friend if I let you know I understood how you felt. I could say, "You must be mad about that!" or "I'll bet you're pretty upset." I could say, "That would really make me mad if it happened to me!"

Transp. #5

There are lots of different ways you can let a person know you understand. Here are some ideas you can use. *Put Transparency #5, "Sentence Starters for Letting Another Person Know You Understand," on the overhead. Go over the list with the class, adding your own and students' ideas.*

I'm going to pretend I'm one of your friends. I'll tell you about something, and I want you to think of a way to let me know you understand how I'm feeling. You may use one of the sentence starters on the transparency, if you like. *Read the following situations and call on two or three volunteers to make statements that reflect your feeling tone:*

- **What a terrible ball game! I made the third out and everyone on my team acted like it was my fault we lost the game.**
- **My friend is having a birthday party Friday and I have to baby-sit my brat brother. My mother says she can't find anyone else!**
- **Look at my new athletic shoes! I've been saving for two months for them. My uncle surprised me and gave me the rest of the money so I could get them now. Aren't they great?**
- **Last weekend I was using my dad's tools to build a treehouse in the vacant lot. His hammer got lost in the tall grass, and now he says I'm grounded for three weeks. I can't believe it!**
- **Because my dad's been out of work, we have to move to a smaller apartment and I'll have to share a room.**

- **My aunt invited me to come spend a week at her house in the summer. She lives near a lake and I can go swimming anytime I want!**
- **I didn't study for the test and my dad said I couldn't go to the concert unless I got an "A."**
- **I've been counting on this trip for months and now we can't go because of my mom's job.**

WHAT TO DO IF FEELINGS AND WORDS DON'T SEEM MATCH

You're getting really good at figuring out how someone is feeling and letting them know you understand. But what do you do if someone acts like nothing is wrong and yet you can tell there is? Do you just jump right in and say something like "Hey! Even though you say you're not mad, I know that you are!" or "You must be feeling left out!" That wouldn't be a friendly thing to do, would it?

When someone is trying to cover up their feelings and you can tell how they're feeling anyway, it's a little bit like having x-ray vision. You have to be very careful not to invade their privacy. This is where you have to use your brain and decide whether to let them know you understand or just to let it go. If the person is a very good friend, you might be able to get them to talk about how they really feel—if not right then, maybe later. If they aren't a close friend, it may be best not to say anything about how you think they're feeling. One way to help you decide what to do is to ask yourself, "What would I want if I were feeling this way?"

CONTINUING TO PRACTICE LISTENING AND WATCHING FOR FEELINGS

Listening for feelings can be a lot of fun. You can ask yourself questions like, "What is this person's face and body telling me? What feelings do I hear in this person's voice? How would I be feeling in this situation?" You may feel a

little like a detective. With practice, you can get really good at it.

Handout #2
Handout #3

There are two things I want you to do for practice. The first is a homework assignment. *Distribute Handout #2, "Sentence Starters for Letting Another Person Know You Understand" and Handout #3, "Guessing the Speaker's Feelings," to each student. If you added any sentence starters to the list on Transparency #5, you may wish to allow time for students to add these to the list on their Handout #2.*

Read the example on Handout #3, explaining to students that they are to read each statement and then write a complete sentence that shows they understand how the speaker is feeling. They may use the sentence starters from Handout #2 if they wish. Tell students that they may find that some of the examples express more than one feeling; for those, they should choose just one of the feelings to write about.

Work for transfer of training to the students' everyday lives by asking them to do the following: **The second thing I want you to do is to choose one person you're going to practice listening and watching for feelings with. It can be someone at school or someone in your neighborhood. You may want to write that person's name in your hand in tiny letters. Use all the detective skills we've talked about—watching their face, watching their body language, and listening to their tone of voice. When you think you know how they feel, say something to let them know you understand. That person is going to be a lucky person to have YOU for a friend this week!**

LESSON REVIEW

Use the Supplementary Activities for your grade level to provide practice of the skills taught in this lesson.

Review the lesson by asking students to complete the following sentence starters:

- *I learned . . . .*
- *I was surprised that . . . .*

- *What I'll remember most is . . . .*
- *I liked . . . .*
- *I'm still confused about . . . .*
- *I think I'll be able to . . . .*

TRANSPARENCY #1

TRANSPARENCY #2

Same Words—Different Meanings

- I'm not doing anything.
- Your new friend is O.K.
- Oh, that's just great.
- Are you sure she said that?
- I don't understand you.
- I am looking for it.
- Would you please do it?
- What are you doing?
- Oh, it was O.K.

TRANSPARENCY #3/HANDOUT #1

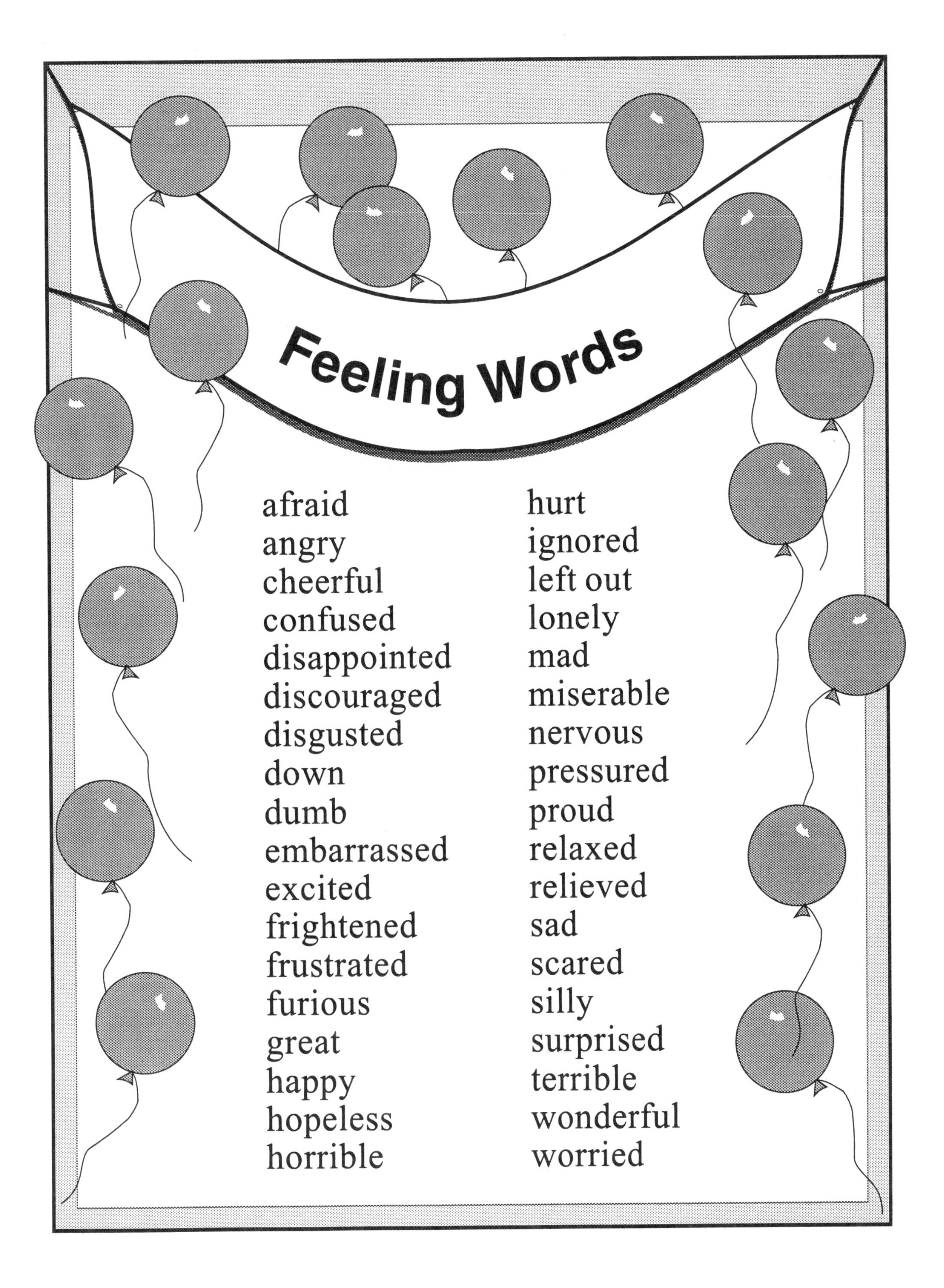

TRANSPARENCY #4

How is This Person Feeling?

angry worried excited scared surprised proud embarrassed left out pleased	curious frustrated delighted angry bashful frightened disapproving miserable relaxed
exhausted proud bored confident discouraged hopeless energetic confused frightened	sad excited lonely silly determined discouraged happy disappointed exhausted

TRANSPARENCY #5/HANDOUT #2

Sentence Starters for Letting Another Person Know You Understand

HANDOUT #3

Guessing the Speaker's Feelings

	What did the speaker say?	How does the speaker feel?
EXAMPLE	"My cat got hit by a car last night. We took him to the vet and she said she wouldn't know until later today if he'll make it or not."	You sound really worried.
1.	"I just found out I made the team."	
2.	"I'll never be good like Mary. I practice and practice and she's still better than I am."	
3.	"Why do I always get sent to the office? **Everybody** was yelling and pushing but she just grabbed me and sent me down there."	
4.	"I don't know if I'm doing this report right. I'm not sure how much she wants, and I can't afford to mess up another assignment."	
5.	"My best friend always spends recess with someone else. She hardly ever talks to me now."	
6.	"Tonight's the night I get my new puppy!"	

SUPPLEMENTARY ACTIVITY #1

This Is How They Might Look

Directions:

Read the situations in the boxes below. Think about how each one might make a person feel. Cut out the faces at the bottom of the page that match how you think a person might look in each situation. Paste the picture(s) in the boxes.

1.	Your friend found out someone was talking about her behind her back!	2.	Your friend was sent to the principal's office for something someone else did.
3.	Your friend's dad has been out of town for a week, and brought your friend back a great present.	4.	Your friend was staying up late watching a horror movie when all of a sudden all the lights in his house went out.
5.	Your teacher asked your friend a question and she didn't know the answer.	6.	Your friend just won an art contest for a drawing she worked really hard on.

SUPPLEMENTARY ACTIVITY #2

How Do They Feel—What Do They Say?

Directions:

Look at the pictures below. Decide what is happening, then draw in the face of each person to show what each one is feeling. When you're done drawing, write in the word balloon what you think the person might be saying.

SUPPLEMENTARY ACTIVITY #3

Match the Faces With the Feeling Words

Directions:

For the pictures below, choose the feeling word from the list at the bottom of the page that you think best describes what each kid is feeling. Write the word beneath the picture. Each picture has several feeling words that would work.

SUPPLEMENTARY ACTIVITY #4

Getting the Meaning Without the Words

Objective Students will listen for inflection and tone of voice to ascertain the feelings behind nonsense words.

Materials None

Procedure List the following feeling words on the chalkboard or overhead.

excited	**scared**
happy	**mad**
sad	**frustrated**

Have students pair up with their Learning Partners and stand with their backs to each other. Have one partner select a feeling from the list above and use only nonsense syllables (nee, rurr, woo, beep, moo, etc.) to express the feeling. The other partner guesses what feeling is being expressed by just listening to the inflection and tone of the nonsense syllables.

SUPPLEMENTARY ACTIVITY #5

Can You Hear Feelings?

Objective To develop skills of recognizing and articulating feelings in the messages people send.

Materials None

Procedure Ask a volunteer to briefly tell about something that happened this (last) week. Ask students whether they can guess what feelings the volunteer had while telling about his or her experience. Check with the speaker to be certain the communication was clear.

Divide the class into Learning Partner pairs. Designate students "A" or "B." "A" begins, speaking on a topic (examples follow). Before "B" speaks, he or she must identify the feeling or feelings expressed in what "A" said. "B" begins by saying, "It sounds like you're feeling . . . ." "A" confirms or denies the feeling.

Sample Topics

1. A vacation I'll never forget
2. Living with my brother or sister
3. Jobs I do at home
4. The time we had a substitute teacher
5. Something that happened to me in P.E.
6. Something my teacher once said to me
7. A time I was really surprised
8. An experience I'll never forget

SUPPLEMENTARY ACTIVITY #6

Find Words to Describe Their Facial Expressions

Directions:

Think of as many words as you can to describe how each of these little kids is feeling. Write the words below the picture. For the last picture, draw in any facial expression you like that is different than the others on this page, then write below one or more words that describe the expression you drew.

SUPPLEMENTARY ACTIVITY #7

Letting Friends Know You Understand How They Feel

Directions:

For each of the following situations, decide what would you say to let your friend know that you understand how they feel and write that in the box.

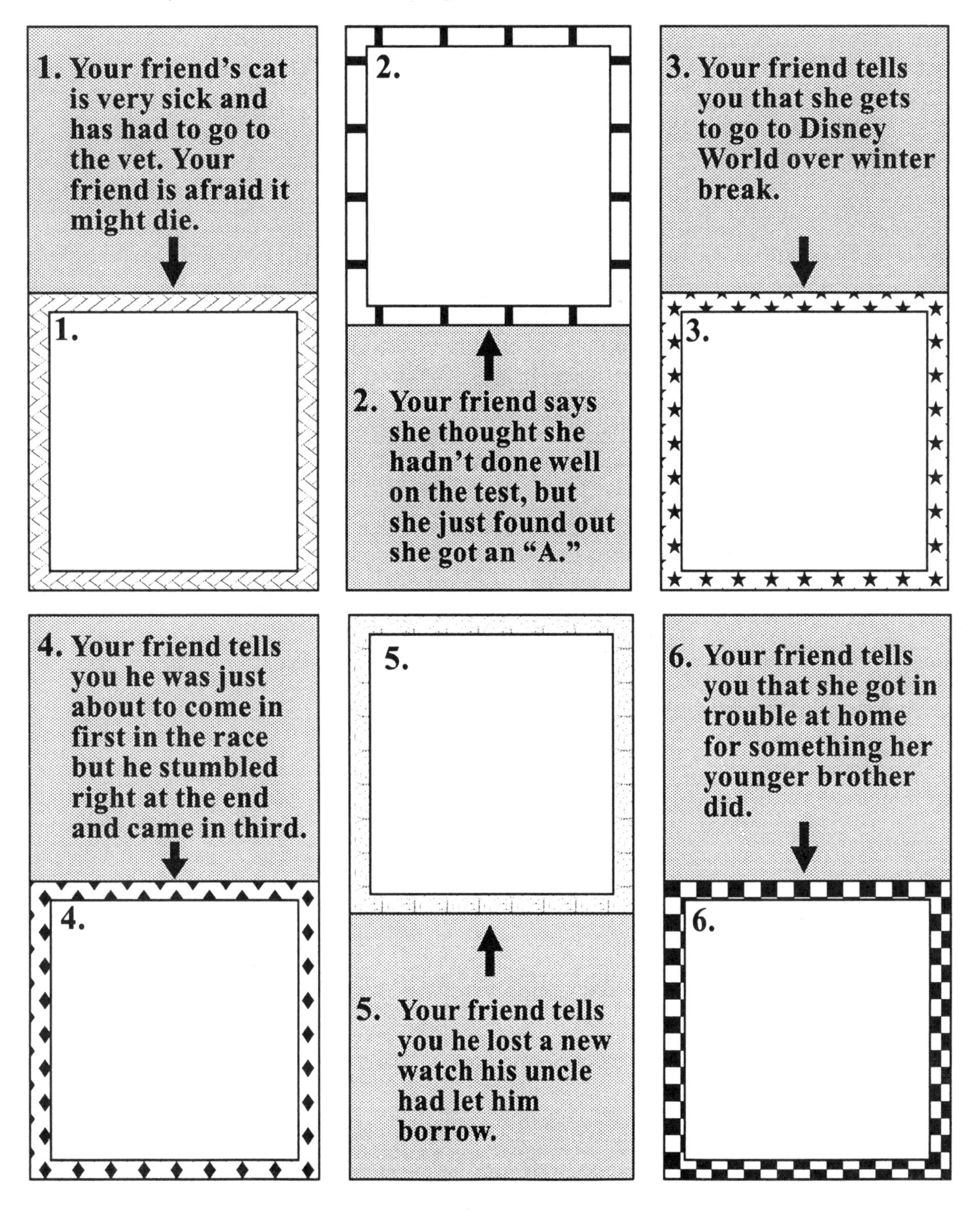

Giving and Receiving Compliments

Objective

Students will learn to give and receive compliments in a sincere manner.

Materials

Transparency #1 - "Everyone Is a Mix of Strengths and Things That Could Be Improved"

Transparency #2/Handout #1 - "Many Kinds of Compliments"

Handouts #2A and #2B - "Examples of Kids' Compliments to One Another"

Transparency #3 - "Giving a Compliment"

Transparency #4 - "Compliment Questionnaire"

Transparency #5 - "Keeping Compliments Out, Letting Compliments In"

Transparency #6 - "Accepting a Compliment"

Transparency #7/Handout #3 - "Compliment Words"

Beanbag, Kushball™, or soft object for throwing

Scratch paper

To the Teacher

It is important for students to understand that being able to give and accept compliments gracefully will help them in making and keeping friends. Being able to communicate appreciation effectively is an excellent way of showing interest in another person and a desire for friendship. The ability to give a sincere compliment is a skill which will also help students interpersonally all their lives.

Many people tend to get embarrassed when giving a compliment. Others either fear rejection and hold back from complimenting, or have simply never learned how to look at the positive qualities of others. In this lesson students learn appropriate areas for giving compliments and then practice sincere complimenting, so that this may become a natural part of their social interaction.

Another obstacle to giving and receiving compliments is the belief of many students that it is immodest to acknowledge a compliment, and that the proper response when complimented is to deny the compliment or quickly return one. In this lesson, students learn how to acknowledge compliments, and then practice both giving and receiving compliments with ease and grace.

If your school uses a grade-leveled approach to this curriculum, the lesson itself can be taught again each year as the concepts bear repeating and students each year will bring a new awareness level, new abilities to process, and new examples to each repeated lesson. Use the following Supplementary Activities at these suggested grade levels:

4th "You're On the Ball!"
(Supplementary Activity #1)
"Compliment Notes"
(Supplementary Activity #2)
"Our Compliment Tree"
(Supplementary Activity #3)

5th "Compliment Sentence Stems"
(Supplementary Activity #4)
"Other Ways to Say Thanks"
(Supplementary Activity #5)

6th "An Alphabetical List of Compliment Words"
(Supplementary Activity #6)
"One Compliment for Everyone"
(Supplementary Activity #7)

Lesson Presentation

Compliments make a difference in a classroom. *Say or paraphrase:* **I'm going to tell you a story of two different classrooms. I want you to listen and see if you can tell what is different about these two classes, and also to decide which one you'd rather be in.**

This is what it was like in Leona's classroom. Leona had on a new brown coat that she was proud of. When she went into the classroom several people noticed her new coat, but no one said anything. Leona hung up her coat and sat down. The teacher handed out the spelling papers. Leona was happy to see that she had made an "A" on her paper. She'd been working really hard to improve her spelling. Her teacher gave her the paper without smiling and went right on handing out papers. At P.E., Leona's class played kickball. Leona kicked a really good one and made it all the way to second base. When Leona crossed home plate, scoring a run for her team, no one said a thing about it.

(continued)

Later, in science, someone spilled water while filling the fish tank. Leona got a paper towel and wiped up the spill. The science teacher saw Leona helping, but didn't comment. Finally, while waiting for the bus after school, a boy in Leona's class dropped his books and papers. Leona helped him pick them up so they wouldn't blow away. The boy took the papers and got on the bus without a word.

That's what it was like in Leona's classroom. Are you noticing anything? Don't tell me yet. Listen to what it was like in Otto's classroom . . . .

Otto felt a little nervous about going into his classroom because he had a new haircut. When he walked into the room, one of the girls said, "I like your haircut, Otto." Otto sat down and waited while the teacher gave back yesterday's math homework. It was story problems; Otto had a hard time with story problems. As the teacher handed him his paper he said, "You got a 'B', Otto. Nice job! You're really improving." In social studies Otto was making a large poster showing different kinds of transportation back in the 18th Century. One of the kids looked over his shoulder and said, "Boy, Otto, you sure can draw!" In P.E. the teacher was having kids shoot baskets. Otto made a basket on his first try. One of the boys shouted, "Good shot!"

That's what Otto's class was like. What was the difference in Leona's class and Otto's class? *Allow for student response. Help students see that Otto's class gave each other compliments while Leona's did not.*

In Leona's class hardly anyone ever got a compliment. How do you think it felt to be in Leona's class? *Lead students to talk about whether they would feel important or noticed and whether they would feel motivated to make an effort to do things well or to be helpful. Discuss whether the classroom would feel like a friendly place to be.*

How do you think it would feel to be in Otto's class? *Lead students to talk about the fact that compliments make us feel good and that when we receive compliments, we feel like giving them, too. Talk about the way compliments help us feel that we matter, that people notice when we try hard or do things that are helpful.*

MANY KINDS OF COMPLIMENTS

I'm sure we'd all rather be in a class like Otto's than one like Leona's. Although our class isn't like Leona's, we can make it a little more like Otto's. We can do that by paying more attention to giving each other compliments.

Transp. #1

You may think at first that there are some people in here you could never compliment! *Show Transparency #1, "Everyone Is a Mix of Strengths and Things That Could Be Improved."* **That's because it's easy to get in the habit of focusing on the things we don't like about someone—looking at their minuses. Everyone is a mix of things that are irritating and things that are neat. You may not like the way someone dresses, but you have to admit she's a whiz in math. You may not like the way someone goofs off in class—but you'll have to admit he's good at everything in P.E.**

Transp. #2

The trick of finding compliments for people is to look for their strong points. There are lots of different areas we can compliment each other on. Let's look at some of them. *Place Transparency #2, "Many Kinds of Compliments," on the overhead, covering all but the first box.*

Handout #1

The first category is "Appearance." It's about the easiest kind of compliment to give. It's easy to see, and you can even give a compliment about appearance to people you don't know very well. When you compliment someone on something they're wearing, you think they have good taste. *Pass out Handout #1, "Many Kinds of Compliments."* **In the box marked "Appearance," jot down all the different things you can think of that you could compliment a person on about their appearance. I'll be collecting your papers at the end of the exercise.** *Pause while students brainstorm compliments on their handout. (This exercise is intended to increase student partici-*

pation and accountability. While it is not necessary for you to read it, it is important that you collect them at the end of the exercise.) **Now let's list our ideas on the transparency. What are some things you could compliment a person on in the area of appearance?** *Write student ideas on the transparency, including hair style or color, eyes, smile, article of clothing, or flair for dressing, etc.*

Good brainstorming! I think you're going to be good at this complimenting business. Let's look at another category. *Uncover the second box on the transparency, "Behavior."* **Another thing we can compliment people on is their behavior. Maybe they act in a way that we like—or maybe there are things they don't do, and we like that! In the second box on your handout, write down different kinds of behaviors you could compliment someone on.** *Pause while students brainstorm.* **I saw lots of writing happening. What are some kinds of compliments you thought of in the behavior category?** *Write student ideas on the transparency, including behaviors such as taking turns, being fair, sharing, helping others, giving others a chance to talk, having a good sense of humor, being a good sport, and not giving put-downs.*

That's a good list! Let's look at another type of compliment you can give. *Uncover the next box on the transparency, "Abilities at School."* **A lot of times we can compliment someone on something they do well at school—it can be something in the classroom or something on the playing field, anywhere at school. In this box on your handout write down all the things you can think of that someone might do well at school. This could be your longest list yet!** *Pause while students brainstorm.*

You seemed to be thinking of a lot of ways to compliment someone on something they do well at school. What were some of your ideas? *Write student ideas on the transparency, including the academic areas, writing, drawing, music, athletic ability, etc. If students offer a behavior, thank them and add it to the "Behavior" category.*

Good job! We ought to be able to find a way to compliment everyone with a list like this! Let's look at one more area

for giving a compliment—things a person does well away from school. *Uncover the last category.* **In the last box on your handout, write as many things as you can think of that are things someone might do well away from school.** *Pause while students brainstorm.* **Let's see what kinds of ideas you had.** *Write student ideas on the transparency. Include areas such as athletic ability in after-school or neighborhood sports, ability to think of fun games and activities, good at video games, fun to spend an overnight with, etc.*

Handout #2A
Handout #2B

You did a very good job brainstorming this compliment list. I think we can use this list to find a way to compliment everyone in our class. I'm also going to give you some handouts with sample compliments on them. When you're having a hard time thinking of what to say, one of the compliments on these handouts might give you an idea. *Distribute Handouts #2A and #2B, "Examples of Kids' Compliments to One Another."*

STEPS FOR GIVING A COMPLIMENT

Transp. #3

Now that we know there are so many different ways to compliment each other, and we have some ideas of what to say, we're ready to start making our classroom an even friendlier place to be. Giving a compliment can be easy, once you decide what to say. *Put Transparency #3, "Giving a Compliment," on the overhead, covering the bottom half. Say or paraphrase:* **What we've been doing is the first step—noticing something you like about a person. It can be something about their appearance, their behavior, an ability at school, or an ability away from school. It can be anything at all. The first step is just to notice something you like. What's the boy on this transparency noticing?** *Allow for student response.* **Yes, he's noticing someone's hitting ability—either at school or away from school.**

Now that he's noticed something he likes, there's only one more step to giving a compliment. *Uncover the bottom half of the transparency.* **Say your compliment in an honest way. If he says it so that the person thinks he's just joking, or is trying to "get in good" with the person, then the whole**

compliment will be wasted. Saying a compliment you don't mean is a lot worse than never giving compliments at all!

PRACTICING WRITING COMPLIMENTS

I'd like you to practice giving compliments by writing some to people you know. Use a piece of scratch paper. Think about someone you could compliment on their appearance; it can be anything about the way they look—their hair, eyes, face, smile, the way they dress, anything. This is step #1, noticing something you like. In this case, it's remembering something you like. *Pause.* **Now, step #2—write a compliment on your paper. Even though they can't hear it, write it so they would know you meant it if they did hear it. Write it in an honest way.** *Pause while students write their compliments.*

Would anyone like to share their compliment with the rest of the class? You can either just read it to the class and not say who it was for, or you can say it to the person you wrote it for if that person is in this room. *Choose two or three volunteers to read their compliments.*

Let's do this practicing again. This time think of someone you could compliment on their behavior. You might even want to pick someone you don't know very well. You can compliment them on a way they act that you like. This is step #1, noticing. Now, write your compliment in an honest way just the way you'd say it to them. *Pause. Allow student volunteers to read their compliments as before.*

Good job! Do you feel as if you're getting the hang of it? When we're not used to complimenting people, it can feel a little awkward and strange at first. Writing it might make it a little easier. So, let's practice this again.

This time I want you to look around the room and find two people to compliment on how well they can do something. Find one person who does something well at school, and another person who does something well away from school. Just for practice, try choosing someone you don't do things

with. Often we don't bother to look at the good things in the people we don't hang around with. We forget that everybody is a mix of strengths and weaknesses. Really great people try to look at the good qualities in other people and not just their weaknesses. So notice two people—one who does something well at school and one who does something well away from school. Then write compliments to each of them on your paper. Write it so they would know you mean it. *Pause while students write their compliments. Ask for a few volunteers to read their compliments as before.*

I'd like to see your papers, so please put your name on them so I can collect them. *You may wish to return those at a later time for inclusion in students' Friendship Folders.*

THE AWKWARDNESS OF ACCEPTING A COMPLIMENT

When someone gives you a gift or offers you a part of their snack or something, what do you do? *Allow for student response. Elicit from students that they accept the offering.* **Yes, when someone gives us something, we hold out our hand and take it—we accept it. It's just the same with a compliment. But, do you know what? Sometimes it's harder to accept a compliment than it is to give one! How many of you have ever heard anything like this:**

You say: **"I like your new jacket."**
And they say: **"It's not new. It was my sister's old jacket."**

or
You say: **"Boy, that was a great goal you kicked in soccer last night!"**
And they say: **"Yeah, finally! I'm usually no good."**

or how about when
You say: **"Your drawing turned out great."**
And they say: **"This isn't really any good. See how I messed up right there?"**

or
You say: **"I like your shoes."**
And they say: **"I like yours, too."**

Allow for student response. **Many of us feel uncomfortable when someone says something nice about us. We may feel awkward and embarrassed. Often we may feel we have to say that what they're complimenting us on is really not so good, or we may feel we have to hurry and give them a compliment back. It's as if we don't let the compliment "sink in." Instead, it just bounces off us.**

Just for the fun of it, let's take a survey and see how we and other people feel and act when we receive a compliment.

Transp. #4

Place Transparency #4, "Compliment Questionnaire," on the overhead, covering the bottom half. **When someone gives you a compliment, what do you think or feel? If I read something that describes you, raise your thumb.** *(During this survey, make some general comments such as:* **Almost everybody has some trouble receiving a compliment.***)*

Uncover the bottom of the transparency and read the last half of the questionnaire, "When you give others a compliment, how do they usually act?" This time have students raise their hands if they've experienced any of the behaviors.

It seems as if we all have trouble accepting compliments from time to time. When we're the ones giving the compliments, we've noticed it's often hard for other people to accept them, even though a compliment is a free chance for them to feel good about themselves. A compliment should make us feel good rather than embarrassed.

WHY IT'S HARD TO RECEIVE A COMPLIMENT

Transp. #5

Why do you think it's so hard to let compliments in? One reason is that when we hear something that doesn't fit what we believe about ourselves, it's hard for us to let it in. *Show Transparency #5, "Keeping Compliments Out, Letting Compliments In," covering the right side.* **People who are critical of themselves or who think they're not O.K. don't believe a compliment because it contradicts what they think they're like. They don't bother to think about whether the compliment could be true or not. When they get a compliment, it**

just bounces right off. It goes "BOING-G-G" *(make exaggerated BOING-G-G sound)* **and plops to the ground.** *Make up two compliments. For each, say it out loud and then use a transparency pen to draw an arrow to the body of the figure. Say "BOING-G-G" as if the arrow was bouncing off and draw a zig-zag as if the compliment was plopping to the ground.*

People who are critical of themselves don't have any trouble letting put-downs in, though, because put-downs fit what they already believe about themselves. Put-downs "POP" right in and go straight to the heart. *Make exaggerated "POP" sound like a cork coming out of a bottle.*

Uncover the right side of the transparency. **People who like themselves find it easier to let a compliment in. Since they know they're O.K., a compliment doesn't contradict what they already believe about themselves. They can let it "POP"** *(make exaggerated "POP" sound)* **right in and make them feel happy inside.** *Make up two compliments. For each, say it out loud and then draw an arrow extending straight to the heart of the figure on the right. Make a "POP" sound as the compliment "gets in."*

STEPS FOR RECEIVING A COMPLIMENT

Transp. #6

Since we all have trouble accepting a compliment at times, I'd like to teach you two steps for accepting a compliment. They're easy to remember, even if they're hard to do. *Put Transparency #6, "Accepting a Compliment," on the overhead, covering the bottom half. Say or paraphrase:* **The first one is obvious—LOOK at the person and THANK them. The boy who made the baseball hit is doing this. He's not saying, "Aw, it was nothing." He's not thinking, "Yeah, but I struck out yesterday"! He's not feeling embarrassed or as if he doesn't deserve the compliment. He's just looking at the person and saying "Thanks!" Most people automatically smile when they do this.**

Now let's look at the second step—it's probably the hardest. *Uncover the bottom half of the transparency.* **Let the compliment SINK IN. He's thinking, "Hey, that really was a great hit!"**

He's letting himself feel good about his hit and feel good that someone complimented him. This boy is letting the compliments "pop" in. He's using his free chance to feel good about himself. Sometimes you can help a compliment sink in by saying to yourself, "I deserve this compliment," or "This person means what they say."

Who's willing to try accepting a compliment? Who's willing to let me give you a compliment? All you have to do is look at me and thank me and let it sink in. *Choose student volunteers to receive compliments. Give students sincere compliments in one of the four categories previously discussed. Help students model letting the compliment sink in by having them take a deep breath after saying "Thank you," as if drawing the compliment in with their breath. Pause for a few seconds during the "sinking in" period, rather than hurrying on to the next volunteer. Ask the rest of the class to make a "pop" sound if they think the volunteer let the compliment sink in. (To model that it is possible to find positives in everyone, you may wish to choose a few of the less popular students to receive compliments.)*

Some people really know how to let compliments sink in. They write them down and keep them in a special place. When they're feeling down, they get them out and read them. This helps them remember their good qualities and makes them feel better. Some of you might decide you want to do this, too.

PRACTICING IN A COMPLIMENT CIRCLE

Now that we all know the steps for giving and receiving a compliment, there's only one thing we need—and that's practice. It may feel weird and awkward at first, but we'll get over that if we practice. And our classroom will be a friendlier, happier place for all of us.

Transp. #7
Handout #3

So you can give really good compliments that describe just what it is you like about a person, I'm going to give you a list of compliment words. *Show Transparency #7, "Compliment Words," and give students Handout #3 (same title). Go over words you think students might not know. Next, have students join you in* *a circle on the floor if this is possible. Say:* **We're going to play a compliment game now. If you want to, you can use the list of compliment words you just received to help play the game.**

The game works like this: The person who has this beanbag *(Kushball™, etc.)* **throws it to someone else around the circle and gives that person a compliment. It can be any kind of compliment. The person who catches the beanbag will follow the two steps for accepting the compliment. It will go like this.** *Throw the beanbag to a student and give him or her a compliment. (If you're concerned that a particular student may be left out until last, throw the beanbag to that student yourself when you begin.) Encourage the receiving student to pause, inhale, and let the compliment sink in after saying "Thank you."*

To the student who caught the beanbag say: **Good job! Now, YOU throw the beanbag to another person and give them a compliment. Remember to notice something you like about the person and say it in an honest way. They will look at you and thank you. Then they will let the compliment sink in. Always throw the beanbag to someone who hasn't had a turn yet. Watch each person carefully when they get their compliment. If we think they let the compliment sink in, let's all go "pop"** *(make a sound like the popping of a cork).* **If we think they didn't really accept the compliment and let it make them feel good, let's go "boing-g-g"** *(make exaggerated "boing-g-g" sound).*

Encourage students to watch closely when someone receives a compliment to see if that person is really letting the compliment "sink in" or if the compliment seems to be "bouncing off" the person. When a student looks embarrassed upon receiving a compliment, encourage him or her to absorb the compliment and to feel good because of it. Remind him or her to look at the giver when saying "Thanks."

Students may throw the beanbag to whomever they wish. Everyone will get a turn. (Because this is a popular activity, you may wish to have the "Compliment Circle" as a recurring "practice" in your room.)

If students need a prompt as they practice giving compliments, you may wish to write sentence starters like the following on a chart or the board:

- *You're really good at . . . .*
- *I like the way you . . . .*
- *I think you're . . . .*
- *One of the things I like best about you is . . . .*

LESSON REVIEW

Review the lesson by asking students to respond to the following sentence stems:

- *It was hard to . . . .*
- *It was easy to . . . .*
- *The part of this lesson I liked best was . . . .*
- *One thing I'll do as a result of this lesson is . . . .*

Use the Supplementary Activities that follow the lesson to provide opportunities for students to practice giving and receiving compliments.

TRANSPARENCY #1

Everyone Is a Mix of Strengths and Things That Could Be Improved

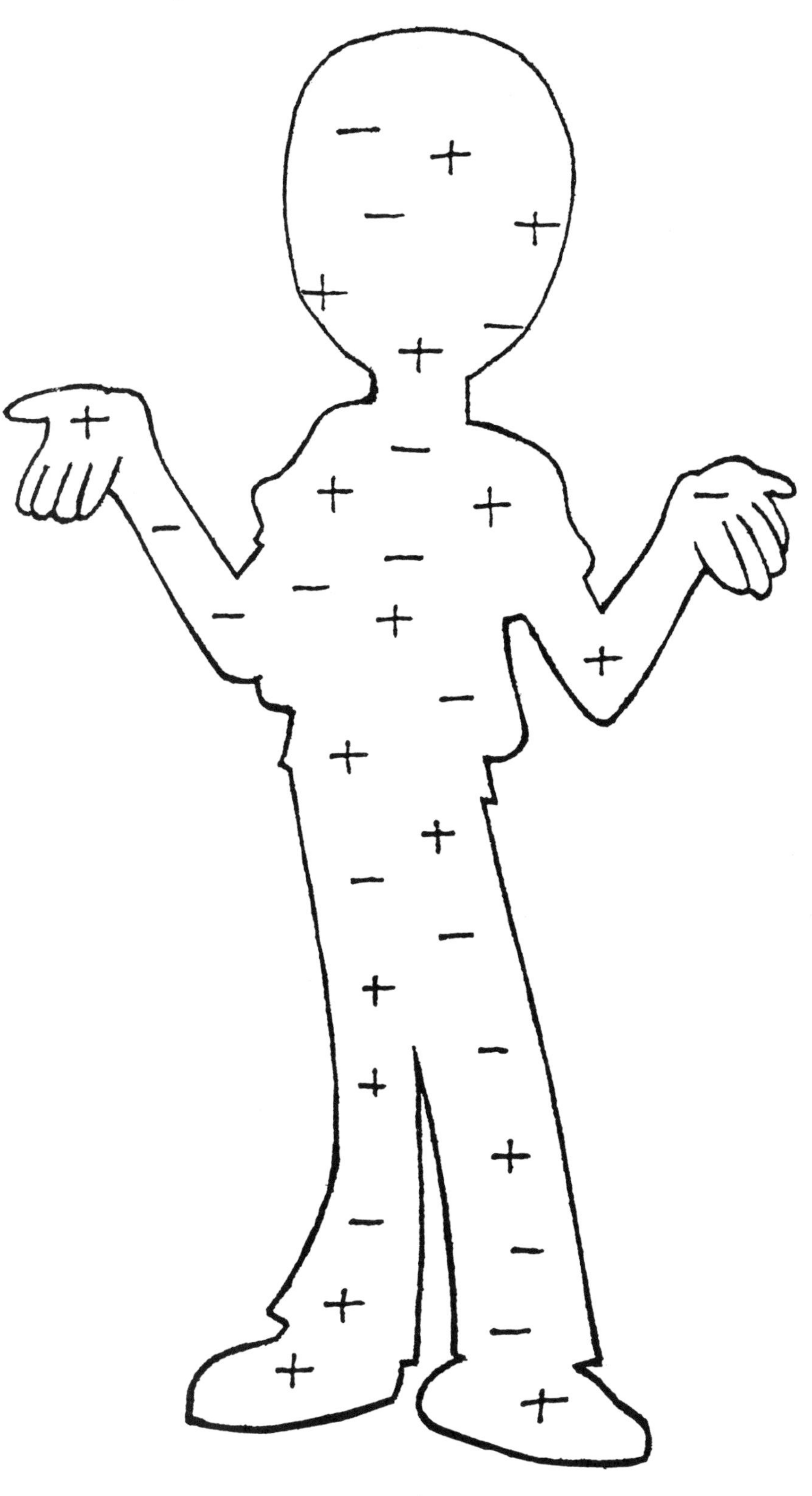

TRANSPARENCY #2/HANDOUT #1

Many Kinds of Compliments

Appearance	Behavior

Abilities at School	Abilities Away From School

HANDOUT #2A

Examples of Kids' Compliments to One Another

Appearance

- You look nice today.
- You're a cool dresser.
- I like your outfit.
- I like the way you smile.
- I like the way you look.
- Wow, that's a great watch!
- Those are really terrific shoes.
- I like the way you fix your hair.

Behavior

- You're always thinking of others' feelings.
- When people make mistakes, you don't put them down.
- You're generous. I like the way you share.
- You have good advice.
- You've got a great sense of humor.
- I like the way you laugh.
- You're such a good listener.
- You're so creative!
- I like the way you always try to be fair.
- I like how you're so self-confident.

HANDOUT #2B

Examples of Kids' Compliments to One Another (continued)

Abilities at School

- You write great stories!
- You're good in cursive writing.
- You're great at making maps.
- You did a good job on your solo in music.
- I thought your report was neat.
- I think it's great how well you do in math.
- You're sure getting good at spelling.

Abilities Away From School

- I think you have great athletic ability.
- You're a really good piano player.
- You're really good at baseball.
- That was the fastest run I've ever seen.
- You've got great taste in music.
- I admire how good you are at chess.
- You're one of the best batters on the team.
- You're getting a lot better at soccer.
- You're so coordinated in gymnastics!
- You're sure a good dancer.

TRANSPARENCY #3

Giving a Compliment

TRANSPARENCY #4

Compliment Questionnaire

When someone gives you a compliment, what do you feel or think?

I often . . .

- Think the person is lying.
- Feel embarrassed.
- Think they're just saying it because they want something from me.
- Feel happy.
- Feel friendly towards that person.
- Wonder what to say.

When you give others a compliment, how do they usually act?

They . . .

- Give a compliment right back.
- Change the subject.
- Say that it isn't really true.
- Put themselves down.
- Look down or pretend they didn't hear it.
- Smile.
- Look pleased and say, "Thanks."

TRANSPARENCY #5

Keeping Compliments Out, Letting Compliments In

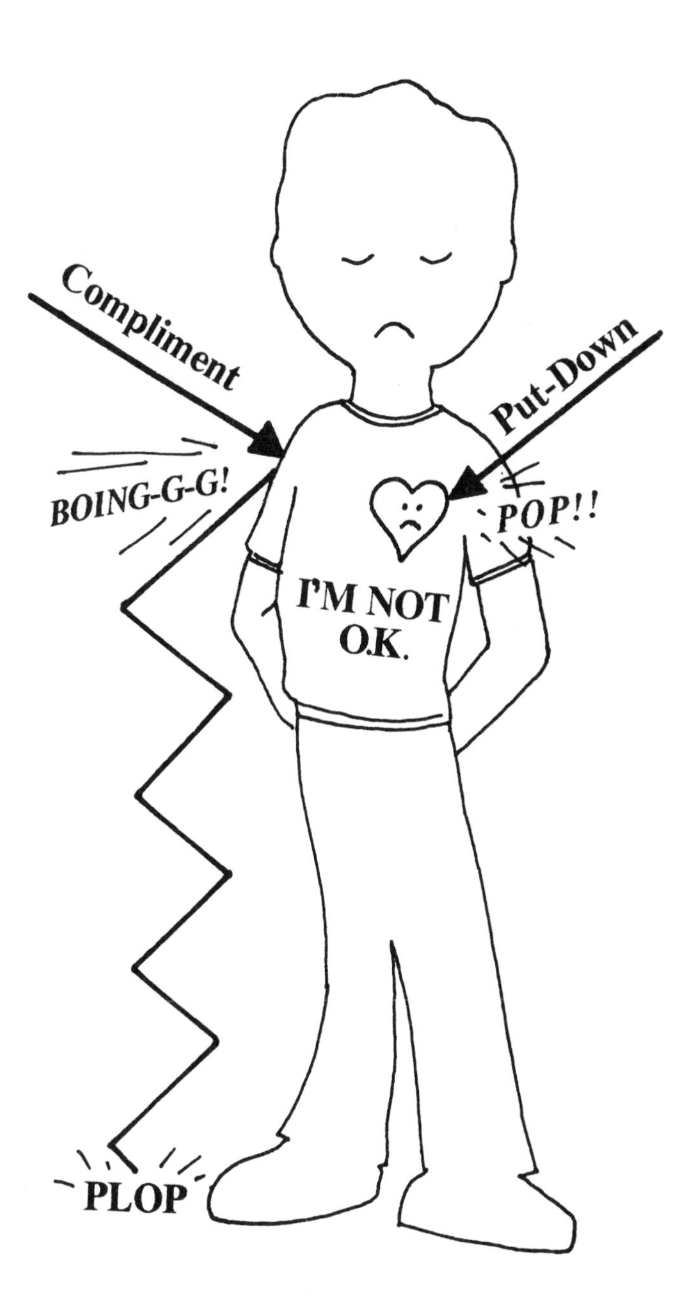

TRANSPARENCY #6

Accepting a Compliment

TRANSPARENCY #7/HANDOUT #3

Compliment Words

Here is a list of words you can use when giving compliments to your friends. If you can think of more, be sure to use those words, too.

adventurous
artistic
athletic
brave
calm
capable
caring
clever
confident
considerate
cooperative
creative
dependable
easy-going
efficient
energetic
fair
fast
flexible
friendly
fun
funny
generous
gentle
genuine
good athlete
good listener
good memory
good sport
graceful
great
helpful
honest
humorous
imaginative
intelligent
interesting
inventive
kind
likable
lively
loyal
mature
musical
neat
optimistic
organized
original
outgoing
patient
playful
positive
problem solver
reasonable
reliable
self-confident
sensible
shares
sincere
smart
special
strong
supportive
talented
thorough
thoughtful
trustworthy
truthful
understanding
unique
unselfish
wise
witty

SUPPLEMENTARY ACTIVITY #1

You're On the Ball!

Objective

Students will learn to give each other positive feedback by writing compliments to each other.

Materials

Supplementary Activity #1 Handout, "You're On the Ball!" for each student

Pencils, scissors

Transparency #2, "Many Kinds of Compliments," from the lesson

Strips of paper with each student's name on one

Procedure

Review with the class the four types of compliments; you may wish to use Transparency #2 from the lesson. Tell them they are going to practice giving each other compliments.

Distribute the "You're On the Ball!" handout to each student. Instruct them to write their names on the blank. Have each student draw a slip of paper with another student and take their handout to that student; wait while the students write a compliment in one of the spaces on the ball that was brought to them. You may wish to limit their compliments to a couple of different categories each time to encourage a variety. Remind students to give some thought to their compliments and to be specific ("You're nice because . . ." instead of "You're nice.")

Collect the name slips and draw again for the second compliment. After the four space are filled on their soccer balls, the students may wish to share their favorite compliment with their Learning Partners or to display them on a class bulletin board.

VARIATIONS

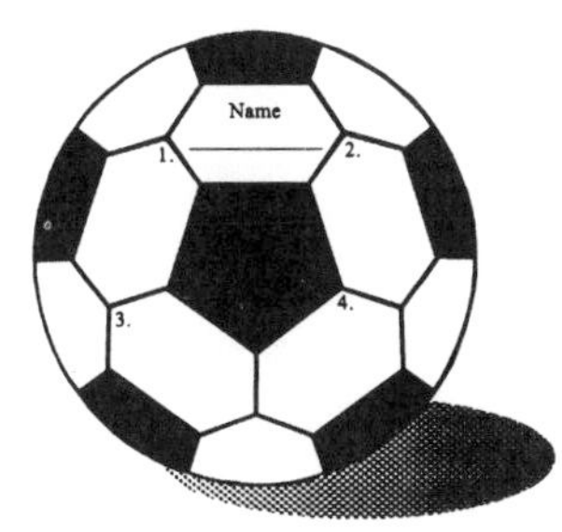

1. You may instruct students in the following manner as they collect their four compliments:
   - Go to your Learning Partner for your first compliment.
   - Go to a friend for your second compliment.
   - Go to someone you don't know very well for your third compliment.
   - Go to anyone you wish for your fourth compliment.
2. You may simply tell students to get their four compliments from whomever they like, beginning when you say "Go!"

SUPPLEMENTARY ACTIVITY #1 HANDOUT

You're On the Ball!

Directions:

Write your name on the blank. Other students will write compliments to you in the numbered spaces, following your teacher's instructions.

SUPPLEMENTARY ACTIVITY #2

Compliment Notes

Directions:

Use these notes to send compliments to others.

SUPPLEMENTARY ACTIVITY #3

Our Compliment Tree

Objective

Students will focus on the strengths of their classmates.

Materials

Supplementary Activity #3 Handouts #1 and #2, "Leaves" and "Birds and Flowers"

Colored paper, scissors

Pens, pencils, or markers

Strips of paper with each student's name on one (optional)

Procedure

With the students' help, construct the tree trunk and branches either by using flat pieces of brown construction paper or by twisting larger sheets of paper to create three-dimensional forms. The construction paper tree can be laminated for greater longevity, but the twisted-paper tree is more fun visually.

Tack the "Compliment Tree" up to a large bulletin board. Have students cut out leaves for the tree, using the ones on Handout #1. Alternately, you may wish to prepare the leaves yourself and laminate them; if students then write their compliments on the leaves with a nonpermanent marker, the leaves can be reused in following years.

Have each student draw two names of fellow classmates, or assign names if you prefer. Students will write compliments on their leaves to the classmates whose names they were given. The leaves are then glued or stapled to the Compliment Tree.

VARIATIONS

For a seasonal variation, consider making the leaves on yellow and orange colored paper for fall, substituting snowbirds for leaves in the winter, using a cluster of pink-paper blossoms in early spring, and making green-colored leaves for late spring. Birds and flowers could also be combined with leaves and used for awards, special compliments, or to recognize exceptional student compliment-givers.

SUPPLEMENTARY ACTIVITY #3 HANDOUT #1

Leaves

SUPPLEMENTARY ACTIVITY #3 HANDOUT #2

Birds and Flowers

SUPPLEMENTARY ACTIVITY #4

Compliment Sentence Stems

Directions:

Think of some positive things about people you know. Finish the sentences below, then cut out the strips and give them to the person you wrote about.

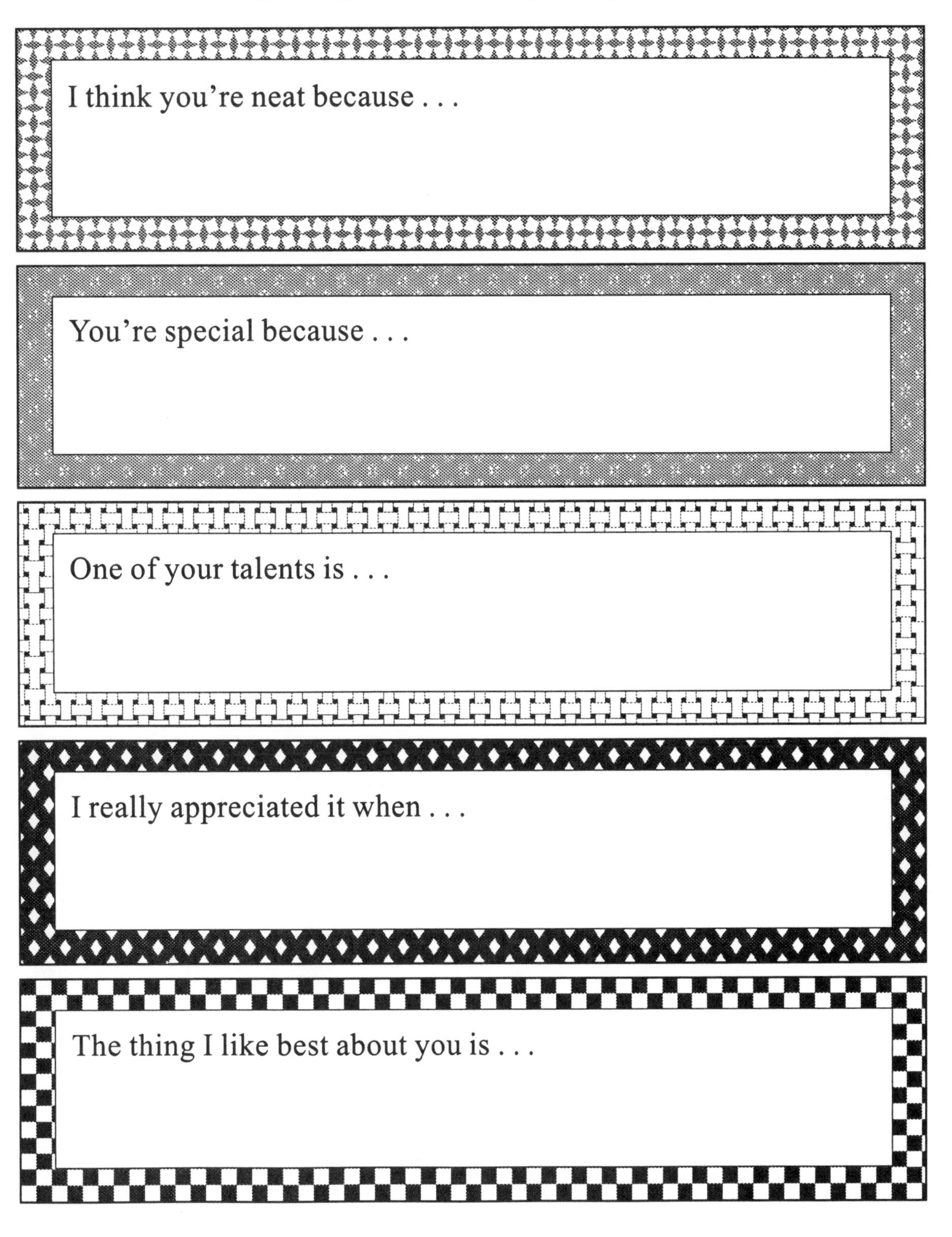

SUPPLEMENTARY ACTIVITY #5

Other Ways to Say Thanks

- Thanks for telling me.
- It's nice of you to say that.
- Thanks for saying so.
- It makes me feel good to hear that.
- Thanks. (and tell him/her something about it, for example: I got it for my birthday.)
- Thanks, I like it, too. (like a new piece of clothing)
- Thanks—I've been working on that a long time.

Directions:

Pretend you receive the compliments below. Write some of the other ways to say "Thanks" under each compliment.

SUPPLEMENTARY ACTIVITY #6

An Alphabetical List of Compliment Words

Objective

Students will increase their vocabulary of compliment words and will use these in giving compliments to others.

Materials

Supplementary Activity #6 Handouts #1A and #1B, "Positive Words Which Describe People"

Supplementary Activity #6 Handout #2, "What's in a Name?"

Paper for signs (optional)

Name tags (optional)

Procedure

Handouts #1A and #1B, "Positive Words Which Describe People" contain an alphabetical list of compliment words. These can be used in the following ways:

OPTION 1

Have students draw each others' names out of a hat. They will then make up a compliment sign for the person whose name they've drawn. They will do this by choosing a word that begins with the same letter as the person's name and which they think best describes him or her (e.g., "Fred is Fantastic" or "Doug is Dependable"). These signs can be mounted on a bulletin board.

OPTION 2

Use the same procedure as Option 1, but have students make a name tag to attach to the desk of the person whose name they've drawn. In this case, use the compliment words as descriptive adjectives (e.g., "Fantastic Fred" or "Dependable Doug").

OPTION 3

Have students complete Handout #2, "What's in a Name?" They will select a friend's name and then write one letter of the name in each of the boxes. They then will find a same-letter compliment word for each letter of their friend's name.

You will probably think of many other applications for the alphabetical compliment word list in your language arts programs. You might want to use the words in spelling or vocabulary building, taking one or two letters each day or week.

SUPPLEMENTARY ACTIVITY #6 HANDOUT #1A

Positive Words Which Describe People

A	Adorable, amazing, articulate, admirable, appreciative, assertive, able, accepting, attractive, affectionate, athletic, ambitious, active, accepting, adventurous, amusing, assuring, artistic
B	Beautiful, bright, brilliant, bubbly, brave, bold
C	Caring, cheerful, considerate, clever, confident, cool, compassionate, courageous, committed, cooperative, capable, conscientious, competent, courteous, calm, cute, creative
D	Daring, delightful, dependable, dedicated, disciplined, dynamic, diplomatic
E	Easy-going, exciting, efficient, enjoyable, expressive, energetic, eager, enthusiastic, effective, even-tempered, exceptional, extraordinary, exuberant, excellent, expert
F	Fantastic, friendly, forgiving, fun, fabulous, flexible, faithful, funny, fair, forthright, fashionable, frisky, fast
G	Great, good-looking, good-natured, giving, gentle, genuine, generous, graceful, good athlete, good listener, good memory, good sport
H	Helpful, handsome, humorous, hopeful, hilarious, happy, hospitable, harmonious, honest, handy
I	Intelligent, interesting, inspirational, incredible, imaginative, inventive, intuitive, industrious
J	Joyful, jolly, jazzy, jovial, jet-propelled, joker
K	Kind, knowledgeable, keen, knowing, knows how to _____ (use any word)
L	Loving, lively, likable, lovable, loyal, leader, lightning-fast
M	Mellow, memorable, modest, mannerly, mature, musical, merry

SUPPLEMENTARY ACTIVITY #6 HANDOUT #1B

Positive Words Which Describe People (continued)

N	Nice, neat, notable, natural, noble, neighborly, nifty, nimble
O	Open, out-of-sight, optimistic, one of a kind, organized, original, observant, outdoorsy, outstanding, outgoing
P	Polite, positive, punctual, pretty, peaceful, prepared, playful, patient, perfect, persevering, pleasant, persistent, peace-making, perceptive, problem solver, perky
Q	Quick, quiet, quotable, qualified, quite _____ (use any word)
R	Restful, reliable, right on, relaxed, realistic, reasonable, risk-taker, refreshing, responsible, racer
S	Stupendous, super, speedy, sensational, sharp, successful, supportive, sensible, smart, strong, sincere, special, sensitive, skillful, self-confident
T	Terrific, trustworthy, thoughtful, truthful, talented, thorough, thrifty, tolerant, tactful
U	Understanding, unique, unforgettable, unbeatable, unselfish, upbeat
V	Verbal, valiant, vivacious, vigorous, valuable, very _____ (use any word)
W	Wonderful, witty, wise, wild, wacky, winning, winsome, warm, worthwhile, whiz
X	"X-ceptional," "X-traordinary," "X-uberant"
Y	Youthful, you are _____ (use any word)
Z	Zestful, zany, zippy, zesty, zealous

SUPPLEMENTARY ACTIVITY #6 HANDOUT #2

What's in a Name?

Directions:

Write a friend's first name in the boxes. (It's O.K. if the name is shorter than the number of boxes.) Then on each line, write a compliment word about your friend that starts with the letter that's in the box. Try not to pick just any compliment word, but one that really fits your friend.

☐ ______________________
☐ ______________________
☐ ______________________
☐ ______________________
☐ ______________________
☐ ______________________
☐ ______________________
☐ ______________________
☐ ______________________
☐ ______________________
☐ ______________________

Example:

S Sensitive
U Understanding
E Energetic

SUPPLEMENTARY ACTIVITY #7

One Compliment for Everyone

Objective

Students will think of one positive thing about each of their classmates.

Materials

A copy of the class list for each student.

Scissors

Handout #3, "Compliment Words," from the lesson

Procedure

Give each student a copy of your class list. The names should be typed double-spaced so students can later cut the list up into strips. Ask students to write a compliment for each person on the list. Remind students that compliments can be about abilities in or out of school, or a person's appearance or behavior. Encourage students to use their list of "compliment words" and to pick just the right compliment for each person. Students may need some time to look for the strengths of classmates they don't know well so you may want to give them several days to complete their list. When everyone is done, ask students to cut up their lists into strips and pass out their compliments.

Making a New Friend

Objective

Students will learn to use a set of six steps for initiating a conversation with a peer they don't know.

Materials

Transparency #1 - "What's the New Kid Like?"

Transparency #2 - "Relax and Say Encouraging Things to Yourself"

Transparency #3 - "Say 'Hi' and Tell Your Name"

Transparency #4 - "Ask a Question About . . ."

Transparency #5 - "How to Get Them Talking"

Transparency #6 - "Tell Something About Yourself"

Transparency #7 - "Suggest You Do Something Together"

Transparency #8A/Handout #1A/Poster #1A and Transparency #8B/Handout #1B/Poster #2B - "How to Talk to Another Person"

Transparency #9 - "How to Make a New Friend"

Handouts #2A and #2B - "Starting a Conversation With Someone You Don't Know"

To the Teacher

Students often find that when they want to make friends with someone they have met for the first time, they feel shy and don't have the skills to initiate conversation. This lesson teaches students how to overcome their sense of shyness with positive self-talk and basic conversation skills.

A simple six-step formula to "break the ice" will be taught. The purpose of these steps is to structure an information exchange so that students can uncover similarities. Students are more likely to progress toward friendship when they discover that they share things in common.

Through role-play, students learn to dialogue and to link their comments to the prior comments of the other person. They also learn to exchange information, find similarities, and establish common ground activities. Finally, students learn that if they think they might "hit it off" with another person, they will need to structure a time to get together again.

The Supplementary Activities for this lesson need to be adapted for nonreaders. All of these activities are appropriate for grades two through five. Supplementary Activity #1 looks at the possibility that sometimes students' efforts may not lead to friendships, and encourages students to take that eventuality in stride.

Lesson Presentation

Transp. #1

Say or paraphrase: **What if we got a new boy in our class today? What if when he came into our room, he said, "My name's Garth, and here's my Information Sheet . . ." and then he handed each one of you something that looked like this transparency.** *Put Transparency #1, "What's the New Kid Like?" on the overhead.*

Garth's Information Sheet tells us a lot of things about Garth. What are some of the things you could learn about him from his Sheet? *Allow for students to guess what the symbols mean. Students could learn that the new boy loves hamburgers, hates math, lives in an apartment building, that his family includes his mother and younger sister, that he likes to draw or do art, has a pet lizard named "Slither," plays soccer, and recently had a birthday and turned nine.* **We'd know a lot about this new kid, wouldn't we?**

O.K. Let's pretend we've finished reading Garth's Information Sheet. He says, "May I have your Information Sheets?" So let's pretend each one of you opens your folder and gives Garth your Information Sheet. What would Garth learn about you? What are some of the things your Information Sheet would say? *Ask students questions about the kinds of topics on Transparency #1.*

A lot of us would have something in common with Garth. It seems he would fit right into our class, doesn't it? Wouldn't it be great if we could really trade Information Sheets with people we didn't know? It would be SO EASY for us to get acquainted that way. It would be easy to know if someone new would be a good friend for us, wouldn't it?

IT'S NOT EASY TO START A CONVERSATION WITH SOMEONE WE DON'T KNOW

But new kids in our class don't come with Information Sheets, do they? If we want to get to know them, what do we have to do? How can we find out if they would make a good friend for us? *Allow for student response. Lead students to see that they will have to get their information by talking to a new person.*

Yes, if we want to find out what a new person is like, we're going to have to talk to them. We'll have to ask them questions about themselves, and we'll have to tell them about ourselves. That way, we'll find out if we have anything in common—if we want to make a friendship. Can any of you remember a time when you started a conversation with someone you didn't know? How did it feel? Were you comfortable? *Allow for student response. Encourage them to share their discomfort with initiating a conversation with strangers.*

Most of us feel shy when we talk to someone we don't know. But, if we don't go ahead and talk to the new person, we may miss a chance to make a new friend. Today we're going to learn some ways to put that nervousness aside and start conversations with someone we don't know.

STEP 1—RELAX AND SAY ENCOURAGING THINGS TO YOURSELF

Transp. #2

When you see someone you don't know, and you think about talking to them, you may think, "Oh, no! I don't know what to say!" That's when you need to relax. Take a deep breath and tell yourself something positive. *Put Transparency #2, "Relax and Say Encouraging Things to Yourself," on the overhead.*

Tell yourself that the new person will be glad to have someone talk to him or her; tell yourself that you are good at being a friend; remind yourself that this is just another kid—not the President of the United States! What are some other things you could say to encourage yourself when you're feeling shy about talking to a new kid? *Allow for* *student response; you may wish to have students model by taking a deep breath before modeling their self-talk. Write some of their responses on the transparency.*

STEP 2—SAY "HI" AND TELL YOUR NAME

Transp. #3

Good ideas! The important thing is to jump right in and DO IT! Just walk right up to the new person and say, "Hi. My name is _____"! *Put Transparency #3, "Say 'Hi' and Tell Your Name," on the overhead.* **And don't forget to . . .** *point to the smile on the transparency or model a big smile . . .* **SMILE! What do you imagine the new person would think if you did this?** *Model saying, "Hi. My name is ______." with a stern or uninterested look on your face.* **How do you think the new kid would feel if I greeted him or her like that?** *Allow for student response. Stress the importance of a friendly face being part of the communication.* **Yes, if we want a new kid to know we're being friendly, our faces have to be friendly, too.**

STEP 3—ASK AN OPEN-ENDED QUESTION

O.K. So you've taken a breath, reminded yourself that you can do this, walked up and introduced yourself with a smile. What do you think would be the next step? *Allow for student response.*

Transp. #4

Yes, you ask a question! This is the trick of talking to someone you don't know—asking questions! You don't have to think of things to say if you ask the new person questions about himself or herself. Probably the best question to ask first is, "What's your name?" After you've found out what the new kid's name is, there are lots of other things you can ask him or her about. *Put Transparency #4, "Ask a Question About . . . ," on the overhead.* **Here are a few of the things you can ask about.** *Point to the various categories around the boys on the transparency, indicating they can ask questions about favorite sports, school, TV viewing, or favorite things to do. (You may have students formulate questions related to each topic.)* **These are just a few of the kinds of things you can ask. Can you think of**

others? *Allow for student response (you may wish to refer to the questions in step #3 on Handout #1A, "How to Talk to Another Person"). Write students' questions at the bottom of the transparency.*

Some questions work better than others when you're trying to talk to someone. Let me show you what I mean. Would someone volunteer to pretend to be a new kid? *Choose a volunteer to answer questions. Whisper instructions to the volunteer to answer only with "Yes" or "No."* **Now, I'm going to try to start a conversation with this new kid by asking some questions.** *Ask the volunteer the following "Yes" or "No" questions:*

- **Are you new around here?**
- **Do you like our school?**
- **Are you in fourth grade?**
- **Do you like baseball?**

Well, I didn't seem to get anywhere. What happened? *Allow for student response. Help students see that questions that are answered "Yes" or "No" don't really help two people to talk together very well.*

When we ask questions that are answered with "Yes" or "No," it sounds more like a quiz than a conversation. It doesn't sound very friendly, does it? Will someone be my volunteer to answer a different kind of question? *Choose another volunteer; instruct the volunteer to answer the following questions:*

- **Where did you move from?**
- **What do you like about our school?**
- **Whose classroom are you in?**
- **What sports do you play?**

Why do these questions work better than the first ones? *Allow for student response.* **These are called "open-ended" questions, or "questions that get kids talking." They sound friendlier, don't they?**

Transp. #5

To help students practice distinguishing between open-ended and closed questions, show Transparency #5, "How to Get Them Talking." Take a piece of paper and cover all but the first "Yes" or "No" Question. Read this to students, then ask them what a better question might be, one that would provide more information than just "Yes" or "No." Accept students' responses, then lower the covering sheet to reveal another possible response that is open-ended and that could be used instead of the first question. Continue in this manner through the rest of the prepared questions on the transparency. Brainstorm with the class some other examples of closed and open-ended questions.

STEP 4—TELL SOMETHING ABOUT YOURSELF

Transp. #6

Using open-ended questions can help you with the next step in talking to someone you don't know. I'll show you how. *Put Transparency #6, "Tell Something About Yourself," on the overhead.* **As you are asking the new kid open-ended questions, you will want to tell him or her something about yourself, too. That's the only way you can both get to know each other. What are some things you could tell a new kid about yourself that have to do with school?** *Allow for student response. Lead students to make statements that give information about what grade they're in, who their teacher is, what they like about their school, subjects they like or dislike, etc. Write some of the responses in the "school" bubble.*

Those would all be good things to tell someone who is just getting to know you. What could you tell the new kid about the movies you like or don't like? *Allow for students to respond about their movie preferences; write these responses in the "movies" bubble.*

Continue the exercise with the "TV shows" and "activities" bubbles. Use the last bubble for any miscellaneous information students think would help a new student in getting acquainted with them.

STEP 5—CONTINUE ASKING QUESTIONS AND TELLING ABOUT YOURSELF

This step is like playing a game of catch. You throw over a question and they toss you an answer back. Then you toss over some information about yourself. They might "throw the ball back" by asking you some questions or telling you some more about themselves.

STEP 6—SUGGEST YOU DO SOMETHING TOGETHER

Transp. #7

So, here you are, asking the new kid questions and telling him or her things about yourself. You're finding out ways you and the new kid are alike and ways you're different. If the kid seems like someone you might like for a friend, there's one more step to take. *Put Transparency #7, "Suggest You Do Something Together," on the overhead.* **You suggest that you and the new kid do something together. That will give you more time to get acquainted. You might ask the new kid to sit with you at lunch.** *Write "Would you like to sit with me at lunch?" in one of the bubbles on the transparency.* **What else could you ask?** *Encourage students to make up questions, such as: "Would you like to play together at recess?"; "Would you like to be on my team?"; "Would you like to come over after school?"; "Do you want to help me make a poster for art?"; "Do you want to go to the ball game together?"; etc. and write them in the bubbles.*

The best way to find out if you can be friends with someone is to spend time together. When you first meet someone, you're only getting a tiny slice of who they are. You're usually both a little nervous talking to each other the first time. It's important to give the other person a chance, and to get to know them better before you decide whether the two of you can be friends.

USING A VOLUNTEER TO MODEL THE SIX STEPS

The steps we've just talked about are not the ONLY ways to start a conversation with someone you don't know, but they're a good way to get started. So let's practice using them. I'd like to have a volunteer—I'll pretend to be the new kid, and I need someone who will start a conversation with me using the steps we've just gone through. *Choose a volunteer you think will model the six steps successfully.* **I'm going to give you each a handout that shows the six steps so you can help our volunteer if he or she needs it.**

Handout #1A
Handout #1B
Transp. #8A

Distribute copies of Handout #1A and #1B, "How to Talk to Another Person," run back-to-back. Put the transparency of the handout (Transparency #8A) on the overhead. Cover all but Step #1.

Are you ready? Step #1 is what? *Have students identify the "relax" step and recall that relaxing can be accomplished by taking a deep breath and saying something encouraging to themselves. Encourage the volunteer to model relaxing and using encouraging self-talk.*

Good! Now, what is Step #2? *Allow for student response. Have the volunteer model the second step. Call on help from other students, if necessary. Remind him or her to smile.*

That was a friendly greeting! *Uncover the third step.* **Now, what question do you want to ask me? There are some suggestions here on the overhead.** *Have the volunteer model asking an open-ended question. Ask the class if the question is open-ended or "Yes" or "No" to keep them involved in the process.*

That's a good question. It can't be answered by "Yes" or "No." Now it's my turn to answer. *Model answering the question.*

Transp. #8B

Put Transparency #8B on the overhead, covering all but Step #4. **Now it's your turn again. What do you do?** *The volunteer should remember to tell the "new kid" something about himself or herself.*

Now the conversation gets to be a little like a ping-pong game. *Uncover Step #5 and read the step aloud.* **You'll continue**

asking me questions and telling me something about yourself. *Read the questions and answers under Step #5 on the transparency.* **Let's see if we can continue with questions and answers just like that.** *Encourage the volunteer to continue asking questions and giving information about himself or herself. Allow the class to offer examples of open-ended questions.*

After several questions, say: **By this time you're probably finding out if I would make a good friend for you. Let's pretend you think we could be friends. What's the last step in making conversation with a new kid?** *Uncover Step #6 and have the volunteer read it aloud.* **Yes! You will want to suggest that we spend more time together. That way we can find out if we like to be together. What could you suggest?** *Have the volunteer formulate a question. Allow the class to offer suggestions, if necessary.*

PRACTICING THE SIX STEPS WITH LEARNING PARTNERS

That was fun! I want you all to get a chance to role-play. Let's practice with our Learning Partners. *Have students sit with their Learning Partners and decide who will be the "New Kid" and who will be the "Conversation Starter." Read the following scenarios to the class to set up the role-play, pausing to allow students time to create their characters. If they are asked for different kinds of information, tell them to make that up however they please.*

SCENARIO ONE

New Kid: You just moved here from the state of _____. You played a sport there; you can decide what it was. You have two pets—one is an ordinary pet; the other is unusual; you decide what they are. There's one thing you're very good at and one thing you're lousy at; you decide what those things are.

Conversation Starter: You've seen the new kid around for the past week. The new kid isn't in your class, so you haven't had a chance to find out anything about him or her. This is your chance to start a ping-pong conversation and find out if you two can be friends.

Guide students through the six steps on Transparencies #8A and #8B. Have the Learning Partners take turns being the New Kid and the Conversation Starter to role-play scenarios like the following:

SCENARIO TWO

New Kid: You've lived in this town all your life, but you just recently moved to this neighborhood. You decide what school you used to go to. Decide what your new teacher's name is and think of something that he or she does in his or her class that you especially like. You live somewhere other than in an ordinary house; you decide where you live.

Conversation Starter: You don't particularly like sports, but there is something else you're VERY good at; as a matter of fact, you're the best in your class. Decide what you're so good at. You're saving your money to buy a very special pet; decide what it is.

SCENARIO THREE

New Kid: You don't live around here. You're visiting your aunt for the summer. Your aunt doesn't have any kids and it gets kind of boring at her house. You've been spending a lot of time doing _____ (you decide) since there's no one to play with at your aunt's house. There's an activity you really like and are very good at, but you need someone else to play it with you; you decide what the activity is.

Conversation Starter: It's summer and you're a little bored because there aren't very many kids in your neighborhood. You've seen the new kid at the pool three times and you've

decided to start a conversation to see if the two of you could be friends this summer.

SCENARIO FOUR

New Kid: You're visiting your cousin from another country; you decide where you're from. Your cousin is having a birthday party, and you don't know anyone there. You're really into music (you decide what kind). You brought a lot of tapes to play at the party but you have no one to talk to.

Conversation Starter: You're at your friend's birthday party. Your friend says, "Hey, come meet my cousin from out of town!" As soon as you walk over to this new person, your friend dashes off to answer the doorbell. You and your friend's cousin are just standing there, looking at each other and feeling weird.

WRITING A SCRIPT FOR CONVERSATION

Transp. #9

That was fun. You all did a good job keeping the conversation going. It doesn't matter if things stop; if it does, you just pick it up and start again, just like ping-pong. This conversation script reminds me of the game we were just playing. *Place Transparency #9, "How to Make a New Friend," on the overhead. Read the cartoon, or have students read it; ask students to identify what is happening in each step.*

We're going to practice being Conversation Starters this week. The more we practice, the easier it will be. Friendships don't just happen; someone has to get them started. When we gather up the courage to start a conversation with someone new, we increase our chances of having another person in our life to have fun with.

I want you to think right now of a specific time this week when you'll use what we've learned today. I'll be checking with you each day to see whether you've had a chance to use the six steps.

Handout #2A
Handout #2B

Use Handouts #2A and #2B, "Starting a Conversation With Someone You Don't Know," as an in-class or homework assignment. Instruct students to write conversations and responses appropriate to the six steps. Suggest they use Handouts #1A and #1B for reference. (You may wish to enlarge Handouts #1A and #1B and display them as posters in the classroom.)

The six steps taught in this lesson are not the only way students can initiate conversations with someone they don't know. However, it is always best for students to learn one thing to master, rather than being exposed to a number of techniques while learning none of them well. After students have become comfortable using the six steps in this lesson, you may wish to broaden their conversation skills by suggesting that they also can initiate conversations by stating an opinion ("The P.E. teacher sure is nice."), giving a compliment ("I really like your jacket."), or stating a fact ("Boy! It sure is raining hard!"). You may also tell students that one of the best ways they can learn to make friends is to watch others who are friendly and to figure out what they do that works so well.

LESSON REVIEW

Use the Supplementary Activities to provide additional practice of the skills taught in this lesson.

TRANSPARENCY #1

What's the New Kid Like?

TRANSPARENCY #2

Relax and Say Encouraging Things to Yourself

Other things you can say to yourself:

- "I'm fun to play with and people like me. This kid will, too."
- "I like meeting new people and can think of good things to say to them."
- "I feel shy, but I can do it."
- "This kid might be shy and really want a new friend."
- "Maybe it'll work out, maybe it won't—I can handle whatever happens."
- "If this person is not nice to me, he or she is missing out—I'm a neat kid!"
- "If he or she doesn't want to be friends I won't die—I'll just try somebody else."

 ______________________________

- ______________________________

TRANSPARENCY #3

Say "Hi" and Tell Your Name

TRANSPARENCY #4

Ask a Question About . . .

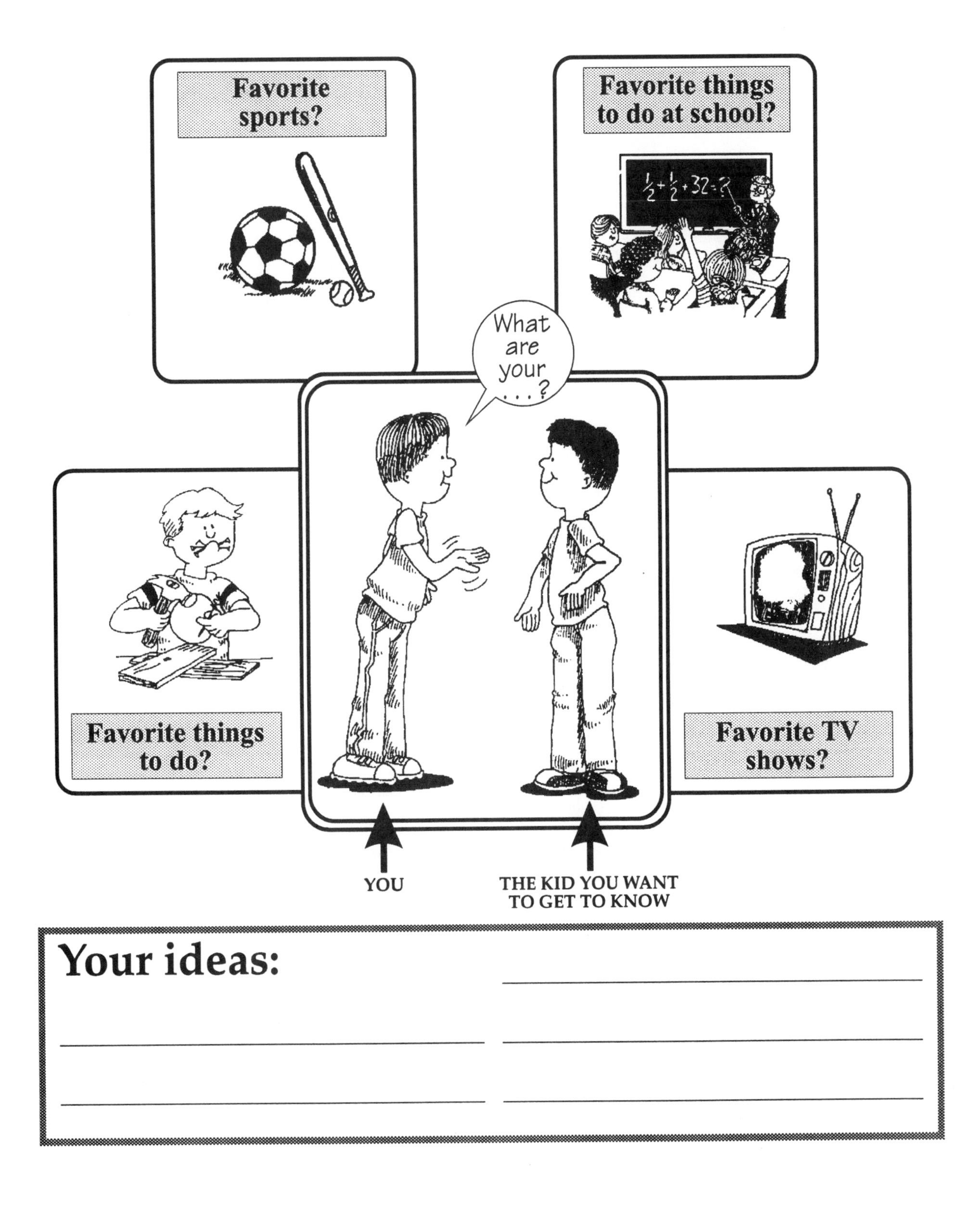

Your ideas:

____

______________________ ______________________

______________________ ______________________

TRANSPARENCY #5

How to Get Them Talking

"Yes" or "No" Questions	Questions That Get Them Talking
Closed questions: These usually start with words like "Do" or "Are."	*Open-ended questions: These usually start with words that begin with a "W" (e.g., "What" or "Where").*
Do you like our school?	What do you think of our school so far?
Are you on a soccer team?	What sports do you like?
Do you like to build models?	What do you like to do for fun?
Do you like to watch music videos?	What kind of music do you like?
Did you used to live around here?	Where else have you lived?

TRANSPARENCY #6

Tell Something About Yourself

TRANSPARENCY #7

Suggest You Do Something Together

TRANSPARENCY #8A/HANDOUT #1A/POSTER #1A

1. Relax and say encouraging things to yourself.

- "I feel shy, but I can do it."
- "If it doesn't work out, I won't die."

2. Say "Hi!" and tell them your name. (Smile!)

3. Ask a question:

- "What's your name?"
- "Where do you live?"
- "Do you know any kids around here?"
- "Where do you go to school?"
- "Do you want to play something?"
- "Do you collect anything?"
- "Do you have any pets?"
- "What sports do you like?"
- "What games do you like to play?"
- "What TV shows do you like?"

TRANSPARENCY #8B/HANDOUT #1B/POSTER #1B

How to Talk to Another Person (continued)

4. Tell the other person something about yourself.

- "I like that game, too."
- "I like to play basketball."

5. Continue asking questions and telling something about yourself.

- "Whose room are you in?"
- "I'm in Mrs. Smith's room."
- "What do you play at recess?"
- "I usually play soccer."

6. Suggest that you do something together.

- "Want to play on the bars?"
- "Want to sit together at lunch?"

TRANSPARENCY #9

How to Make a New Friend

HANDOUT #2A

Starting a Conversation With Someone You Don't Know

Directions:

Write in the bubbles a conversation between these kids who don't know each other.

STEP

HANDOUT #2B

Starting a Conversation With Someone You Don't Know (continued)

Directions:

Write in the bubbles a conversation between these kids who don't know each other.

SUPPLEMENTARY ACTIVITY #1

When Trying to Make a New Friend Doesn't Work Out

Objective

Students will learn that not all efforts at making friends are rewarded by a new friendship.

Students will think of examples of positive self-talk to use in situations where their friendly overtures are not returned and choose between positive and negative courses of action.

Materials

Blank transparency and pen

Supplementary Activity #1 Handout, "When Trying to Make a New Friend Doesn't Work Out," for each student

Procedure

Tell the class that you want to read them a story about a girl just their age named Darlinda who had been learning about making friends with someone new. Tell them that Darlinda was confused because, even when she had followed all the steps, things hadn't worked out. Read the following story aloud:

When Shannon joined her class in the middle of the year, Darlinda wondered what it would be like to be friends with her. Shannon was friendly and outgoing; she was good at reading and math and could draw anything! Darlinda admired her talent and thought it would be fun to have her for a friend.

Darlinda tried for several weeks to make friends with Shannon. She smiled and asked her to sit by her at lunch. She offered to share her new colored markers and complimented Shannon's artwork. She did everything she had learned about how friends treat each other, but Shannon never really seemed to want to be friends with Darlinda. Shannon wasn't mean or rude; she just didn't seem to care if Darlinda was there or not.

Ask the class how they think Darlinda felt. Ask them to share experiences where they tried to make friends with someone and it hadn't worked out. Ask them what they did to try to establish the friendship, what the disappointing results were, and how they felt about it. Continue reading the story:

> **Darlinda was feeling pretty blue. "I wonder why Shannon doesn't like me . . ." she thought. "Maybe she doesn't want to be my friend because I don't have as many clothes as some of the other girls. I bet she'd like me more if I wasn't such a loser!"**

Ask the class what mistake they think Darlinda is making. Help students see that Darlinda has interpreted Shannon's lack of interest to mean that there's something wrong with Darlinda. Talk about the fact that there are some people we are drawn to and some we are not, even when there's nothing "wrong" with them or us.

Ask the class how Darlinda is hurting herself with her self-talk. Discuss the negative, self-deprecating quality of it. (You may wish to reread the last paragraph of the story.) Ask the class to help Darlinda think of things to say to herself to make herself feel better, such as:

- "Just because she doesn't want to be friends, doesn't mean there's something the matter with me."
- "I'll live, even if she doesn't want to be friends."
- "There are a lot of other people who want to be my friend even if she doesn't."
- "There are a lot of neat things about me, even if she can't see them."
- "She's missing out on a good friendship."
- "I don't need every single person to be my friend."

List these on a blank transparency.

Give students the Supplementary Activity #1 Handout and instruct them to help Darlinda decide what to do next. Tell them to cross out the thoughts they think would not be good choices. Have them choose one of the good choices and write why they think it would be a good choice on the lines at the bottom of the handout.

SUPPLEMENTARY ACTIVITY #1 HANDOUT

When Trying to Make a New Friend Doesn't Work Out

Darlinda has been trying to make friends with Shannon, but it hasn't worked out. Below are some of Darlinda's thoughts about what to do next.

- **Cross out** those thoughts that you think **would NOT be good choices** for her to take.
- **Pick one** of the remaining choices that you think **would be** a good solution to her problem. **Circle** it, and **write** why you think this would work on the lines below.

____

____

____

____

SUPPLEMENTARY ACTIVITY #2

The Getting to Know Someone Conversation Game

Objective

Students will practice asking open-ended questions to find out about a person they don't know by interviewing each other.

Materials

Supplementary Activity #2 Handout, "Getting-to-Know-Someone Conversation Form," for each student

Pencils

Transparency made from "Getting-to-Know-Someone Conversation Form" (Supplementary Activity #2 Transparency)

Procedure

Tell the class they are going to practice their conversation skills by interviewing their Learning Partners. Tell students that they will each be making up their character; they will choose a different name for themselves and decide where they lived before they moved here. Give them some suggestions to spur their creativity: Where do they live—in a house, apartment, mobile home, condo, on a farm or ranch, in a log cabin? Who do they live with—parent(s), aunt, uncle, grandmother, grandfather, brothers or sisters? What kind of pets do they have or did they have—dog, cat, horse, snake, parakeet, pig? Put the transparency on the overhead and go over the different topics, giving them a chance to think about them while they make up their character.

Remind the students about the question and answer skills they learned in the lesson—asking a question, listening to the answer, and then giving some information about themselves. Tell the Learning Partners to decide who will be the "Questioner." Questioners will ask their partner a question, write down the partner's answer, and then tell their partner some similar information about themselves. Their partner will write that information down on his or her own Getting-to-Know-Someone Conversation Form.

After the "getting-to-know-someone conversation" is completed, allow students to introduce their partners, using the information from their conversations.

In order to give the Learning Partners who didn't ask the questions a turn, have them exchange places with someone else who didn't ask questions. They will be the Questioner this time with their new Learning Partners. Distribute new Getting-to-Know-Someone Conversation Forms.

VARIATION

You may wish to have students working in triads, with one student acting as the "Observer." The Observer would notice if the questions were open-ended or "Yes" or "No" and whether the Questioner was smiling. Observers would give feedback at the end of each session, either to the pair or to the class. Triads would rotate roles.

SUPPLEMENTARY ACTIVITY #2 HANDOUT/TRANSPARENCY

Getting-to-Know-Someone Conversation Form

Questioner's Name ______________________________

From ______________________________

Other Person's Name ______________________________

is from ______________________________

lives ______________________________

family ______________________________

pets ______________________________

interests ______________________________

____

activities ______________________________

____

likes ______________________________

doesn't like ______________________________

favorite food ______________________________

favorite TV show ______________________________

SUPPLEMENTARY ACTIVITY #3

Tossing the Conversation Ball

Objective

Students will practice the six steps of having a conversation with someone they don't know by tossing a ball back and forth with another student who is role-playing a "new kid."

Materials

Tennis ball, Nerf™ ball, or paper wad for each pair of students

Posters #1A and #1B, "How to Talk to Another Person," from the lesson

Supplementary Activity #3 Handouts #1A and #1B, "New Kid Cards," cut apart, folded, and placed in sack or jar

Procedure

Students play in pairs seated across from each other. You may have two students or the whole class playing this game in pairs. Duplicate enough New Kid Cards so that there is at least one card for each pair playing; it doesn't matter if some pairs have duplicate cards.

Have partners designated as "New Kids" draw a New Kid Card to give them information about their character. (If you like, you may divide them according to probable sex so that no student draws a card that seems to be for the opposite sex.) The student designated as "Conversation Starter" acts out the first step, "Relax," and then smiles and introduces himself or herself. He or she then asks the first question, tossing the ball to the New Kid. The question should be an open-ended, rather than a "Yes or No" question. The New Kid answers the question, tossing the ball back to the Conversation Starter. The Conversation Starter tells something about himself or herself and then asks another question, tossing the ball to the New Kid.

Allow the question and answer period to continue for six or eight rounds, and then instruct the Conversation Starter to complete the last step, suggesting they get together another time.

Collect the New Kid Cards and reshuffle them. Partners change roles and the New Kids draw another New Kid Card. Students who draw the same card twice can draw a second time. (You may wish to add more New Kid Cards of your own or ask interested students to do so.)

SUPPLEMENTARY ACTIVITY #3 HANDOUT #1A

New Kid Cards

You are the "new kid." You moved here three weeks ago from Hawaii. You are a very good swimmer and were learning to surfboard when your family moved away from Hawaii. You like the new school, but you can't get used to the cold winters here. Your cat just had kittens, but you had to give them all away before you moved.
You are the "new kid." You lived in a small town in Michigan before you moved here, and you loved to ski and snowmobile. The town you lived in was smaller than this one, and you find it strange that there are so many people who don't know each other. Your family is living in an apartment building while they're looking for a house. You have three hamsters and a golden retriever.
You are the "new kid." Your family moved here from Queens in New York City. Your mother is an artist, and you have drawn all your life. You can usually draw better than anyone in your class. Math is hard for you, but you like reading. You have a white fluffy cat and are a very good swimmer. Your mom is making you take piano lessons and you hate to practice.
You are the "new kid." You moved here from a ranch in West Texas. You grew up riding a horse and helping your uncle with the cattle. When your uncle died, you had to move here. The people are friendly here, but you miss your horse and old friends. You like the sports at this school and found out you're really good at baseball.
You are the "new kid." Your dad is in the military and has been stationed in Germany most of your life. You're having fun getting used to living in the United States. There are so many neat-looking clothes and lots of places to eat hamburgers and pizza! You've already made a couple of friends and think this is a friendly school.
You are the "new kid." You're visiting your dad for a month and would like to make a friend who enjoys swimming and listening to music. You like to go shopping and also play video games. You live with your mom in a big city a long way from here. No pets are allowed in your apartment, but you'd really like to have a dog.

SUPPLEMENTARY ACTIVITY #3 HANDOUT #1B

New Kid Cards (continued)

You are the "new kid." This is your first time to go away to a summer camp, and most of the other kids seem to know each other. You love water sports and would like to find someone to be your canoe partner. You are a pretty good pitcher in softball, but you strike out more often than you get a hit. You have an iguana at home and really like to take nature hikes.
You are the "new kid." You used to go to a school not far from here, but your family just moved. Your parents are divorced and you live with your mom and step-father. You argue with him sometimes, but he helps you with your science homework and is pretty cool most of the time. You have a collection of old comic books and like to trade them with other kids. Your favorite foods are tacos and enchiladas. Your little sister has a yappy little dog that you hate.
You are the "new kid." You are what they would call "born to shop." In the town where you used to live, you lived in an apartment right across the street from a mall. You and your friends used to go over there on Saturday. This town is smaller and you haven't found anyone to do things with yet. Your mom is always bugging you to turn off the TV and do something else. But what is there to do? Homework? Yuk!
You are the "new kid." You just moved here last week from a town in California. You like to collect baseball cards and go to baseball card shows. You usually play baseball in the summer and are a pretty good hitter. You have a baseball signed by three of your favorite players. Baseball is your life!
You are the "new kid." You just moved here from Mexico City and think this is a neat town, even though it's not as big as Mexico City is. One of the things you like best here is the music, even though your mom won't let you go to any concerts until you're a teenager. You also really like to go to the movies. There are several you'd like to see right now. You have a kitten that wandered up to your door. It was hungry so you fed it and gave it a home.

SUPPLEMENTARY ACTIVITY #4

How Other Kids Make a New Friend

Directions:

The following are real suggestions made by students like you about how to make a friend. Read them and underline the ideas you like most, then answer the "Dear Abby" letter at the end, giving what you think would be the best advice.

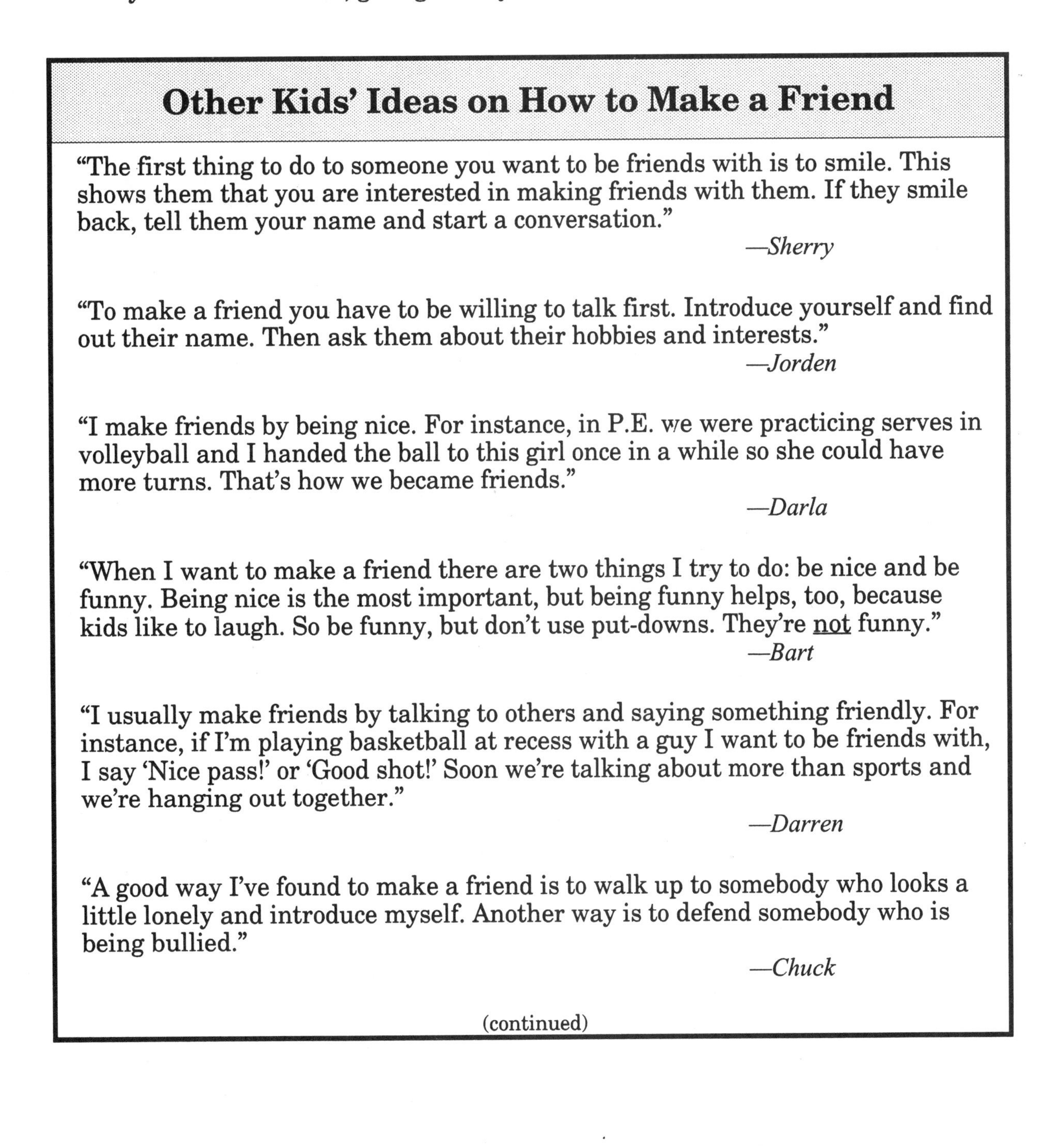

Other Kids' Ideas on How to Make a Friend

"The first thing to do to someone you want to be friends with is to smile. This shows them that you are interested in making friends with them. If they smile back, tell them your name and start a conversation."

—*Sherry*

"To make a friend you have to be willing to talk first. Introduce yourself and find out their name. Then ask them about their hobbies and interests."

—*Jorden*

"I make friends by being nice. For instance, in P.E. we were practicing serves in volleyball and I handed the ball to this girl once in a while so she could have more turns. That's how we became friends."

—*Darla*

"When I want to make a friend there are two things I try to do: be nice and be funny. Being nice is the most important, but being funny helps, too, because kids like to laugh. So be funny, but don't use put-downs. They're not funny."

—*Bart*

"I usually make friends by talking to others and saying something friendly. For instance, if I'm playing basketball at recess with a guy I want to be friends with, I say 'Nice pass!' or 'Good shot!' Soon we're talking about more than sports and we're hanging out together."

—*Darren*

"A good way I've found to make a friend is to walk up to somebody who looks a little lonely and introduce myself. Another way is to defend somebody who is being bullied."

—*Chuck*

(continued)

How Other Kids Make a New Friend (continued)

"I like to ask questions to see if we have anything in common. If we do, I say something like, 'Maybe we can do something together sometime.'"

—Kuniko

"I say 'How's it going?' to strike up a conversation. A few days later I ask them if they want to sit by me at lunch. I try and do this with people I'm pretty sure I won't get turned down by, otherwise I'd just end up getting hurt."

—Rick

"The way I make friends is to try to notice the kids who smile at me or talk to me. Then I ask them if they'd like to work on a school project with me or come to my house."

—Tracy

Dear Abby:

I have just moved to a new school and have not made any friends yet. There is one group at school that seems really neat and just the kind of kids I want to be friends with. There are a couple of kids in particular I'd like to get to know. I would feel dumb just asking them if I could join them. Do you know of some ways I could get into this group without being embarrassed?

Signed,
Want To Belong

Dear "Want To Belong,"

Yours truly,
Abby

What's one thing you would <u>never</u> do if you wanted to make a friend?

Being a Good Friend Isn't Always Easy

Objective

Students will demonstrate an understanding of how to deal with some of the common difficulties encountered in friendships, including being honest but kind, keeping secrets and promises, apologizing and forgiving, and letting a friend have other friends.

Materials

Blank transparencies and pen

Transparency #1 - "Being a Good Friend Isn't Always Easy"

Transparency #2A/Handout #1A and Transparency #2B/ Handout #1B - "Being Honest but Kind"

Transparency #3 - "Once You Tell Someone's Secret, You Can't Stop It From Spreading"

Handout #2 - "Should You Ever Tell a Secret?"

Transparency #4 - "Sometimes It's Hard to Apologize"

Transparency #5 - "Apologizing Doesn't Always Mean You Were Wrong—It Means You're Sorry"

Transparency #6 - "Apologizing Means You're Growing Up"

Transparency #7 - "Three Steps to Apologizing"

Transparency #8 - "The Parts of Forgiveness"

Transparency #9 - "Feeling O.K. About Your Friends Having Other Friends"

To the Teacher

This lesson focuses students' attention on those keys to friendship that particularly require them to consider another's point of view, that is, to empathize. The four areas given particular emphasis in the lesson are: (1) being honest but kind, (2) keeping secrets and promises, (3) apologizing and forgiving, and (4) letting friends have other friends. These are often areas where students find that being a friend isn't always easy.

Empathizing is an ability that develops gradually. This lesson provides numerous scenarios for discussion where, by listening to the comments and social reasoning of students in higher stages of social development, less mature students can learn to empathize. Then, by engaging in role-plays, students can practice responses which take into account the perspective of others.

This lesson begins by helping students cultivate their ability to express their feelings honestly, but to do so with sensitivity and kindness. While it is important that students recognize and accept their own feelings, it is also important that they consider the feelings of others. Asking questions such as those suggested in the lesson provides students with an opportunity to identify and practice "honest but kind" expressions of feelings and opinions.

The inability to keep secrets or the breaking of promises are frequent causes of friendship problems or even termination. The fate of a friendship usually depends on whether trust can be maintained. Revealing a secret shared between friends erodes and often destroys trust. Students need to take seriously the request to keep a secret. This is a difficult thing to do, especially after friends have had a fight or when someone else is pressing them for information.

In this lesson, students are led to reflect on how they have felt when one of their secrets was revealed. Remembering those feelings will often help students stop themselves when they are tempted to reveal the secret of a friend. The lesson also emphasizes that once a secret is told, one has no control over keeping it from spreading.

Students are encouraged to use the criterion of judging whether someone is in danger or is being hurt as their guide in deciding when a secret should be revealed. They are asked to debate a number of situations using this concept as a guide.

Making and accepting apologies is a skill that is difficult for many students because they often equate an apology with an admission of being wrong, or they are afraid that their apology will not be accepted. The premise of this part of the lesson is that an apology means that you're sorry about something, whether you're wrong or not. Students are taught that apologies are appropriate even if they did not deliberately offend another person. Students learn a simple formula for apologizing. Students are encouraged to view an apology as a sign of maturity, rather than as a sign of weakness, especially when it might mean risking having to face a friend's anger. Students also learn to accept apologies gracefully, even when they are still feeling some anger themselves.

Forgiveness is presented in the lesson as trying to see things from another's point of view, not seeking revenge, and not trying to get even by hurting back. It is stressed that forgiveness doesn't absolve the offending person of responsibility for what they've done, but simply allows them a second chance. Students who learn to forgive yet not become a "doormat" for others to walk on have an easier time both with friendships and with other challenges in life.

One of the most difficult things of all for students is to curb possessiveness and allow their close friends the freedom to form other friendships. Although this is a later stage friendship skill, students in earlier stages want and even demand this freedom from one another. The lesson asks students to brainstorm things they can say to themselves that can

help them deal with uncomfortable feelings that may occur when one of their friends wants to play or do something with someone else.

If your school uses a grade-leveled approach to this curriculum, you may teach the lesson itself each year as it contains life skills that benefit from repeated practice and from students' increasing cognitive ability to empathize. Use the following Supplementary Activities at these suggested grade levels for additional skills practice:

4th
"More Practice in Being Honest But Kind" (Supplementary Activity #1)
"Some Questions About Secrets" (Supplementary Activity #2)
"Dear Abby Letters" (Supplementary Activity #3)

5th
"How I Feel About Honesty Between Friends" (Supplementary Activity #4)
"How to Keep a Friendship When You Fight With a Friend" (Supplementary Activity #5)
"Times I Was a Winner by Apologizing" (Supplementary Activity #6)

6th
"Your Opinions About Friendship" (Supplementary Activity #7)
"True or False Statements About Friendship" (Supplementary Activity #8)

Lesson Presentation

SOMETIMES FRIENDSHIP ISN'T EASY

Transp. #1

Today we're going to talk about some of the things that friends do for one another that can sometimes be hard. *Show Transparency #1, "Being a Good Friend Isn't Always Easy."* **By the end of this lesson you'll be able to do a better job of saying what you honestly feel or think without hurting your friend's feelings, of keeping secrets and promises, of**

apologizing to a friend or forgiving them, and of letting a friend have other friends.

BEING HONEST BUT KIND

Say or paraphrase the following: **First we'll talk about being "honest but kind." Raise your hand if you can remember a time when you wished you could tell a friend what you were thinking, but you knew that your friend would have a hard time hearing what you had to say.** *Pause.* **Who can think of some situations where it might be hard for a friend to hear the truth about something?** *Allow for student response.* **Let's look at some examples of these kinds of situations and see if we can decide what we might say.**

Transp. #2A
Transp. #2B
Handout #1A
Handout #1B

Show students Transparencies #2A and #2B, "Being Honest But Kind," and give them Handouts #1A and #1B of the same title. Say or paraphrase: **Here are some tough situations where you really have to think about what to say if you want to be honest but also kind. A good way to figure out what to say is to put yourself in the place of your friend and imagine how you would like someone to tell you the truth in this situation.**

Let's brainstorm some honest but kind things to say in these examples. I'll write on the transparencies the things you all agree are kind ways to tell the truth. You write on your handouts the things to say that you think are the best for each situation.

Let's take the first situation. Your friend calls and asks you to come over. You've already promised to play with someone else. Put yourself in the place of your friend. How would you like the problem to be handled? Would you want to be lied to? What way of explaining the situation would feel best to you? *Allow for student response. Write on the transparency those responses which students agree are honest but kind. Ask students to pick their favorite response or responses to write on their handouts. Continue in this manner. Choose only those examples you think your students will relate to.*

Summarize by saying: **Most kids are very good at telling when their friends are lying. They usually want their friends to be honest with them, even if it's a little hard to hear the truth at times. Real friends try to be honest in a kind way, doing the best they can not to hurt a friend's feelings.**

KEEPING SECRETS AND PROMISES

Say or paraphrase the following: **Let's talk now about keeping secrets and promises. We'll talk about keeping secrets first. I'd like each of you to think of a secret you have; something you would never tell or would only tell to someone you trust very much. You're not going to be asked to tell it to anyone—just to think of it for a few seconds.** *Pause for a few seconds.*

Blank Transp.

O.K., now what would it take for you to feel safe in telling the secret to someone in our class? *Write student comments on a blank transparency and tally those that are the same. Use students' comments along with suggestions of your own to allow you to summarize by saying or paraphrasing:* **So, it looks as if in order for you to feel safe in sharing a secret, you'd need to feel sure that the person who you told your secret to wouldn't tell anyone else.**

Would you feel safe if the person said that they would tell only ONE of their friends? Why or why not? *Allow for student response, then give students the following analogy.*

HOW SECRETS SPREAD: THE FEATHER ANALOGY

Transp. #3

Show Transparency #3, "Once You Tell Someone's Secret, You Can't Stop It From Spreading." **Imagine a person taking a large feather pillow or down comforter full of feathers, making a hole in it, and shaking it outside on a very windy day. Feathers would fly everywhere! They could even fly miles away.**

Once you tell someone's secret, you can't be sure you can stop it from spreading any more than you can stop feathers

from blowing away in a strong wind. The person you tell it to might think it would be O.K. if they just told it to one of their best friends, even though you asked them not to tell anyone. That person might not like the person who told you the secret, or they just might not be good at keeping secrets, and they might tell a lot of people. Pretty soon the secret could be spreading all over, just like the feathers in this picture. It would be hard, but still possible, to go out and try to pick up all these feathers, but you can <u>never</u> get someone's secret back once you let it out.

WHEN A SECRET SHOULD AND SHOULDN'T BE TOLD

Handout #2

Ask students if they think there are times when a secret <u>does</u> need to be told. Ask them to give examples. Point out that it is appropriate to tell a secret if someone is in real danger or is being hurt. Give students Handout #2, "Should You Ever Tell a Secret?"

Have your students form teams of four to debate the situations on the handout. Assign each team of four one of the situations or have them make up a situation of their own. Assign two of the students from each team the task of presenting arguments FOR telling each secret and the other two students the task of presenting arguments for NOT telling each secret. Point out that in a debate a person doesn't have to agree with the side they are asked to take, only to come up with what they think are the best reasons or arguments why someone would take that side. Students can trade positions with someone else in their group if they want. Have each team present a summary of the arguments for each side of their situation to the class. Have the rest of the class act as judges for the debate.

KEEPING PROMISES

Blank Transp.

Breaking a promise is a lot like telling a secret, because when you break a promise you hurt a person's feelings and you damage his or her trust in you. Who would like to share a time when a friend didn't keep a promise? Don't use names, just tell the situation. *Allow for student response.* **Let's write down some words that describe what we've felt like**

when someone didn't keep a promise to us. *Allow for student response. Write the feelings students suggest on a blank transparency.*

It's very important in making promises to be sure that you can keep the promise you make. Sometimes keeping a promise is hard, but if you remember how you felt when someone broke a promise to you, it will help you keep the promises you make to others.

APOLOGIZING

Transp. #4

Now let's talk about something else that's hard to do—apologizing. *Show Transparency #4, "Sometimes It's Hard to Apologize."* **Here is someone who is really mad and who is chewing out his friend. The friend knows that most of what's being said is true, but he's having a really hard time apologizing. What are some of the things the person on the left might be mad about? Why do you think it might be so hard for the person on the right to apologize?** *Allow for student response. Help students talk about their negative feelings about apologizing, such as: the person might not accept your apology and might stay angry; the person might take advantage of you if you apologize; you might feel a sense of injustice because you think the other person is partly to blame and should also apologize (or should apologize first); you may be frustrated that you're being accused of more than is true; you may feel attacked and want to fight back instead of apologizing; you may not like to admit being wrong; etc. Write on the transparency in the "thought bubble" space over the boy on the right some of the things he may be thinking regarding how hard it is to apologize.*

APOLOGIZING DOESN'T NECESSARILY MEAN YOU WERE WRONG OR WERE THE ONLY ONE WHO WAS WRONG

Transp. #5

One hard thing about apologizing can be the feeling that if you apologize for something, it's like saying out loud that you were the only one who was wrong. It might feel like

you're saying you're 100% WRONG and the other person is 100% RIGHT. Apologizing doesn't really mean this—it just means you're sorry. *Put Transparency #5, "Apologizing Doesn't Always Mean You Were Wrong, It Means You're Sorry," on the overhead.*

Let's pretend you promised to bring a friend in class a music tape he or she wanted to use for a class project, but you forgot to bring it. Your friend gets mad at you and says, "You promised you'd bring that tape! You're always saying you'll do things and you never keep your promises!" Of course, it's not true that you never keep your promises, but it is true that you didn't keep your promise this time. That's the part to apologize for. *Write the apology in the "I'm sorry I . . . " conversation bubble.* **You are sorry, but you're not someone who is always wrong. When you apologize, it helps if you say something to yourself to remind yourself that you're not a bad person—you're just human.** *Write, "I slipped up this time, but I usually keep my promises." in the thought bubble.*

Is anyone willing to share a time when you were able to tell a friend you were sorry, even though it was hard to do that? *Offer an example of your own to establish a climate of safety, then allow for student response. Ask students what they could have said to themselves right after they apologized which would have kept them from feeling that they were bad or 100% wrong. Give students acknowledgment for their personal examples.*

APOLOGIZING MEANS YOU'RE GROWING UP

Transp. #6

Another hard thing about apologizing is that the other person might get mad at you, or might stay mad at you even though you're apologizing for what you did. It takes courage to apologize! *Put Transparency #6, "Apologizing Means You're Growing Up," on the overhead. Say:* **Having the courage to apologize is a sure sign that you're growing up or getting more mature. Have you ever heard a baby or a spoiled brat apologize?** *Point to the baby on the transparency. Elicit responses from students that reflect the naturally selfish nature of babies or immature children.*

When kids get older and start to become mature, they start changing how they act when they do something that hurts another person's feelings. They start being able to think about other people instead of only about themselves. When they make a mistake, they're able to say, "I made a mistake; I'm sorry about it." It's not easy to do, but kids get better at it as they mature. Ask yourself if you're mature enough to admit it when you're wrong. *Pause.*

THREE STEPS TO APOLOGIZING

Transp. #7

Let me show you three easy steps to making an apology. *Place Transparency #7, "Three Steps to Apologizing," on the overhead. Cover all but the first step.* **After you've decided it would be a good thing to apologize, make your apology simple and sincere. Usually the other person can tell if you don't mean it. Kids have an amazing ability to spot a phoney.** *Write on the transparency some words of apology the girl might say.*

The second part of the apology is to decide if there's anything you can do to make up for what you did. If there is, offer to do it. If you broke or lost something, you might offer to fix it or replace it; if you took more than your share, offer to make it up to the person. Offer to do whatever it takes to make things right or fair.

Sometimes it will be obvious what you should do to make up for your mistake. Who can think of an example? *Allow for student response.* **Sometimes there won't be anything you can do except apologize. Who can think of some examples of times like this?** *Allow for student response.*

There's one last step to apologizing. *Uncover the last point and indicate the girl thinking to herself.* **Give yourself credit for being grown up enough to apologize to someone! It's one of the hardest things to do, and YOU DID IT! It's important to take a second to compliment yourself on your maturity.**

PRACTICING APOLOGIZING USING ROLE-PLAY SCENARIOS

Let's practice these three steps by doing some role-plays. *Choose volunteers to enact the scenarios following. Use the transparency to prompt students through the three steps. Help students determine whether or not there is anything they need to do to set things right (Step #2). Remind them that there may be times when there isn't much that can be done except to say that it won't happen again. For Step #3, suggest some self-statements students could use to give themselves credit for being mature and courageous enough to apologize.*

Scenarios

1. **You thought your friend was through with her library book, so you borrowed it without asking. When you see her the next day she's mad at you because the book was due the day you borrowed it and now she owes a fine.**
2. **When everyone got their test papers back, your friend didn't want you to see his. You made a big deal of seeing it and then said in a loud voice, "You got a D!" Your friend is really mad at you.**
3. **You were so slow getting ready that you and your friend were late to the end-of-the-soccer-season pizza party. There was almost no pizza left when the two of you finally got there, and your friend is mad at you.**

After completing these examples, have students role-play the following scenarios with their Learning Partners. Say or paraphrase: **I'd like you now to practice the three steps of apologizing with your Learning Partner. Get together, and then decide which of you is the taller person.**

I'm going to read you a situation. Taller Learning Partner, I want you to pretend that you're the person in the situation who needs to make the apology. When I've finished reading the story, make a simple and sincere apology. Then, decide if there's something that you can do to make up for the problem. If so, tell your Learning Partner what you'll do.

Finally, give yourself a compliment for being mature enough to make an apology. In a real situation you'd say this compliment to yourself. For this practice situation, I'd like you to say it out loud.

While the taller partners are doing these three steps, I'd like all the shorter partners to look at them, listen, and then accept the apology. After you're both done, we'll switch places and the shorter partner will be the one to apologize in the next situation.

Ready, taller partner? Here's the first situation:

- **Your friend asked to borrow some lunch money for the third time in one week, and you said, "What's the matter? Are you POOR or something?" Your friend was really embarrassed and has stayed away from you since then. Later on that week you heard your mother mention that your friend's dad had just lost his job. You feel terrible!**

Allow students time to complete the role-play, then say: **Now it's the shorter partner's turn to practice apologizing. Here's your story:**

- **After yesterday's ball game you were so frustrated that you hadn't gotten to play much that you called your friend a "ball hog." Your friend is angry about it.**

Alternate partners for the rest of the scenarios:

- **You found a plate of brownies in the refrigerator. No one was home to ask, so you ate some. When your sister got home she hit the ceiling because she'd promised to bring the brownies to a meeting.**
- **You were over at your friend's house and you were in a silly mood. You kept goofing off, playing practical jokes, and teasing your friend until he got all hyper. He was grounded for making too much noise.**
- **You told your friend you couldn't go shopping with her because you had company from out of town. Now she's found out you went to a party she hadn't been invited to. She's really hurt that you lied to her.**

- **When you sat down in the cafeteria, you bumped someone's arm and he spilled his chocolate milk. His favorite concert T-shirt has chocolate all over it and he's really mad.**

WHAT IF SOMEONE DOESN'T ACCEPT YOUR APOLOGY?

Sometimes peoples' feelings can be so strong that it takes them a while to be ready to accept an apology. If someone is still mad at you after you've apologized, just remember, FEELINGS CHANGE! The best thing you can do is to remind yourself that you were mature to apologize, and that the other person probably needs some cooling off time before your apology can sink in.

FORGIVENESS

It's not easy to apologize to someone when he or she isn't ready to listen to you, is it? What would you LIKE to have happen when you apologize to someone? *Allow for student response.*

What we'd like when we apologize, really, is forgiveness, isn't it? Another part of friendship that's just as important as apologizing is knowing how to forgive.

When others do something that hurts us or makes us mad, we sometimes want to hurt them back or "make them pay" for what they did. We want them to know that we're in the right and they're wrong. For some of us, forgiving can be hard to do.

If we forgive a person, it can feel like we're somehow saying what he or she did to us is O.K.; it can feel like we're letting the other person get away with what happened. That's not what forgiveness really means, though. Forgiveness doesn't mean you're saying the other person isn't responsible for what he or she did.

Transp. #8

Show Transparency #8, "The Parts of Forgiveness." Say or paraphrase: **What forgiving means is that you try to understand the other person's point of view, that you don't try to get even or hurt them back, and that you're willing to give them or the friendship another chance.**

Trying to see things from the other person's point of view makes it easier to forgive someone. Seeing things from their point of view is like getting inside them and feeling the way they feel. When you understand a little about what the other person is feeling inside, you can usually forgive a little.

Here's an example. Maybe a friend acts really mean toward you one day, and you find out later that his dad chewed him out for no good reason earlier that day. He shouldn't have taken his anger out on you, but if you understand that he was feeling really bad himself it makes it easier to forgive him. Can you think of another example where understanding why the person did something that bugged you helped you to forgive the person? *Allow for student response. Remind students not to use names.*

You can forgive others but still tell them you don't like what they did that made you mad and that it's not O.K. for them to do it again. You can even stay mad for awhile. You just won't try and get even. Forgiveness means you don't try to hurt the other person back. It means you're willing to try to forget about what the other person did and give the friendship another chance.

Let me give you an example of this. Let's say that you and your grandfather made a model together, and one day your friend is fooling around with it and accidentally breaks it. You might feel really mad. You could let those angry feelings cause you to do something to hurt your friend or to try to make him or her feel bad or embarrassed for a long time for breaking the model.

If you forgive your friend, you might say something like, "I'm really mad that you broke my model, even though I

know you didn't mean to. I want to keep on being friends, but I don't want you to fool around with my stuff."

Can any of you think of a time when someone did something to you and you were able to forgive them? When you give your example, don't use names. *Allow for student response. Summarize by saying:* **So in all these examples we can see that forgiving means that even though you feel hurt or mad: (1) you try to see things from the other person's point of view, (2) you don't try to get even or hurt the other person back, and (3) you're willing to give the friendship another chance.**

When we refuse to forgive each other, we all waste a lot of time being mad and we miss out on the fun we could be having with each other.

LETTING A FRIEND HAVE OTHER FRIENDS

One of the very hardest things to do in a friendship is to let your friends have other friends. Let's talk about this for a minute.

Everyone likes to have a friend who wants to do things with them more than with anyone else. Sometimes, though, you might find yourself wanting your friend to <u>only</u> do things with you. Part of growing up is learning to let your friends have other friends, too.

Transp. #9

Even when you realize this, it's still not easy when your friend chooses to do something with someone else instead of with you. *Show Transparency #9, "Feeling O.K. About Your Friends Having Other Friends."* **Let's brainstorm some things you could say to yourself that could make you feel better when this happens.** *Allow for student response. Write helpful responses on the transparency and prioritize these by having students vote for their favorites.*

LESSON REVIEW

Summarize the lesson by doing a "whip" around the class, asking students to complete one of the following sentence starters:

- *I learned . . . .*
- *I was surprised . . . .*
- *This can help me because . . . .*
- *The part of this lesson I liked best was . . . .*
- *A way I'm going to use what I learned today is . . . .*

Use the Supplementary Activities to provide further practice of lesson concepts. Appendix E contains posters of behaviors useful for making and keeping friends. If you have not already displayed these posters in your classroom, you may wish to select the poster(s) that relate to this lesson and hang these up as a reminder of lesson concepts.

TRANSPARENCY #1

Being a Good Friend Isn't Always Easy

Good friends try to:

1. Say what they honestly feel or think without hurting their friend's feelings—they are honest but kind.
2. Keep secrets and promises.

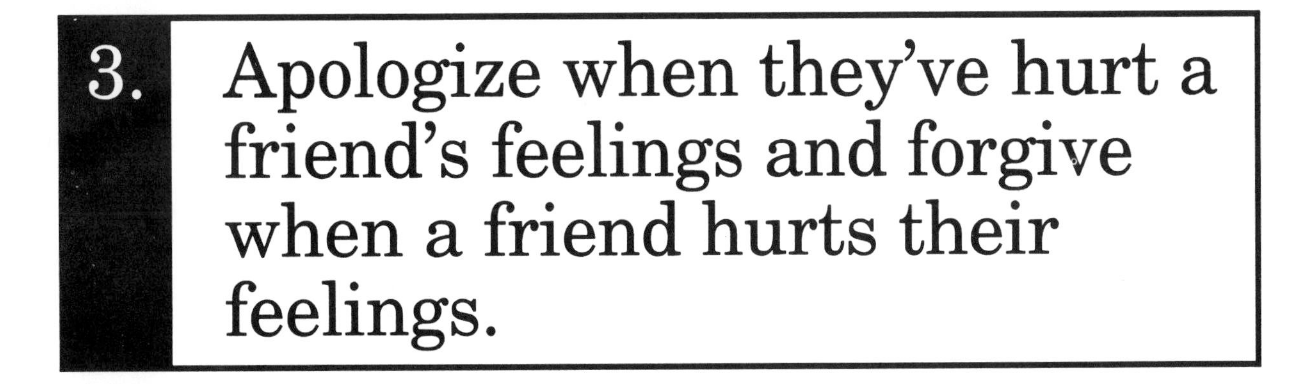

3. Apologize when they've hurt a friend's feelings and forgive when a friend hurts their feelings.
4. Let their friends have other friends.

TRANSPARENCY #2A/HANDOUT #1A

Being Honest But Kind

1. Your friend calls and asks you to come over. You've already promised to play with someone else.

2. Your friend sits next to you. During tests, he or she asks you for answers. You don't like this, and you also worry about being caught.

3. Your friend just bought a new jacket. He or she wears it to school for the first time and says, "How do you like my jacket?" You don't!

4. Most of the kids in your class don't like your friend because she is so bossy. She isn't bossy very often with you. She tells you that she's feeling hurt because several other kids don't like her.

5. It's your friend's birthday. She is expecting you to give her a gift, but you forgot about it. You don't have anything to give her.

6. Your friend likes to put down an unpopular student. You don't think the person is that bad and you think your friend is being mean.

TRANSPARENCY #2B/HANDOUT #1B

Being Honest But Kind (continued)

7. The last time your friend borrowed something from you he broke it. Now he wants to borrow something else. You don't want to lend him anything, but still want to keep him as a friend.

8. Your friend is horsing around and keeps poking you. You don't like it.

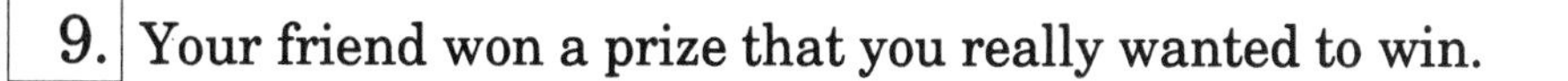

9. Your friend won a prize that you really wanted to win.

10 You promised your friend you'd sit with him or her at lunch everyday. Now you want to make some new friends, too.

11. Your friend asks if he or she can bring another person to your birthday party. You don't like the person your friend wants to bring.

12. Your friend brags a lot. It really bugs you and you wish that he or she would stop.

13. You promised your friend you'd come over Saturday. Somebody else invites you skiing. You love to ski.

TRANSPARENCY #3

Once You Tell Someone's Secret, You Can't Stop It From Spreading

HANDOUT #2

Should You Ever Tell a Secret?

Directions:

For each of the secrets below, pretend a friend told you the secret and asked you not to tell anyone. Decide whether you would tell the secret or not. Check the box that shows what you would do and give your reasons.

Secrets	Would you tell?	Who would you tell?	Explain why.
Your friend tells you that two other kids are going to fight each other after school.	❑ YES ❑ NO		
Your friend has just told you that his parents are getting a divorce.	❑ YES ❑ NO		
Your friend tells you the name of a boy in class who she really likes.	❑ YES ❑ NO		
Your friend shows you some pills he got from an older kid.	❑ YES ❑ NO		
Your friend tells you that his dad often drinks too much and yells at everyone in the house until they are crying.	❑ YES ❑ NO		
Your friend tells you she hates a certain person in the class.	❑ YES ❑ NO		
Your friend tells you her older brother drinks their parents' alcohol when they aren't at home. She says that her brother has said he'd beat her up if she told anyone.	❑ YES ❑ NO		
You went shopping with your friend. After you leave the store, he says, "Can you keep a secret?" and shows you candy he has stolen.	❑ YES ❑ NO		
Give another example of a secret that you would or would not keep and explain why.			
	❑ YES ❑ NO		

TRANSPARENCY #4

Sometimes It's Hard to Apologize

TRANSPARENCY #5

Apologizing Doesn't Always Mean You Were Wrong— It Means You're Sorry

TRANSPARENCY #6

Apologizing Means You're Growing Up

TRANSPARENCY #7

Three Steps to Apologizing

1. Make a simple and sincere apology.

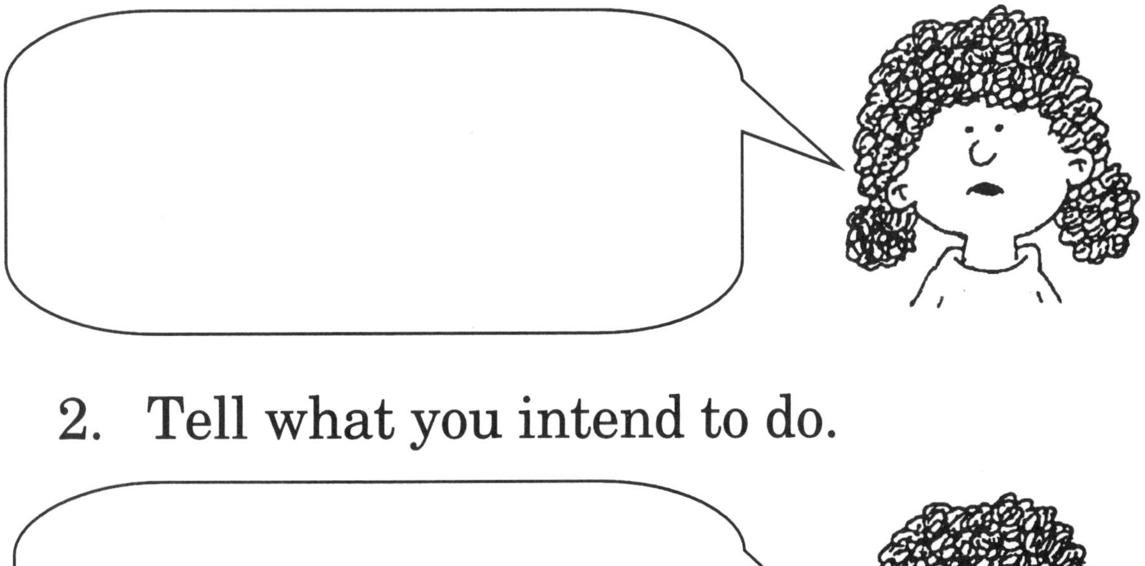

2. Tell what you intend to do.

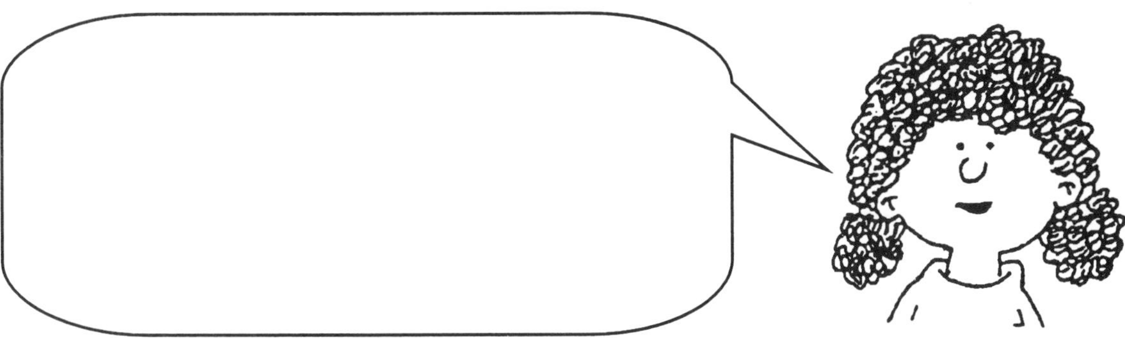

3. Tell yourself you're growing up.

TRANSPARENCY #8

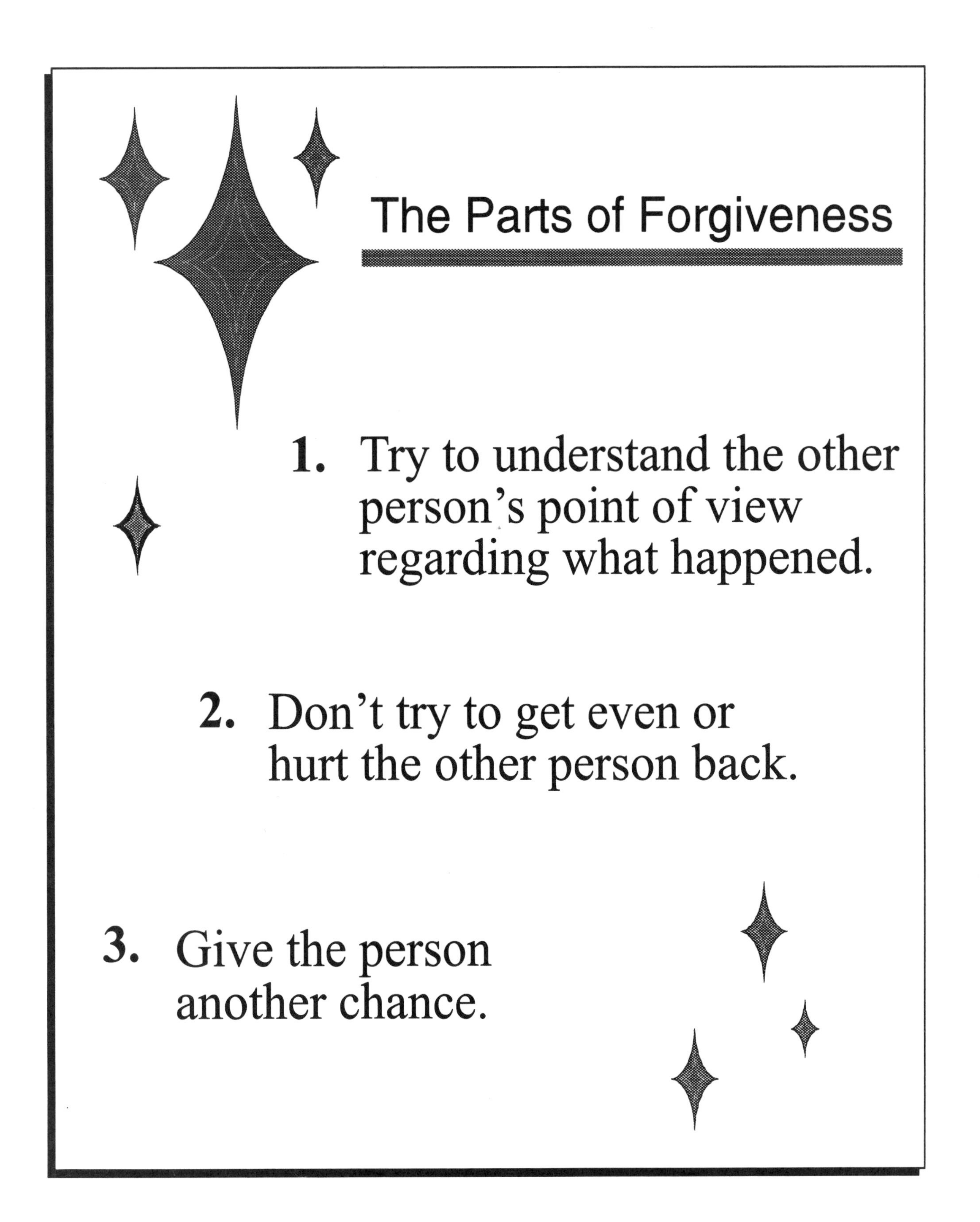

TRANSPARENCY #9

Feeling O.K. About Your Friends Having Other Friends

SUPPLEMENTARY ACTIVITY #1

More Practice in Being Honest But Kind

1. Your friend paints a picture which you think looks awful. He or she asks you what you think of it.

   What do you say?

   ____

   ____

2. You gave your friend a nice present and he or she doesn't seem to appreciate it.

   What do you say?

   ____

   ____

3. Your friend asks you to tell his or her parents that he or she was with you after school, so that your friend won't get into trouble. Your friend wasn't with you, and you don't want to lie.

   What do you say?

   ____

   ____

4. Your friend promised to help you do something you needed to get done. Your friend never came over to help as he or she promised.

   What do you say?

   ____

   ____

5. Your friend wants to use your new bike. You don't want to lend it.

   What do you say?

   ____

   ____

More Practice in Being Honest But Kind (continued)

6. You meet your friend after you heard that he or she had said some mean things about you.

   What do you say?

   ___

   ___

7. You lent your friend your radio. He or she breaks it!

   What do you say?

   ___

   ___

8. Your friend always talks about others behind their backs. You like some of the kids he or she talks about.

   What do you say?

   ___

   ___

Directions:

Pick three of the situations above and ask yourself: If these situations were reversed, what would you want your friend to say to you?

Situation #1 ___

___

___

Situation #2 ___

___

___

Situation #3___

___

___

___

___

SUPPLEMENTARY ACTIVITY #2

Some Questions About Secrets

1. Have you ever told someone a secret and later found out that they told someone else? YES ☐ NO ☐

2. If yes, how did you feel? __________________________________

3. Did the secret spread to other people? YES ☐ NO ☐

4. If yes, was there any way you could have stopped the secret from spreading? YES ☐ NO ☐

5. Have you ever told someone else a secret that you were told to keep? YES ☐ NO ☐

6. Did the secret spread to other people? YES ☐ NO ☐

7. If you had it to do over again, would you tell the secret? YES ☐ NO ☐

8. Is it O.K. to tell someone else's secret to one of your friends who you trust? YES ☐ NO ☐
   Why or why not? __________________________________

9. Is it good to tell someone a secret when there are other people standing nearby? YES ☐ NO ☐

10. If two of your friends whispered secrets to each other in front of you, how would you feel? __________________________________

11. Is it fair to try to get someone to tell another person's secret? YES ☐ NO ☐

12. How do you feel when someone tries to get you to tell a secret someone else told you? __________________________________

SUPPLEMENTARY ACTIVITY #3

Dear Abby Letters

Objective Students will increase their skill at dealing with friendship problems.

Materials Pencil and paper

Procedure Explain to the students that they will be doing some group problem solving on typical friendship difficulties. To do this, they will be brainstorming solutions to the problems stated in "Dear Abby" letters they will write.

Have students write their own Dear Abby letters on typical friendship problem situations. Students may draw from their own experiences or ones they have heard about. Ask them not to use the real names of people in their letters. They should be careful not to say anything about others that could be hurtful. They should sign the letter with a made up name such as "Frustrated" or "Confused."

Collect the letters and select those relevant to your students for group problem solving.

SUPPLEMENTARY ACTIVITY #4

How I Feel About Honesty Between Friends

A time when my friend was dishonest with me:	
How I felt:	
What I would have done in their place:	
A time when my friend had the courage to be honest with me:	
How I felt:	

SUPPLEMENTARY ACTIVITY #5

How to Keep a Friendship When You Fight With a Friend

Directions:

Decide if these ideas are helpful or not helpful things to do when you and a friend are fighting about something.	**Helpful**	**Might be Helpful**	**Not Helpful**
1. Give in, even if you think you're right.	☐	☐	☐
2. Suggest taking turns.	☐	☐	☐
3. Threaten to do something mean.	☐	☐	☐
4. Complain until you get your way.	☐	☐	☐
5. Explain how you feel.	☐	☐	☐
6. Try to make a compromise so that each gets part of what they want.	☐	☐	☐
7. Hit the person.	☐	☐	☐
8. Change the subject.	☐	☐	☐
9. Apologize (if you were wrong).	☐	☐	☐
10. Tattle on the person.	☐	☐	☐
11. Ask someone else to help you both work it out.	☐	☐	☐
12. Listen to the other person's point of view.	☐	☐	☐
13. Call the person names.	☐	☐	☐
14. Brainstorm a list of ways to solve the problem.	☐	☐	☐
15. Flip a coin (if you both want the same thing).	☐	☐	☐
16. Tell the other person what they are thinking or feeling.	☐	☐	☐

SUPPLEMENTARY ACTIVITY #6

Times I Was a Winner by Apologizing

These are some times I was a winner—because even though I was wrong, I admitted it and said I was sorry.

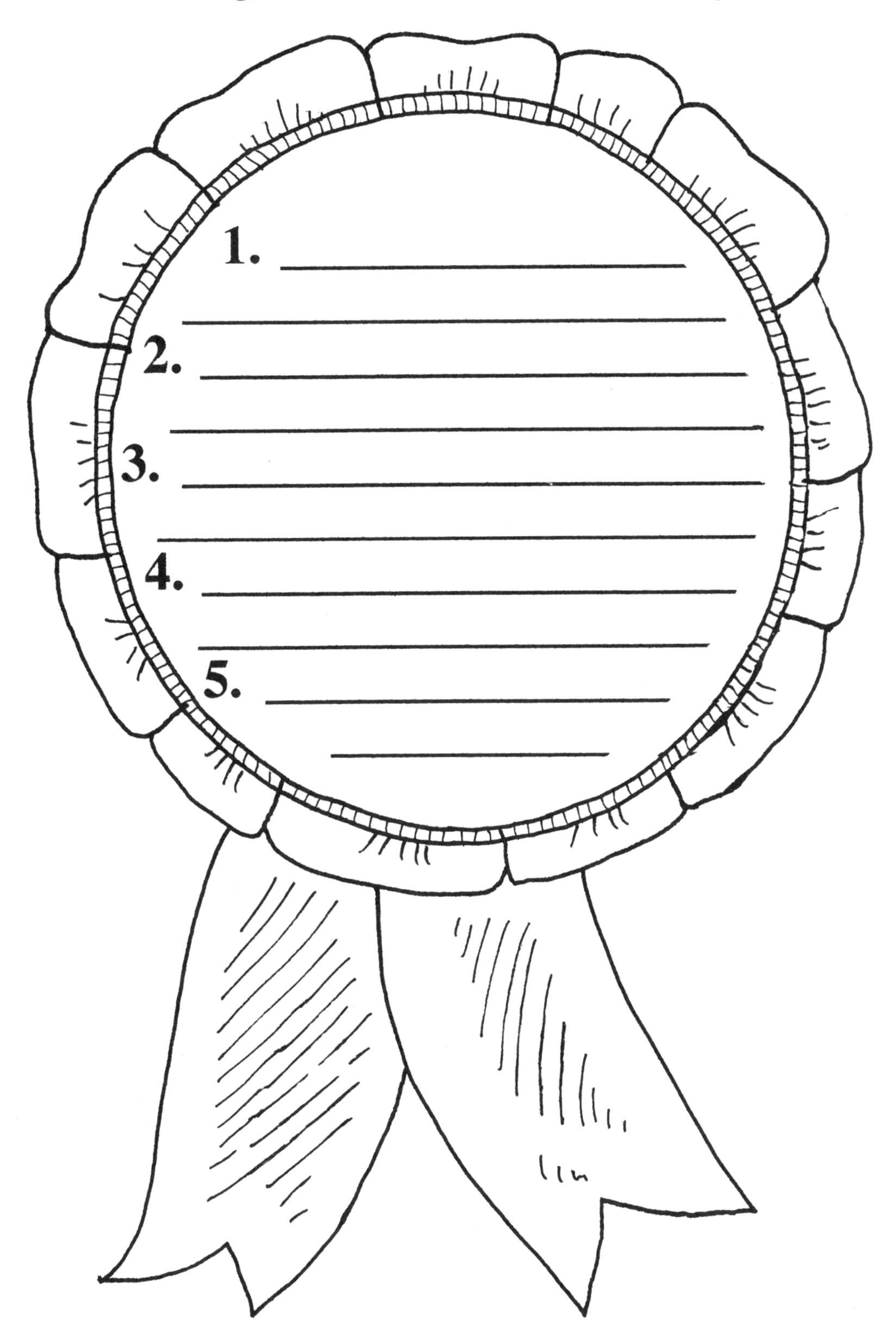

SUPPLEMENTARY ACTIVITY #7

Your Opinions About Friendship

Directions:

Decide whether you would do each of these things or not and give your reasons.

1. Would you lend a friend your lunch money even if it meant you would have to go without lunch?

2. Would you let a friend copy your paper and get credit for your idea?

3. Would you tell your friend the truth if the reason you didn't want to go somewhere with him or her was because you wanted to play with someone else?

4. Would you loan your allowance to a friend, even if he or she wouldn't tell you why he or she needed to borrow it?

5. Would you stop being friends with someone if he or she borrowed a CD or cassette tape from you, then lost it and acted as if he or she didn't care?

6. Would you continue to buy presents for a friend who never bought presents for you, even though he or she could afford to?

7. Would you tell a friend if you didn't like a present he or she gave to you?

8. Would you remain friends with someone who told one of your secrets after promising that they wouldn't tell?

9. Would you remain friends with someone who constantly put down your other friends?

10. Would you rather be friends with someone who was really popular even though it meant you didn't have time to be friends with someone else you liked better who wasn't as popular?

SUPPLEMENTARY ACTIVITY #8

True or False Statements About Friendship

Objective Students will share opinions on friendship issues.

Materials Supplementary Activity #8 Handout, "True or False Statements About Friendship"

Procedure Give students the handout. After they have had time to complete it, lead a discussion in which students are asked to share their responses to the items and the reasons for their choices. See how many items students can come to agreement on as a group. For those items where students disagree, allow students to share their reasons for their opinions.

Following completion of the discussion, ask if any students changed their mind about an answer because of new thoughts they had as a result of the class discussion.

VARIATION

When conducting this activity, sometimes it's fun to invite students to do a standing vote. Have students who agree with the statement line up on the left side of the room, those who disagree line up on the right side, and those who feel neutral or unsure stand in the middle of the room. This way students can see immediately how their classmates feel about a friendship issue.

SUPPLEMENTARY ACTIVITY #8 HANDOUT

True or False Statements About Friendship

Directions:

Put a "T" on the lines next to those statements you think are true, an "F" on the lines next to those you think are false, and a "U" on the lines for those statements you're unsure about. Be prepared to give reasons for your opinions.

1. ____ To keep friends, you can't hurt their feelings.
2. ____ You can be mad at someone and still be their friend.
3. ____ You can only have one very close or "special" friend at a time.
4. ____ It's impossible to be best friends with two other people who know each other.
5. ____ You should be able to share your deepest secrets with your best friend.
6. ____ You should say you "hate" the same people your friend does.
7. ____ Friends should never make fun of each other.
8. ____ You should "forgive and forget" when a friend hurts you in some way.
9. ____ You should let a best friend borrow anything of yours that they need.
10. ____ Once you tell someone's secret to another person, it's hard to keep it from spreading.
11. ____ It's normal to feel badly when your best friend plays with someone else.
12. ____ A person can be your friend even if you don't trust him or her.
13. ____ It helps to use your imagination to understand your friend's point of view.
14. ____ Your friends can say mean things to you and still like you.

A Multiple Intelligences Friendship Center

You can provide students with a variety of activities which reinforce friendship behaviors by setting up a Multiple Intelligences Friendship Center in your classroom.

Dr. Howard Gardner of Harvard University, in his book *Frames of Mind: The Theory of Multiple Intelligences**, suggests that it is more accurate to think of a person as having seven different intelligences rather than a single intelligence that encompasses verbal and math abilities. This concept can readily be seen in the classroom, where students often experience greater interest in and insight of a subject when they can explore it by using one or more of their areas of aptitude.

The activities in this center are designed to provide students with a variety of interpersonal skill-building activities in each of the seven intelligences: Linguistic, Mathematical-Logical, Musical, Kinesthetic, Visual-Spacial, Interpersonal, and Intrapersonal. (While many of these activities actually require a combination of different intelligences, they have been categorized under the intelligence that is being utilized the most.) Before introducing students to the center, you may want to teach the ASSIST lesson "Discovering the Ways You Are Smart: Looking at Multiple Intelligences." This can be found in the forthcoming ASSIST manual *Building Self-Esteem in the Classroom*.

* Basic Books, Inc., New York, 1983

Setting Up the Center

To set up the center, designate an area of the classroom where center displays and materials can be located. Use a bulletin board or cardboard to create a backdrop or a three-panel screen. The center itself can be created by using a table or two desk tops on which you can place the center materials. If the activities you select require bulky materials or "kits" of collected objects, you may want to put these into cardboard boxes near or below the table.

Using the Center

To help students learn how to use the center, it is advisable to demonstrate how each activity is done. For some activities, it may be helpful to display a completed project near the activity to serve as a model.

Explain to students your rules for when and how they are to use the center. Since some of the activities involve crafts, you may wish to discuss clean up rules or procedures.

Before students start using the center, decide on a plan for how you'll acknowledge their efforts. You may want to establish a system for giving students feedback regarding activities they do at the center. You might set aside classroom time for students to present to the class those projects they do at the center. You could also set aside bulletin board space on which to post some of the products resulting from center activities.

Selecting Activities at the Center

There are a number of ways you can set up activities at the center. One way is to start with two activities from each of the seven intelligences. These can be mounted on cards. Stock the center with the necessary materials to do these activities. You can change center activities on a weekly basis. (See Illustration A.)

Another approach to establishing the center is to laminate all the following pages of activities and place these "activity cards" in a box with dividers for each of the seven intelligences. You may choose not to cut the pages containing two cards so all pages in the boxes will be the same height. You can have all the materials needed to do the activities in boxes under the activity table. If you choose this approach, duplicate the reproducible handouts and have these available in another box, again grouped by intelligence. (See Illustration B.)

It would also be helpful to have a copy of the intermediate friendship word list permanently mounted at the center.

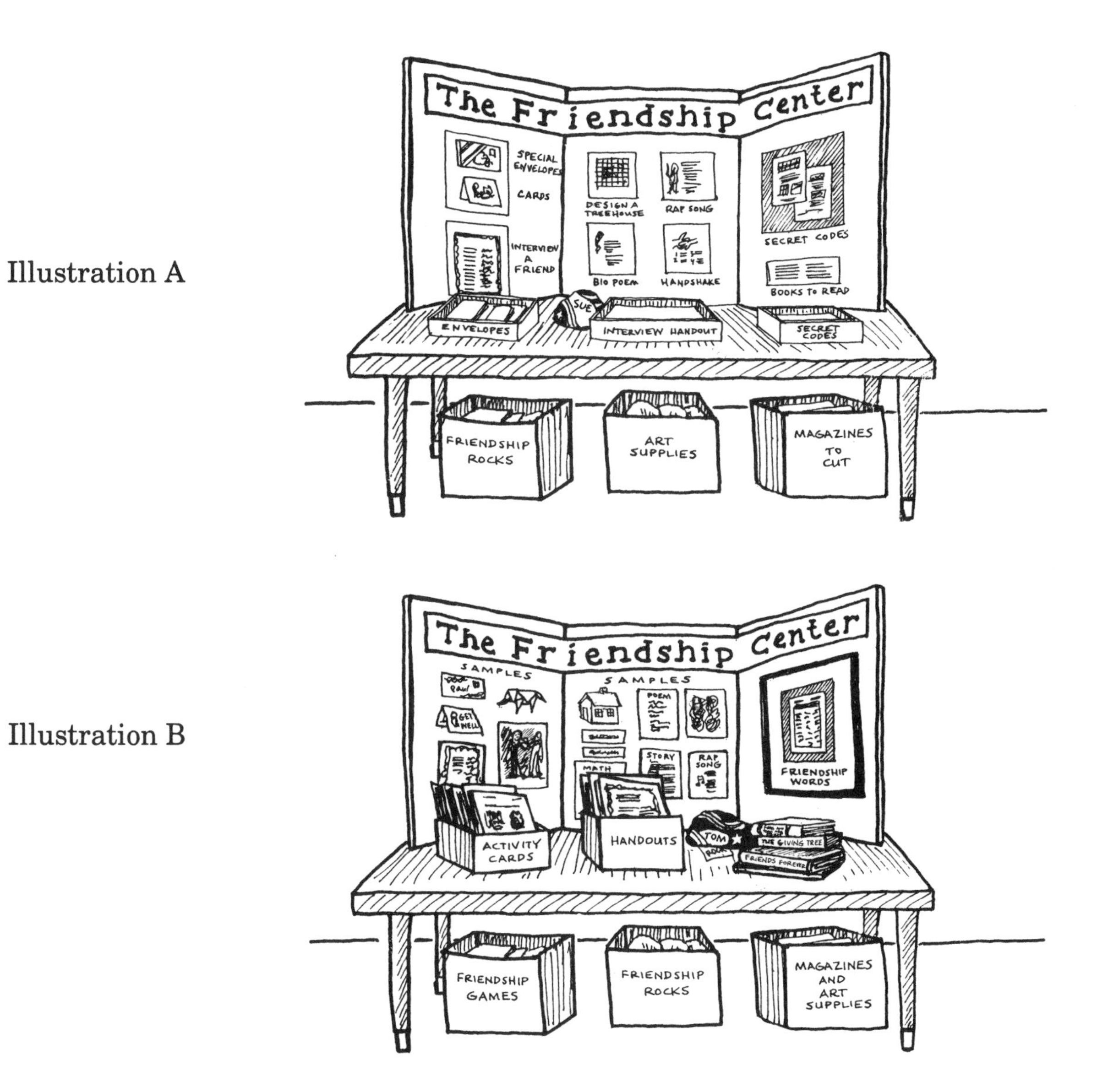

Scheduling Student Use of the Center

You may wish to make use of the center a scheduled activity, a free time option, or both. The center can also be used as a reward for good friendship behavior or as an activity center for students who finish other classwork early.

Using Books, Games, and Lesson Handouts at the Center

You might like to include at your center a rotating selection of library books that relate to the topic of friendships. You can use the books suggested in Appendix B, "Using Literature to Enhance Students' Understanding of Friendship." The activity card for Activity 2 in this Appendix has suggested questions students can answer regarding the friendship book that they read.

You can also duplicate and set out the friendship games which are found in Appendix C, "Friendship Games." You can ask students to color the games and then have these laminated. The activity card for Activity 42 in this Appendix suggests that students play these games.

The lesson handouts and supplementary activities from each lesson in this manual also make great center activities. If you use any of these, simply make up your own activity cards to include in the center.

A Multiple Intelligences Friendship Center

Table of Activities

Activities are listed by the primary intelligence used most. Those which have handout(s) are indicated by an asterisk.

"Friendship Words" Poster for the Friendship Center

Linguistic (Language)

1. A Cooperative Story About Friendship
2. Read a Book About Friendship
* 3. Write a Letter to a Friend
4. Writing About Friendship
5. Put Your Friend Into the Story
* 6. Saying Thanks to a Friend in Many Languages (Grateful-Grams)
7. Word Search
8. Kind Crosswords for Friends
9. Bio Poems
10. Writing About Friendship Day by Day

Mathematical-Logical

11. A Million Dollars for Friendship
12. Analyzing the Behavior of Kids Who Are Well-Liked
13. The Ways You and Your Friend Are Alike and Different
* 14. A Secret Code for You and Your Friend
* 15. Friendship Puzzles
* 16. Go Figure!

Musical

17. Sharing the Beat
18. Focus on Friendly Sounds
19. Turn an Old Song Into a New Friendship Song
20. A Friendship Rap
21. Tune In to Friendship
22. A Friendship Round

Kinesthetic (Physical)

23. Hands of Your Friends
24. A Friendship Handshake
25. A Dance for Friendship
26. Walk Like a Friend
27. A Footrace With a Friend
28. Friendship Rocks

Visual-Spatial (Artistic)

29. Make a Coloring Book for Your Friend
30. A Picture of My Best Friend
* 31. A Wish for a Friend
32. Send a Card to a Friend
33. A Collage About Friendships
* 34. Make a Special Envelope for Your Friend
35. Design a Treehouse or a Clubhouse
36. Make an Origami Gift for a Friend
37. Draw a Picture of You and Your Friend
38. Friendship Wish Collage

Interpersonal (Social)

* 39. Friendship Awards
* 40. Friendship Coupons
* 41. Noticing What a Friend Did
42. A Puppet Play About Friends
43. Play a Friendship Game
* 44. Friends of All Ages
45. A Friendship Thought Balloon
46. Body Language
47. Solve These Friendship Problems
* 48. Interview a Classmate You Don't Know Well
* 49. Let Me Tell You About My Friend
* 50. How Well Do You Know Your Friends?
* 51. Pen Pals

Intrapersonal (Self)

52. What Kind of Friend Do I Really Want?
53. The Reasons Why Someone Would Want Me for a Friend
54. A Letter to an Imaginary Best Friend
55. A Timeline of Your Friends
56. How Good a Friend Am I to Others?
57. Know Yourself

POSTER FOR THE FRIENDSHIP CENTER

Friendship Words

adventurous
artistic
athletic
brave
calm
capable
caring
clever
confident
considerate
cooperative
creative
dependable
easy-going
efficient
energetic
fair
fast
flexible
friendly
fun
funny
generous
gentle
genuine
good athlete
good listener
good memory
good sport
graceful
great
helpful
honest
humorous
imaginative
intelligent
interesting
inventive
kind
likable
lively
loyal
mature
musical
neat
optimistic
organized
original
outgoing
patient
positive
problem solver
reasonable
reliable
self-confident
sensible
sensitive
shares
sincere
skillful
smart
special
strong
supportive
talented
thorough
thoughtful
trustworthy
truthful
understanding
unique
unselfish
wise
witty

ACTIVITY CARD FOR THE FRIENDSHIP CENTER

1. INTELLIGENCE: LINGUISTIC (LANGUAGE)

A COOPERATIVE STORY ABOUT FRIENDSHIP

Everyone can share in writing a part of this story, which will make it more interesting.

Directions:

On a piece of paper, write an exciting beginning to a story about friendship. Include any picture you might want to draw. Leave the story unfinished so that someone else can add to the story.

On the bottom half of the page, paste or tape an envelope. On the envelope, write a message asking others to continue or finish the story. They should write what they want to add on another piece of paper and put it in the envelope for you and others to enjoy.

Ask your teacher where you should place your cooperative story so that others can see it to write their additions to the story.

ACTIVITY CARD FOR THE FRIENDSHIP CENTER

2. INTELLIGENCE: LINGUISTIC (LANGUAGE)

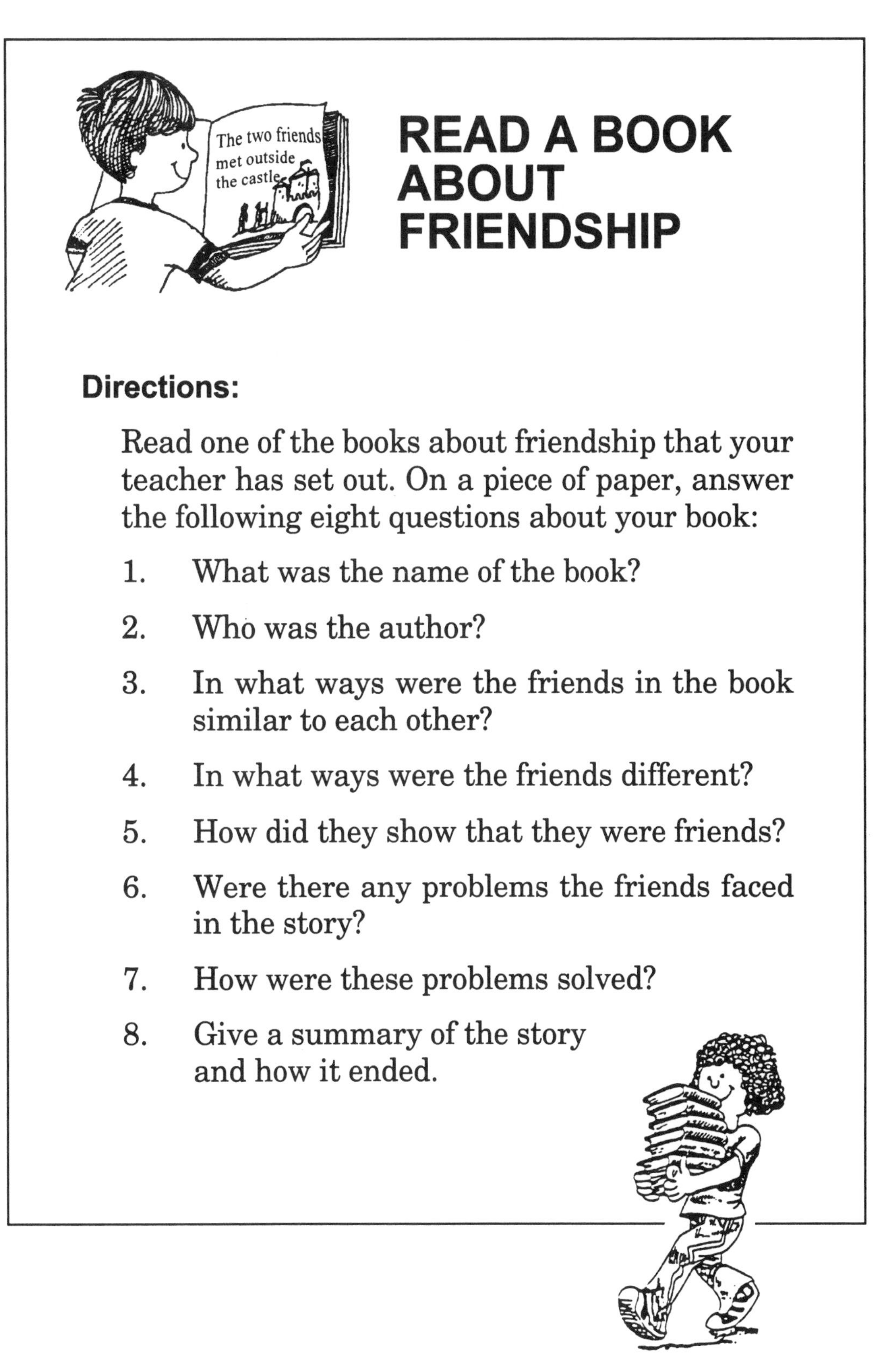

READ A BOOK ABOUT FRIENDSHIP

Directions:

Read one of the books about friendship that your teacher has set out. On a piece of paper, answer the following eight questions about your book:

1. What was the name of the book?
2. Who was the author?
3. In what ways were the friends in the book similar to each other?
4. In what ways were the friends different?
5. How did they show that they were friends?
6. Were there any problems the friends faced in the story?
7. How were these problems solved?
8. Give a summary of the story and how it ended.

ACTIVITY CARD FOR THE FRIENDSHIP CENTER

3. INTELLIGENCE: LINGUISTIC (LANGUAGE)

WRITE A LETTER TO A FRIEND

Directions:

It's fun to be allowed to write to a friend during class time! It's also fun to write a letter to someone you don't know well but would like to be friends with. Use the handout to write your letter, and be sure to remember to put in a sincere compliment or two. Then give your letter to your friend.

You'll need: a pencil and the "Dropping You a Line" handout for boys or for girls.

Dropping You a Line

ACTIVITY 3 HANDOUT #1A FOR THE FRIENDSHIP CENTER

Dropping You a Line

ACTIVITY 3 HANDOUT #1B FOR THE FRIENDSHIP CENTER

Dropping You a Line

ACTIVITY CARD FOR THE FRIENDSHIP CENTER

4. INTELLIGENCE: LINGUISTIC (LANGUAGE)

WRITING ABOUT FRIENDSHIP

Directions:

Choose ONE of the following ways to write a paragraph or two about friendship.

1.	No Friends	Pretend you know a person who told you that he or she didn't have any friends. Write what you would say to him or her that would be helpful.
2.	Similar and Different	Describe the similarities and differences between (choose one): • The weather and friendship • The ocean and friendship • Money and friendship
3.	Which One?	If you could have it only one way, would you rather have a friend who always says what he or she thinks or a friend who is a good listener? Give reasons for your decision.
4.	Agree or Disagree	Choose one of the statements below and tell whether you agree or disagree with it. Give at least three reasons for your opinion. • "It's important to be popular." • "You have to work at friendship." • "Not everyone is going to like you."
5.	A Short Poem	Write a six-line poem about friends. Start each line of the poem with "Friends are ____________."
6.	Detective Report	Pretend you're a private detective. You've been following "The Most Friendly Person in the World" around for several days. Now, write your detective report telling about all the friendly things this person did and said to others.

ACTIVITY CARD FOR THE FRIENDSHIP CENTER

5. INTELLIGENCE: LINGUISTIC (LANGUAGE)

PUT YOUR FRIEND INTO THE STORY

Directions:

1. Make up a story and have your friend be one of the people in it, or take a story you know well and change it to put your friend into it. If you like, you can have both you and your friend be a part of the story.
2. Use some facts about your friend in the story.
3. Draw pictures to illustrate the story. If you can get small pictures of your friend, paste these onto the drawings.
4. Staple the pages together into a book. Show it to your teacher, then give it to your friend.

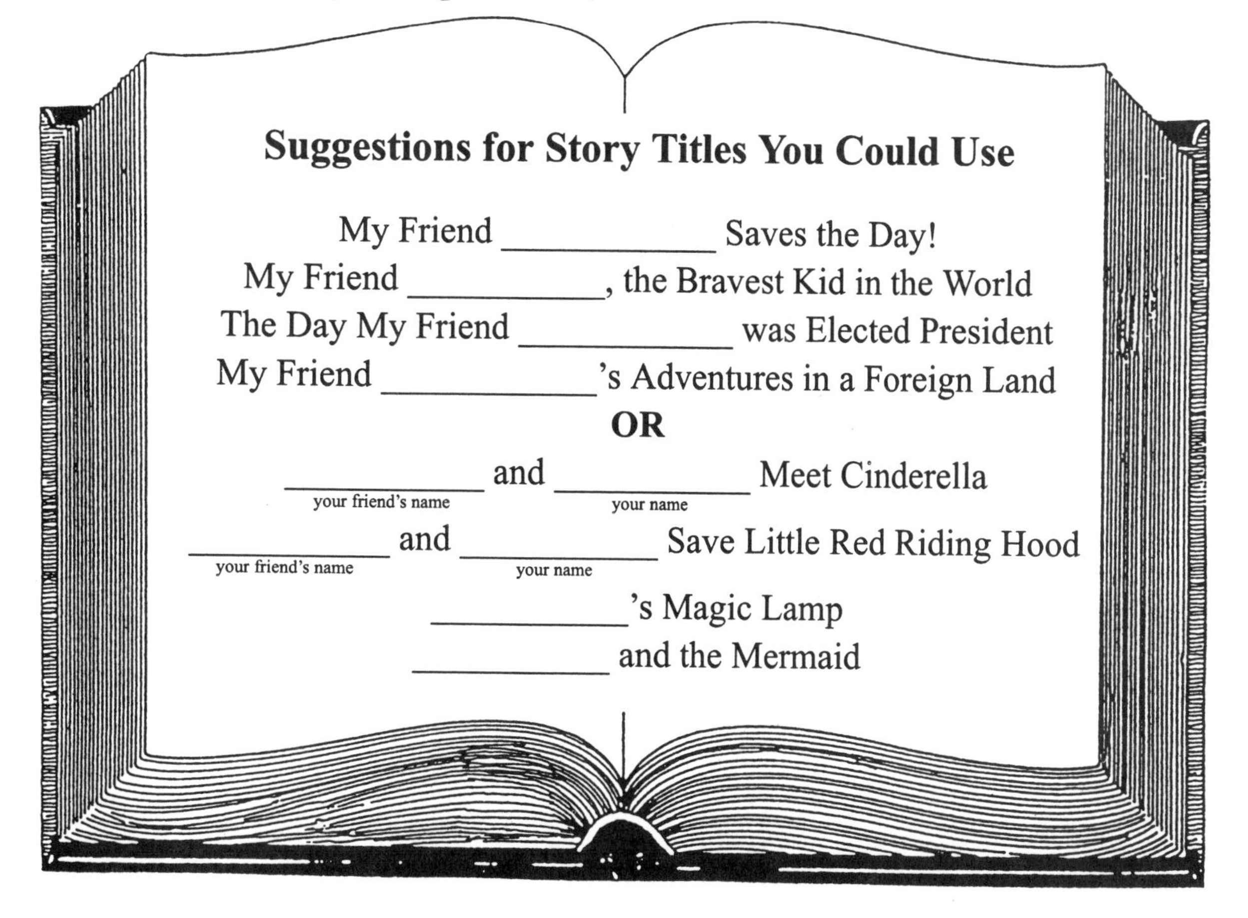

ACTIVITY CARD FOR THE FRIENDSHIP CENTER

6. INTELLIGENCE: LINGUISTIC (LANGUAGE)

Grateful Gram

GRAZIE!
ARIGATO!
MERCI!
GRACIAS
THANKS!

To my friend ________
Name
Thank you for ________

Your friend, ________
Name

MANGE TAKKE! Danke Schön! TAKE SOMEKE

SAYING THANKS TO A FRIEND IN MANY LANGUAGES (GRATEFUL-GRAMS)

Directions:

Think about something a friend has done that you appreciate or are thankful for. Use the Grateful-Gram on the handout to write down for your friend what he or she did that you liked and to say THANKS! Then give the Grateful-Gram to your friend.

You'll need: a pencil and the Grateful-Gram handout (cut in half).

Grateful Gram
GRAZIE! ARIGATO! MERCI! GRACIAS THANKS!
To my friend ________ Name
Thank you for ________
Your friend, ________ Name
MANGE TAKKE! Danke Schön! TAKE SOMEKE

Grateful Gram
GRAZIE! ARIGATO! MERCI! GRACIAS THANKS!
To my friend ________ Name
Thank you for ________
Your friend, ________ Name
MANGE TAKKE! Danke Schön! TAKE SOMEKE

ACTIVITY 6 HANDOUT FOR THE FRIENDSHIP CENTER

Grateful Gram

GRAZIE!
ARIGATO!
MERCI!
GRACIAS
THANKS!

To my friend ______________________
Name

Thank you for ______________________

____

____

____

____

____

Your friend, ______________________
Name

MANGE TAKKE! **Danke Schön!** TAKE SOMEKE

Grateful Gram

GRAZIE!
ARIGATO!
MERCI!
GRACIAS
THANKS!

To my friend ______________________
Name

Thank you for ______________________

____

____

____

____

____

Your friend, ______________________
Name

MANGE TAKKE! **Danke Schön!** TAKE SOMEKE

ACTIVITY CARD FOR THE FRIENDSHIP CENTER

7. INTELLIGENCE: LINGUISTIC (LANGUAGE)

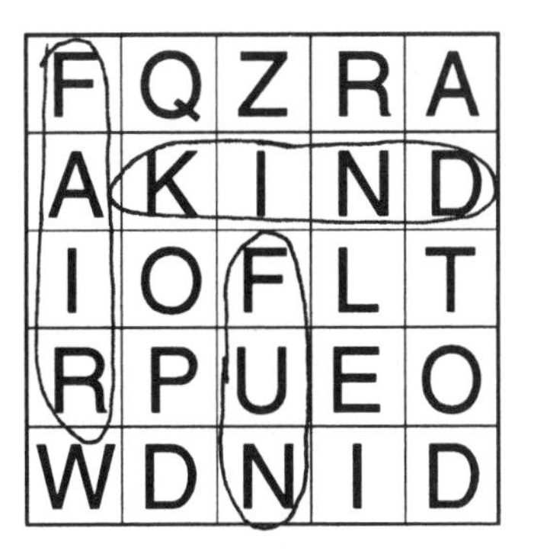

Directions:

Make up a word search game for your friend. Your friend will try to find the words you've hidden that tell about your friendship.

You'll need: a pencil and two pieces of graph paper.

1. Take two pieces of graph paper. Draw the same size grid on each paper. On the first one, make up the word search and circle the answers. This is your answer key. Next, copy in the letters on the second sheet. This is what you'll give your friend.
2. Fill in the grid by first putting in somewhere in the grid the first names of you and your friend. Then pick words that will remind your friend of special things you've done for each other or things you like about your friend. You can also pick other friendship words.
3. It's easier to make your word search if you put the longest words into the empty grid first and then do shorter and shorter words. After you put in all your words, put other letters in the remaining squares of the grid.
4. Write the words you've hidden at the bottom of the page. This will let your friend know what words to search for.

ACTIVITY CARD FOR THE FRIENDSHIP CENTER

8. INTELLIGENCE: LINGUISTIC (LANGUAGE)

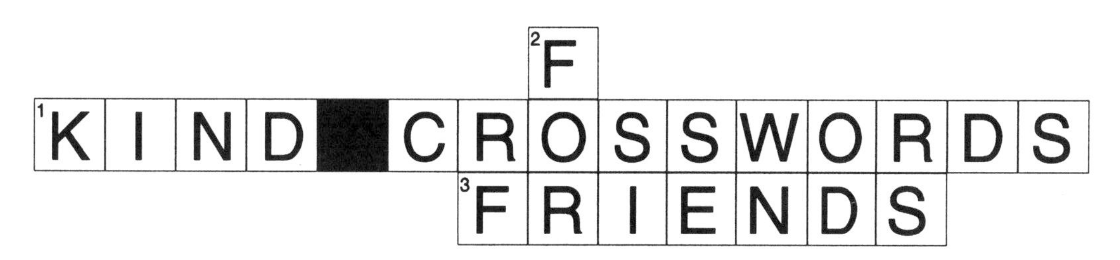

Directions:

Create a crossword puzzle for a friend! Your friend will use the clues you give to find the words that you have chosen about him or her.

You'll need: a pencil and two pieces of graph paper.

1. Take two pieces of graph paper. On the first one, you'll make up your crossword puzzle with all the answers filled in. This will be your answer key. Then you'll copy it without the answers on the second sheet for your friend.

2. To make your crossword, it's easiest if you fill in the words first. Then you can go back, number them, and write down the clues.

3. Have one clue be to fill in your name and another to fill in your friend's name. Then make up clues about those friendship qualities you like in your friend.

   For example, these might be:

   11 Down — What you do when you have a big snack and I am with you. (*Answer:* S H A R E)

   or

   15 Across — What I like best when I ask your opinion. (*Answer:* H O N E S T Y)

4. It's easier to make your crossword puzzle if you put the longest words into the empty grid first and then do shorter and shorter words. After you put in all your words, make other words if you can and then black out the remaining squares.

ACTIVITY CARD FOR THE FRIENDSHIP CENTER

9. INTELLIGENCE: LINGUISTIC (LANGUAGE)

BIO POEMS

Directions:

In this activity you'll create a biographical poem about your friend: a poem that tells a story of who your friend is. Share your poem with your friend.

Make your poem in this way:

FIRST line –	Write **your friend's first name**.
SECOND line –	Write **three positive adjectives** that describe your friend.
THIRD line –	Write **"Who likes . . ."** and two to four things your friend likes.
FOURTH line –	Write **"Who feels . . ."** and a short phrase to finish the thought.
FIFTH line –	Write **"Who needs . . ."** and a short phrase to finish the thought.
SIXTH line –	Write **"Who would like to see . . ."** and a short phrase to finish the thought.
SEVENTH line –	Write **"Who enjoys . . ."** and a short phrase to finish the thought.
EIGHTH line –	Write **"Who likes to wear . . ."** and a short phrase to finish the thought.
LAST line –	Write **your friend's first name** again.

Two examples are:

John.
Laughing, friendly, and easy to get along with.
Who likes airplanes, bicycles, his dog, and his family.
Who feels good, shy, and sometimes bad.
Who needs more time to practice sports and math.
Who would like to see himself fly a plane to faraway places.
Who enjoys his family and being different.
Who likes to wear jeans, blue shirts, and red socks.
John.

Nancy.
Happy, tall, kind.
Who likes horses, Madonna, and going to the beach.
Who feels love, excitement, and a little sad.
Who needs to talk and be heard.
Who would like to see castles, China, and a cleaner environment.
Who enjoys music, eating ice cream, and TV.
Who likes to wear purple, red, and black.
Nancy.

ACTIVITY CARD FOR THE FRIENDSHIP CENTER

10. INTELLIGENCE: LINGUISTIC (LANGUAGE)

WRITING ABOUT FRIENDSHIP DAY BY DAY

Directions:

During the next four weeks, write about the topic suggested for each day.

	Monday	Tuesday	Wednesday	Thursday	Friday
Week One	A friend is someone who	A way I found to get to know someone I wanted to be friends with was	Some nice things a friend has done for me are	I can trust my friend to	The best times I've had with a friend were when . . .
Week Two	What I like best about my friend is	A time I lost a friend was when	A time I was honest with a friend was when	My friend deserves a medal for	The nicest thing I've ever done for a friend is . . . .
Week Three	Ways my friend and I are alike are	Ways my friend and I are different are	A perfect day with a friend would be	A time my friend and I had a fight was when . . . . We made up because	A gift I'd like to give my friend is . . . .
Week Four	Some words that describe my friend are	If I could make three wishes for my friend, I'd wish for	The hardest thing about being a friend is	Kids would have more friends if only they would	It can be tricky to be with two friends because . . . .

ACTIVITY CARDS FOR THE FRIENDSHIP CENTER

11. INTELLIGENCE: MATHEMATICAL-LOGICAL

A MILLION DOLLARS FOR FRIENDSHIP

Directions:

If you were given $1,000,000 to spend on helping people become friends with each other, how would you spend this money? Make a list of all the different ways you would spend the money. Tell why you chose these ways.

12. INTELLIGENCE: MATHEMATICAL-LOGICAL

ANALYZING THE BEHAVIOR OF KIDS WHO ARE WELL-LIKED

Directions:

Observe two or three of your classmates who are well-liked and have many friends. Watch the way these kids treat others. Observe carefully what they do or say. See if you can find four things that all these kids do that are the same—four ways that they are similar. List these similarities on a piece of paper. Decide if these similar behaviors are part of the reason why these kids are so well-liked. Give reasons for your answer.

ACTIVITY CARD FOR THE FRIENDSHIP CENTER

13. INTELLIGENCE: MATHEMATICAL-LOGICAL

THE WAYS YOU AND YOUR FRIEND ARE ALIKE AND DIFFERENT

Directions:

On a piece of paper, draw overlapping circles like the ones below (or trace these). Write your name and your friend's name in the circles, then write all the ways you can think of that you and your friend are different and alike.

Example:

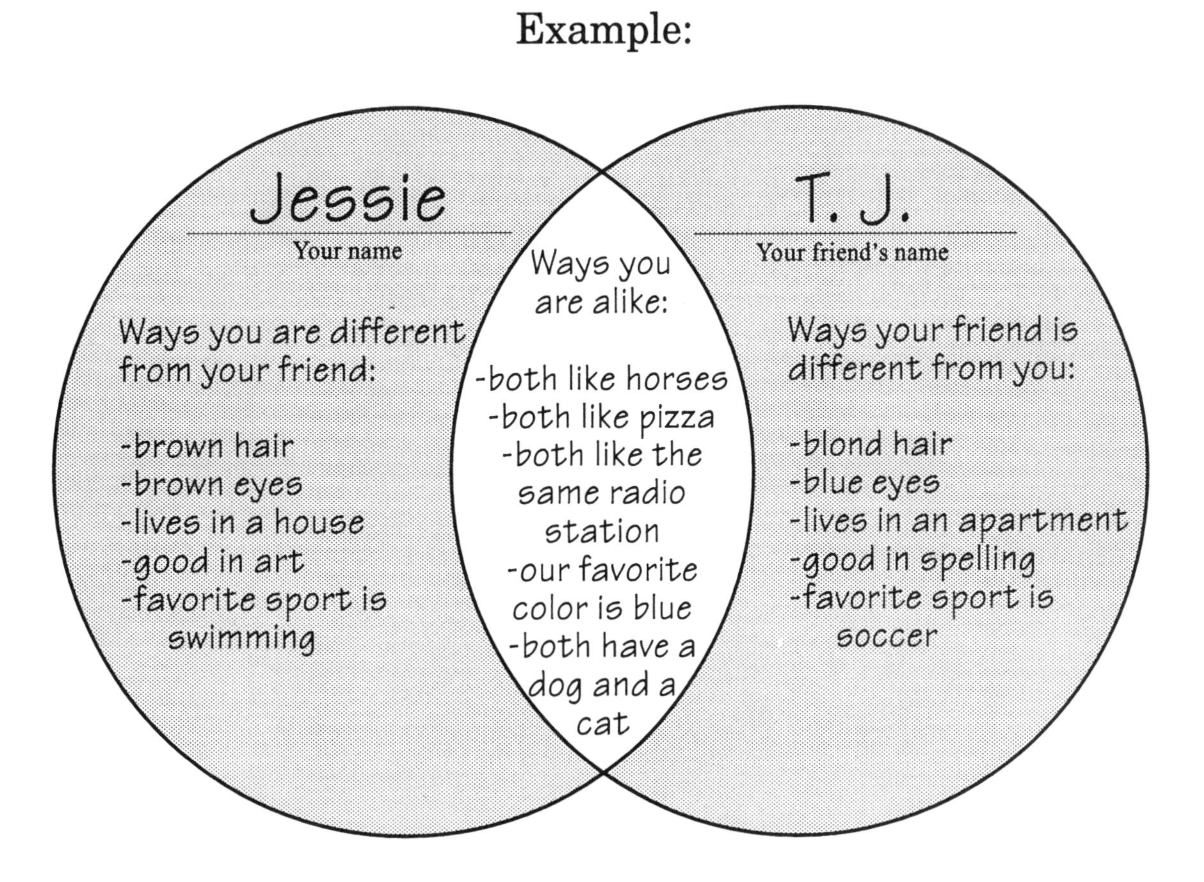

ACTIVITY CARD FOR THE FRIENDSHIP CENTER

14. INTELLIGENCE: MATHEMATICAL-LOGICAL

A SECRET CODE FOR YOU AND YOUR FRIEND

Directions:

Create a secret code that only you and your friend will share. Give your friend the secret code card along with your message.

You'll need: a pencil and the Alphabet Code Sheet handout.

ALPHABET CODE SHEET

To put ***your message*** into code:

Real Message	A	B	C	D	E	F	G	H	I	...
Code Letter	d	m	o	e	x	z	r	s	a	...

Directions:

For each letter of the alphabet put a different symbol or letter. One easy way to do this is to simply write the alphabet down again, but start several letters away, like this:

A	B	C	D	E	F	G	...
Y	Z	A	B	C	D	E	...

You can also use numbers or symbols:

A	B	C	D	E	F	G	...
*	#	%	&	$	@	+	...

Also, your school or community library will have books on making codes.

To decode ***your friend's*** message:

All you have to do is find the letter, number, or symbol on the code line and look up to find and write down the letter of the real message.

For You

Our Secret Code

A	B	C	D	E	F	G	H	I

J	K	L	M	N	O	P	Q	R

S	T	U	V	W	X	Y	Z

For Your Friend

Our Secret Code

A	B	C	D	E	F	G	H	I

J	K	L	M	N	O	P	Q	R

S	T	U	V	W	X	Y	Z

ACTIVITY 14 HANDOUT FOR THE FRIENDSHIP CENTER

ALPHABET CODE SHEET

To put *your message* into code:

Real Message	A	B	C	D	E	F	G	H	I	...
Code Letter	d	m	o	e	x	z	r	s	a	...

Directions:

For each letter of the alphabet put a different symbol or letter. One easy way to do this is to simply write the alphabet down again, but start several letters away, like this:

A	B	C	D	E	F	G	...
Y	Z	A	B	C	D	E	...

You can also use numbers or symbols:

A	B	C	D	E	F	G	...
*	#	%	&	$	@	+	...

Also, your school or community library will have books on making codes.

To decode *your friend's* message:

All you have to do is find the letter, number, or symbol on the code line and look up to find and write down the letter of the real message.

For You

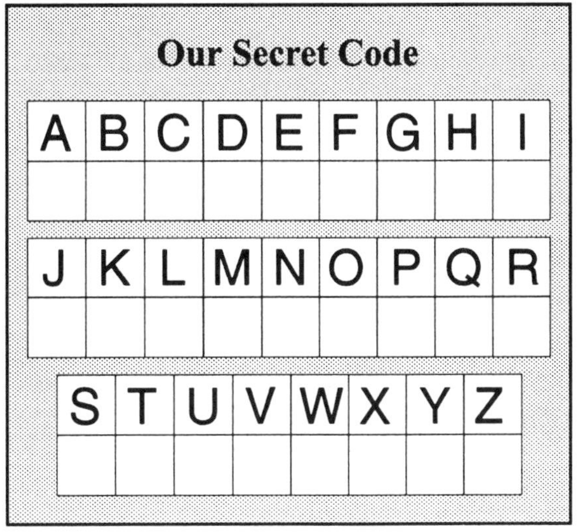

Our Secret Code

A	B	C	D	E	F	G	H	I

J	K	L	M	N	O	P	Q	R

S	T	U	V	W	X	Y	Z

For Your Friend

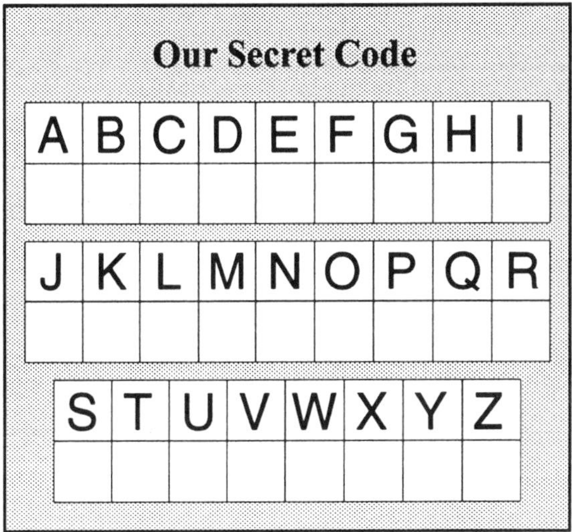

Our Secret Code

A	B	C	D	E	F	G	H	I

J	K	L	M	N	O	P	Q	R

S	T	U	V	W	X	Y	Z

ACTIVITY CARD FOR THE FRIENDSHIP CENTER

15. INTELLIGENCE: MATHEMATICAL-LOGICAL

FRIENDSHIP PUZZLES

Directions:

Can you figure out these friendship puzzles?

Use the handout to
s t r e t c h
your brain!

Then, use the answer sheet to check your answers.

You'll need: a pencil, the "Friendship Puzzles" handout, and the "Friendship Puzzles Answer Sheet" handout.

FRIENDSHIP PUZZLES

Directions:

Exercise your thinking skills with these puzzles.

1. A group of friends has been collecting free coupons to go on a roller coaster ride. It takes 12 coupons to get into a roller coaster car. The car seats 2 people. Which of these friends should sit together so that everyone can go on the ride?

Juanita has 2 coupons	Mary has 5 coupons
Mei Lin has 3 coupon	Jane has 7 coupons
Jennifer has 10 coupons	Amy has 9 coupons

2. Sarah is new at school. To try to help make friends, she decides to learn the names of all the kids in her class as soon as she could. On the first day she learns 3 names. The next day she learns 7 names, and the day after that she learns 11. If there are 31 kids in Sarah's class and she keeps learning at the same rate as the last three days, how many more days will it be before she knows all the kids' names?

3. 6 friends are sitting on the school bus. Each seat holds 2 kids.

Carlos is 2 rows ahead of Alex.
Simon is right behind Jamaal.
Alex isn't sitting next to Suwat or Simon.
Tim is sitting in a window seat.

How are the friends seated on the bus?

ACTIVITY 15 HANDOUT #1 FOR THE FRIENDSHIP CENTER

FRIENDSHIP PUZZLES

Directions:

Exercise your thinking skills with these puzzles.

1. A group of friends has been collecting free coupons to go on a roller coaster ride. It takes 12 coupons to get into a roller coaster car. The car seats 2 people. Which of these friends should sit together so that everyone can go on the ride?

Juanita has 2 coupons	Mary has 5 coupons
Mei Lin has 3 coupon	Jane has 7 coupons
Jennifer has 10 coupons	Amy has 9 coupons

2. Sarah is new at school. To try to help make friends, she decides to learn the names of all the kids in her class as soon as she could. On the first day she learns 3 names. The next day she learns 7 names, and the day after that she learns 11. If there are 31 kids in Sarah's class and she keeps learning at the same rate as the last three days, how many more days will it be before she knows all the kids' names?

3. 6 friends are sitting on the school bus. Each seat holds 2 kids.

   Carlos is 2 rows ahead of Alex.
   Simon is right behind Jamaal.
   Alex isn't sitting next to Suwat or Simon.
   Tim is sitting in a window seat.

   How are the friends seated on the bus?

ACTIVITY 15 HANDOUT #2 FOR THE FRIENDSHIP CENTER

FRIENDSHIP PUZZLES
ANSWER SHEET

1. This is how the friends should sit:

Juanita and Jennifer	2 + 10 = 12
Mei Lin and Amy	3 + 9 = 12
Mary and Jane	5 + 7 = 12

2. Sarah will need 5 more days.
She learns 4 new names per day (after the first day, when she only learned 3 names). So far she's learned 11 names.

So, the next day	11 + 4 = 15
Second day	15 + 4 = 19
Third day	19 + 4 = 23
Fourth day	23 + 4 = 27
Fifth day	27 + 4 = 31

(Did you notice? It doesn't change the answer, but since Sarah is in a class of 31 kids, she really only needs to learn 30 names, because she is the 31st kid herself!)

3.

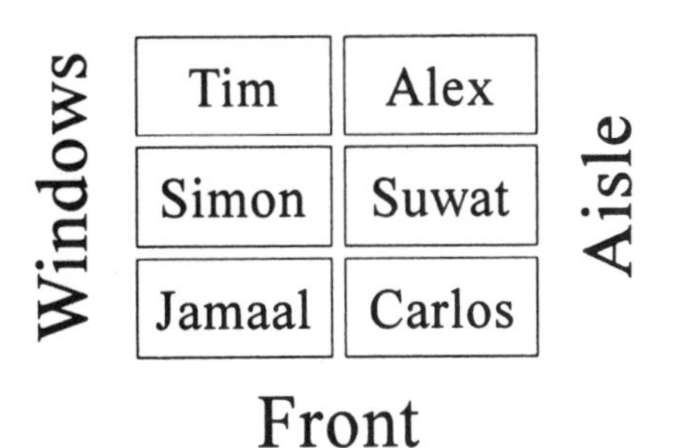

ACTIVITY CARD FOR THE FRIENDSHIP CENTER

16. INTELLIGENCE: MATHEMATICAL-LOGICAL

GO FIGURE!

How's your brain for figuring things out?

The "Go Figure!" handout has some puzzle problems about friendship that will give your math-logic skills a workout!

GO FIGURE!

Directions:

See if you can solve these puzzles.

1. Twenty friends decided to go to a concert together, and all but seven went. How many **weren't** able to go?
2. Rachel and Krista play at the same ballpark after school. Not counting herself, half of the other players at the ballpark are Rachel's friends. For Krista, one-third of the players (not counting herself) are her friends. If Krista has six friends there, including Rachel, then how many friends does Rachel have at the ballpark? What's the **total** number of kids there?
3. Sam and John have birthdays on the same day. They both plan to h their birthday party at the **same time** that day. Josh is a friend of Sam and John, and wouldn't want to hurt either friend's feelings being at that friend's party. Josh isn't worried about it, though, does plan to be at each friend's party. How can he do this?
4. Six girls are eating lunch together. They are all sitting together al side of a long table. Only friends are sitting next to each other. Us following clues, can you figure out which girls are sitting next other? Draw on your answer sheet how they are sitting at the tab
   - Tiffany is not a friend of Melinda or Jessica.
   - Allison likes Tammy and Jessica, but isn't friends with eith them yet.
   - Tammy is a friend of Tiffany.
   - Jessica is not sitting next to Melinda, Tammy, or Allis
   - Robin likes Tiffany, but they're not friends yet. Robin are friends.
   - Melinda has only one friend in the group and it's r
   - Melinda always sits on the left side of the table.
5. If you have four friends, and each of them has four friends other and each of their four friends also has an additional four fri many friends does that make in all?

ACTIVITY 16 HANDOUT #1 FOR THE FRIENDSHIP CENTER

GO FIGURE!

Directions:

See if you can solve these puzzles.

1. Twenty friends decided to go to a concert together, and all but seven went. How many **weren't** able to go?

2. Rachel and Krista play at the same ballpark after school. Not counting herself, half of the other players at the ballpark are Rachel's friends. For Krista, one-third of the players (not counting herself) are her friends. If Krista has six friends there, including Rachel, then how many friends does Rachel have at the ballpark? What's the **total** number of kids there?

3. Sam and John have birthdays on the same day. They both plan to have their birthday party at the **same time** that day. Josh is a friend of **both** Sam and John, and wouldn't want to hurt either friend's feelings by not being at that friend's party. Josh isn't worried about it, though, and he does plan to be at each friend's party. How can he do this?

4. Six girls are eating lunch together. They are all sitting together along one side of a long table. Only friends are sitting next to each other. Using the following clues, can you figure out which girls are sitting next to each other? Draw on your answer sheet how they are sitting at the table.

- Tiffany is not a friend of Melinda or Jessica.
- Allison likes Tammy and Jessica, but isn't friends with either of them yet.
- Tammy is a friend of Tiffany.
- Jessica is not sitting next to Melinda, Tammy, or Allison.
- Robin likes Tiffany, but they're not friends yet. Robin and Jessica are friends.
- Melinda has only one friend in the group and it's not Tammy.
- Melinda always sits on the left side of the table.

5. If you have four friends, and each of them has four friends other than you, and each of their four friends also has an additional four friends, how many friends does that make in all?

GO FIGURE!
ANSWER SHEET

1. Since "all but seven went," that means that **seven** friends weren't able to go!

2. Krista's six friends = 1/3 of the kids there, **other than herself**.
6 x 3 = 18 kids, + 1 (Krista) = **19 kids total** at the ballpark.
Rachel is friends with half the kids, not counting herself.
19 total kids - 1 (Rachel) = 18 kids. Half of 18 = **9 friends for Rachel**.

3. Sam and John are twins **OR** Sam and John are simply having their birthday parties together!

4. The girls are sitting in the following order:

Melinda	**Allison**	**Tiffany**	**Tammy**	**Robin**	**Jessica**
on the left side; one friend; not next to Tammy	not next to Tammy or Jessica	not next to Melinda or Jessica	a friend of Tiffany	not next to Tiffany; a friend of Jessica	not next to Melinda, Tammy, or Allison

5.

1	(yourself)
+ 4	(your friends)
+ (4 x 4 =) 16	(their friends)
+ (4 x 16 =) 64	(their friends' friends)
85	**total**

17. INTELLIGENCE: MUSICAL

Directions:

Find a friend and share making music together without instruments. First, you'll start by softly tapping out a beat on your knees. Next, create a combined rhythm with your friend by asking your friend to start up his or her own beat that's different from yours but that will combine with it.

18. INTELLIGENCE: MUSICAL

Directions:

Next time you go out for recess, find a place to stand or sit quietly and just listen to all the sounds around you. Are they mostly friendly sounds or unfriendly sounds? Write down some examples of the friendly and unfriendly sounds that you heard.

ACTIVITY CARDS FOR THE FRIENDSHIP CENTER

19. INTELLIGENCE: MUSICAL

TURN AN OLD SONG INTO A NEW FRIENDSHIP SONG

Directions:

Take a song that you know well and make up new words to create a song about your friend.

20. INTELLIGENCE: MUSICAL

A FRIENDSHIP RAP

Directions:

Write a rap song
about what you know
about how to keep a friend.
Work with a partner if you like.

ACTIVITY CARDS FOR THE FRIENDSHIP CENTER

21. INTELLIGENCE: MUSICAL

TUNE IN TO FRIENDSHIP

Directions:

- Make up a tune to go along with one of the two sets of lyrics below.
- Write your tune in musical notation on a sheet of paper. Make up more verses of the lyrics if you want to, and give your song a title.
- Find a friend to sing your song with!

22. INTELLIGENCE: MUSICAL

A FRIENDSHIP ROUND

Directions:

Find two friends. Decide together on a single song you all know, like "Three Blind Mice," "Row, Row, Row Your Boat," or "Are You Sleeping?" Sing it as a round by having one friend start singing the song, the next friend start singing when your first friend gets to the second line, and you start singing when your second friend begins singing the second line. Perform the round for the class. (If you want to be more creative, make up new words about friendship for the song you choose.)

ACTIVITY CARD FOR THE FRIENDSHIP CENTER

23. INTELLIGENCE: KINESTHETIC (PHYSICAL)

HANDS OF YOUR FRIENDS

Here's a way for you and your friends to give each other a hand!

Directions:

You'll need: two or more friends, pencil and paper, crayons or markers.

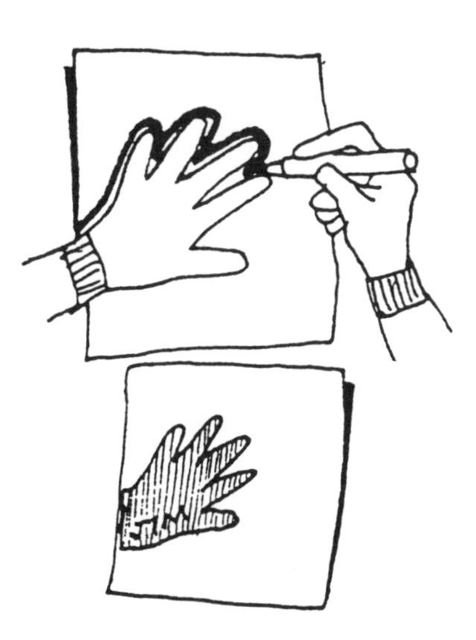

1. Put your hand on the paper and trace around it with a pencil, crayon, or marker.

2. Color in the hand on the paper. Write your name on it.

3. Pass the paper on to a friend. Have him or her do the same thing you just did. (It's O.K. to have the hands go on top of each other—just be sure you can read your names.)

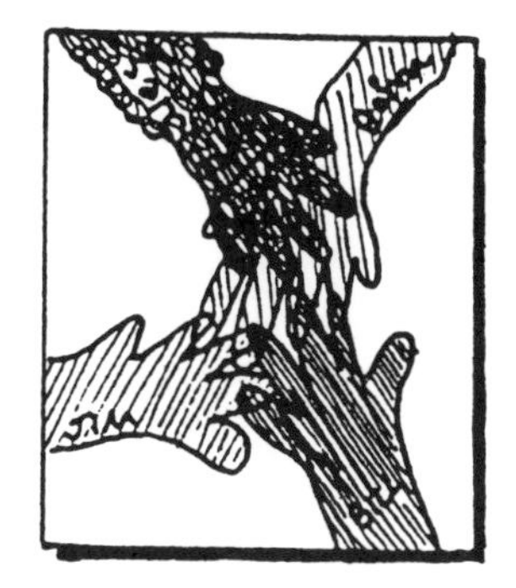

4. Repeat this with as many more friends as you like. Then choose a compliment word that best describes each of your friends and write it on his or her "hand." Ask your teacher to display the hands on the bulletin board.

24. INTELLIGENCE: KINESTHETIC (PHYSICAL)

A FRIENDSHIP HANDSHAKE

Directions:

Friends can share a secret handshake! Invent a special friendship handshake for you and your friend, then try it out with your friend.

25. INTELLIGENCE: KINESTHETIC (PHYSICAL)

A DANCE FOR FRIENDSHIP

Directions:

Design a special dance that demonstrates your ideas about friendship.

26. INTELLIGENCE: KINESTHETIC (PHYSICAL)

WALK LIKE A FRIEND

Directions:

Most people have a distinct way of moving their body, walking or running that is slightly different from everyone else's. Pick a good friend and study how he or she moves, walks, or runs. How do they hold their body and head? How do they move their hands? When they walk, do they look straight ahead or up or down? When you think you can imitate them exactly, show them. Be careful you don't exaggerate anything that would hurt their feelings. Then ask them if they would like to study and imitate you.

27. INTELLIGENCE: KINESTHETIC (PHYSICAL)

A FOOTRACE WITH A FRIEND

Directions:

Next recess, find a friend and have a footrace! If you can't find a place where you can run, have a fast-walking race instead.

ACTIVITY CARD FOR THE FRIENDSHIP CENTER

28. INTELLIGENCE: KINESTHETIC (PHYSICAL)

FRIENDSHIP ROCKS

Is your friendship solid as a rock?
Here's a way to say so!

Directions:

You'll need: a rock with a smooth side that faces up, soap and water, colored pencils, tempera paint, newspaper, a paintbrush, shellac, and some paintbrush cleaner for the shellac (or use a spray can of shellac instead).

1. Wash your rock with soap and water. Let the rock dry.
2. Draw your design on the rock with colored pencils.
3. Put down newspapers to protect your desk or the floor, then paint over your drawing. Let the rock dry overnight.
4. Paint or spray the whole rock with shellac. Be sure to clean your paintbrush if you used it to apply the shellac.
5. Give your rock to a special friend!

29. INTELLIGENCE: VISUAL-SPATIAL (ARTISTIC)

MAKE A COLORING BOOK FOR YOUR FRIEND

Directions:

Make up a coloring book for your friend that shows things he or she likes or activities he or she likes to do.

When you're done, show it to your teacher and then give it to your friend.

You'll need: paper you can staple or fold into a book, a pen or markers.

---

30. INTELLIGENCE: VISUAL-SPATIAL (ARTISTIC)

A PICTURE OF MY BEST FRIEND

Directions:

Paint or draw a picture of your best friend. Give it to your friend as a gift!

You'll need: a pencil, drawing paper, coloring or painting materials.

ACTIVITY CARD FOR THE FRIENDSHIP CENTER

31. INTELLIGENCE: VISUAL-SPATIAL (ARTISTIC)

A WISH FOR A FRIEND

What would you like to give your friend if you could give him or her anything at all?

Directions:

Use the handout to draw two things that you wish your friend could have, then give your friend the drawing.

You'll need: a pencil and the "A Wish for a Friend" handout.

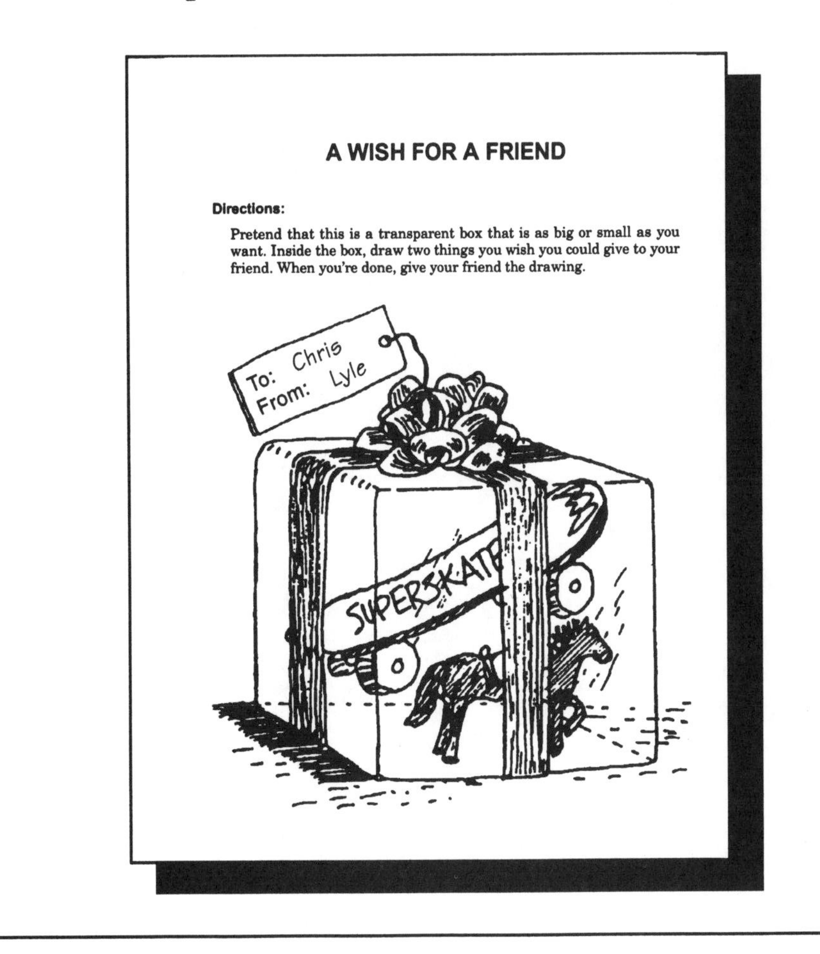

A WISH FOR A FRIEND

Directions:

Pretend that this is a transparent box that is as big or small as you want. Inside the box, draw two things you wish you could give to your friend. When you're done, give your friend the drawing.

ACTIVITY 31 HANDOUT FOR THE FRIENDSHIP CENTER

A WISH FOR A FRIEND

Directions:

Pretend that this is a transparent box that is as big or small as you want. Inside the box, draw two things you wish you could give to your friend. When you're done, give your friend the drawing.

ACTIVITY CARDS FOR THE FRIENDSHIP CENTER

32. INTELLIGENCE: VISUAL-SPATIAL (ARTISTIC)

Directions:

It really feels good to get a card from a friend, especially when that friend took the time to make a card especially for you. Design a card or cards like these to give to your friend!

You'll need: heavy paper and drawing, coloring, or painting materials.

33. INTELLIGENCE: VISUAL-SPATIAL (ARTISTIC)

A COLLAGE ABOUT FRIENDSHIPS

Directions:

Create a collage showing what makes a good friend. To make your collage, you can use objects, drawings, pictures cut from magazines, words, symbols, phrases, and photographs. For fun, hide your name somewhere in the collage. When you're done, show it to your teacher and he or she will tell you where you can display it so others in the class can see it.

You'll need: a large sheet of heavy paper and any or all of the materials mentioned above.

CARD FOR THE FRIENDSHIP CENTER

34. INTELLIGENCE: VISUAL-SPATIAL (ARTISTIC)

Envelopes are like "gift wrapping" for a letter. In this activity you will create a special decorated envelope for your notes to friends.

Directions:

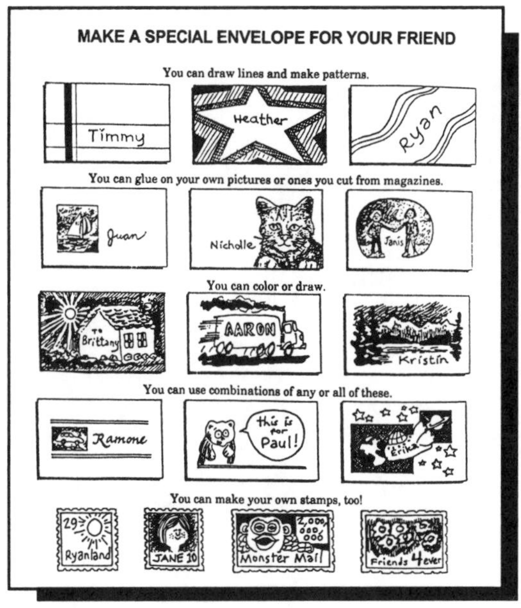

Use one or more of the ideas shown in the examples on the handout to decide which fun way you'll use to make your envelope. Be creative!

You'll need: the "Make a Special Envelope for Your Friend" handout, an envelope, and then any or all of the following, depending on what you choose to do to make your envelope: colored pens, colored pencils (especially silver or gold colored pencils), crayons, paints; magazines to cut; scissors and paste (or a gluestick); a ruler; glitter, rubber stamps, and anything else that comes to mind!

When your envelope is ready, write a special note to a friend and tuck it in his or her desk when he or she is not looking so it will be a surprise.

ACTIVITY 34 HANDOUT FOR THE FRIENDSHIP CENTER

MAKE A SPECIAL ENVELOPE FOR YOUR FRIEND

You can draw lines and make patterns.

You can glue on your own pictures or ones you cut from magazines.

You can color or draw.

You can use combinations of any or all of these.

You can make your own stamps, too!

35. INTELLIGENCE: VISUAL-SPATIAL (ARTISTIC)

DESIGN A TREEHOUSE OR A CLUBHOUSE

Directions:

Design a plan for a treehouse or a clubhouse for you and your friends. Put in every detail you'd like to have there. Show your plan to your friends so they can suggest or add other details.

OPTIONAL: You could make a drawing of your treehouse or clubhouse to scale, showing the measurements. You could also describe the materials and colors you would use.

36. INTELLIGENCE: VISUAL-SPATIAL (ARTISTIC)

MAKE AN ORIGAMI GIFT FOR A FRIEND

Directions:

Use a pattern from an origami instruction book to make a special gift for a friend. Fold thin colored paper into the animal, bird, or other figure you choose. Attach your name to your origami figure with a small name tag, then surprise your friend by hiding your gift in his or her desk.

You'll need: a pencil, an origami instruction book, colored paper, and a name tag.

37. INTELLIGENCE: VISUAL-SPATIAL (ARTISTIC)

DRAW A PICTURE OF YOU AND YOUR FRIEND

Directions:

Draw a picture of you and your friend! When you're done, show it to your teacher and then give it to your friend.

You'll need: colored pencils, drawing paper, coloring or painting materials.

---

38. INTELLIGENCE: VISUAL-SPATIAL (ARTISTIC)

FRIENDSHIP WISH COLLAGE

Directions:

Create a collage of things you would like to give to your friends. Don't just include material things, but things like "happiness," "good grades," and "scoring the winning goal in a big soccer game," too.

Cut words and pictures from magazines, or draw the things you wish for your friends now or in the future. You can either make up a special wish collage for just one friend and give it to him or her, or you can make a collage of your wishes for all your friends and keep this in your Friendship Folder.

You'll need: Oversize or heavy paper for the collage itself, magazines to cut, scissors, paste or a gluestick, and drawing materials as needed.

ACTIVITY CARD FOR THE FRIENDSHIP CENTER

39. INTELLIGENCE: INTERPERSONAL (SOCIAL)

FRIENDSHIP AWARDS

Make someone feel special with a Friendship Award!

Directions:

Fill in the hand-out, cut out the award, and give it to your friend!

You'll need: a pencil and the "Friendship Award" handout.

Friendship Award

To: ____________________

From: ____________________

For: ____________________

____

____

ACTIVITY 39 HANDOUT FOR THE FRIENDSHIP CENTER

FRIENDSHIP AWARD

ACTIVITY CARD FOR THE FRIENDSHIP CENTER

40. INTELLIGENCE: INTERPERSONAL (SOCIAL)

FRIENDSHIP COUPONS

Friendship

I promise to do the following this week for the person who gets this coupon:

____

____

____

Your friend,

____

Coupon

Directions:

A good way to develop friendships is to do something helpful or kind for another person.

Think of someone you'd like to do something nice for. Decide what you think they might like. Fill out the friendship coupon with something you can do for that person. Some examples are: carrying that person's books to the bus for a week, cleaning someone's desk for them, helping that person practice his or her spelling words.

When you have filled in the coupon, roll it up and tie it with a piece of ribbon. At recess, hand it to the person you selected.

You'll need: a pencil, the "Friendship Coupons" handout (cut in half), and a piece of ribbon.

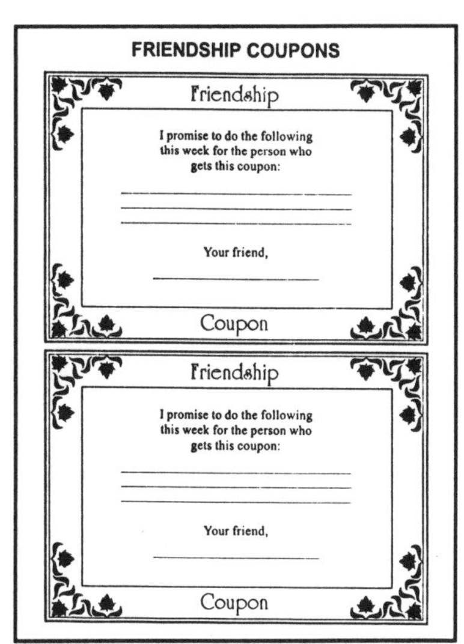

FRIENDSHIP COUPONS

Friendship

I promise to do the following this week for the person who gets this coupon:

Your friend,

Coupon

Friendship

I promise to do the following this week for the person who gets this coupon:

Your friend,

Coupon

ACTIVITY 40 HANDOUT FOR THE FRIENDSHIP CENTER

FRIENDSHIP COUPONS

Friendship

I promise to do the following
this week for the person who
gets this coupon:

____

____

____

Your friend,

____

Coupon

Friendship

I promise to do the following
this week for the person who
gets this coupon:

____

____

____

Your friend,

____

Coupon

ACTIVITY CARD FOR THE FRIENDSHIP CENTER

41. INTELLIGENCE: INTERPERSONAL (SOCIAL)

Directions:

Make a special card to give to your friend. Use this to let them know about something they did that you liked or, better still, to let them know that you noticed something good they did which no one said anything about. Write what you noticed him or her do, color the card so it looks the way you want, and then give it to your friend.

You'll need: a pencil, something to color with, and the "My Friend Didn't Think I Noticed, But . . . " handout.

MY FRIEND DIDN'T THINK I NOTICED, BUT . . .

Directions: Cut along the heavy black line, then fold along the dashed line to make a card for your friend.

Fold along this line

Dear:

I really liked it when you

Your friend,

ACTIVITY 41 HANDOUT FOR THE FRIENDSHIP CENTER

MY FRIEND DIDN'T THINK I NOTICED, BUT . . .

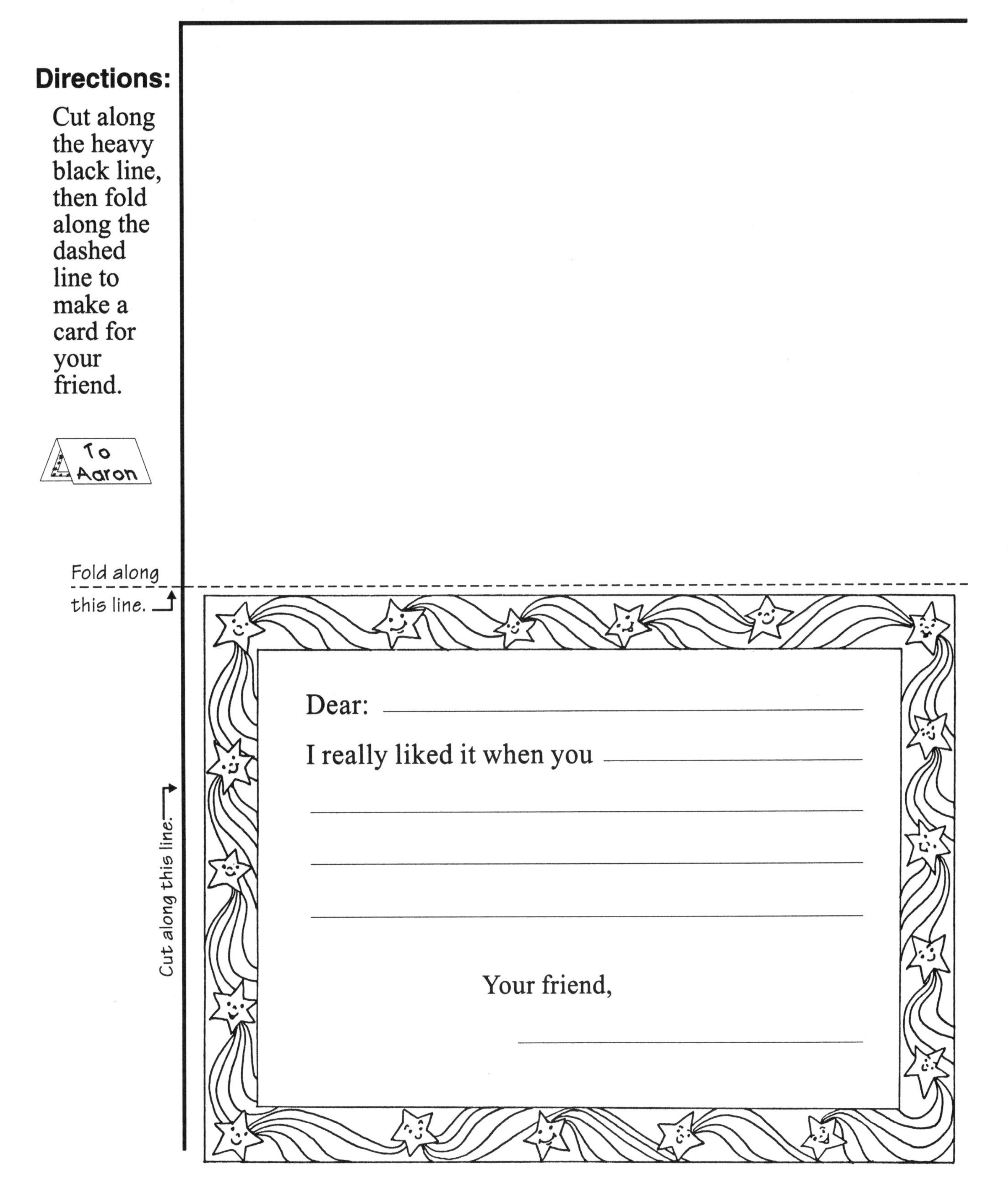

ACTIVITY CARDS FOR THE FRIENDSHIP CENTER

42. INTELLIGENCE: INTERPERSONAL (SOCIAL)

A PUPPET PLAY ABOUT FRIENDS

Directions:

Make up a puppet play about two friends. Have a beginning, middle part, and end to your play. You might want your play to be about a friendship problem that gets solved in the end. Or, you could use puppets to act out the story in a book about friendship.

You'll need: a pencil and paper to write down your play and puppets.

---

43. INTELLIGENCE: INTERPERSONAL (SOCIAL)

PLAY A FRIENDSHIP GAME

Directions:

If your teacher has set out one of the ASSIST friendship games, find someone to play it with you. Write down some ways you think the game could be improved, if you have any, and mail your ideas to this address:

ASSIST Project
7024 North Mercer Way
Mercer Island, WA 98040

ACTIVITY CARD FOR THE FRIENDSHIP CENTER

44. INTELLIGENCE: INTERPERSONAL (SOCIAL)

FRIENDS OF ALL AGES

Our friends come in all ages! Many people have friends who are older or younger than they are. Having different age friends lets you share and do different things than you can with kids your own age.

Directions:

In this activity, you'll take time to think about what you like about two friends, one who is at least two years older than you and one who is at least two years younger. Use the handout to write a paragraph about these friends.

You'll need: a pencil and the "Friends of All Ages" handout.

FRIENDS OF ALL AGES

Directions:

Write in the name and age of an **older** friend. Then write something about this friend or a special time you shared together.

Older Friend

Name: ______________________ Age: ________

Write in the name and age of a **younger** friend. Then write something about this friend or a special time you shared together.

Younger Friend

Name: ______________________ Age: ________

ACTIVITY 44 HANDOUT FOR THE FRIENDSHIP CENTER

FRIENDS OF ALL AGES

Directions:

Write in the name and age of an **older** friend. Then write something about this friend or a special time you shared together.

Older Friend

Name: ______________________________ Age: __________

____

____

____

____

Write in the name and age of a **younger** friend. Then write something about this friend or a special time you shared together.

Younger Friend

Name: ______________________________ Age: __________

____

____

____

____

45. INTELLIGENCE: INTERPERSONAL (SOCIAL)

A FRIENDSHIP THOUGHT BALLOON

Directions:

Cartoon characters use a "thought balloon" like the one in the picture on the left to show what they're thinking. In this activity you'll use a real balloon to share your thoughts with a friend!

Here's how it works: Choose someone in the class you don't know very well and don't usually play with. Write a compliment or friendly message to that person on a small piece of paper. Fold the message up even smaller and put it into a balloon. Blow up the balloon, tie a string on it, and give it to the person at recess.

You'll need: a pencil, small piece of paper, a string, and a balloon.

---

46. INTELLIGENCE: INTERPERSONAL (SOCIAL)

BODY LANGUAGE

Directions:

How people look and how they hold their bodies can tell us as much about what they are thinking and feeling as what they say in words. This is called "body language."

Try to guess what someone is thinking or feeling by watching their face and body. Do this at least five times. Each time, check out how good you are at this by asking the person if you were right.

ACTIVITY CARD FOR THE FRIENDSHIP CENTER

47. INTELLIGENCE: INTERPERSONAL (SOCIAL)

SOLVE THESE FRIENDSHIP PROBLEMS

1. Karen has two friends who don't like each other. They both want Karen to play only with them. They also talk unkindly about each other to Karen. Karen likes both girls and hates it when they each try to get her on their side. She wishes she could get them to like each other. She would like all of them to be able to play together. Can you think of two things Karen could say or do to solve this problem?

2. Dirk promised a friend he'd go to the movies with him Saturday night. Saturday afternoon a boy Dirk would really like for a friend called and asked him to go to a baseball game. Dirk loves baseball and hardly ever gets a chance to go to a game. What should Dirk do?

3. You're having a birthday party. A friend you invited calls and asks you if she can bring two more people. You don't want her to.

4. Your friend tells you he feels like nobody likes him. You know that some people don't like him because he is bossy and likes to be the center of attention. Should you tell your friend what you think? If so, how could you tell him without hurting his feelings? If not, what would you say to him instead?

5. Your best friend asks you to tell her if another friend of yours has been talking about her behind her back. Your other friend said some unkind things about her because she was really mad at her, but she asked you not to tell her. What should you say to your best friend?

ACTIVITY CARD FOR THE FRIENDSHIP CENTER

48. INTELLIGENCE: INTERPERSONAL (SOCIAL)

INTERVIEW A CLASSMATE YOU DON'T KNOW WELL

Directions:

Here's a chance for you to get to know someone better! Use the handout to ask the person questions and jot down the answers. You may be surprised at the answers and find you have things in common.

You'll need: a pencil, the "Interview a Classmate You Don't Know Well" handout, and someone to interview.

INTERVIEW A CLASSMATE YOU DON'T KNOW WELL

Directions:

Here's a chance for you to get to know someone better! Ask these questions and jot down the person's answers. You may be surprised at his or her answers and find you have unexpected things in common.

Your name: ____________

Your classmate's name: ____________

Questions to Ask

Where were you born? ____________

Where is your favorite place to go? ____________

Do you have any pets? ____________

Do you have any collections? ____________

What is your favorite color? ____________

What is your favorite food? ____________

What is your favorite radio station? ____________

What is your favorite music group or singer? ____________

What is your favorite TV show? ____________

What is your favorite book? ____________

What is your favorite sport? ____________

What is something that bugs you? ____________

If you could be anyone for a day, who would you be, and why? ____________

What is the best advice you've ever received? ____________

ACTIVITY 48 HANDOUT FOR THE FRIENDSHIP CENTER

INTERVIEW A CLASSMATE YOU DON'T KNOW WELL

Directions:

Here's a chance for you to get to know someone better! Ask these questions and jot down the person's answers. You may be surprised at his or her answers and find you have unexpected things in common.

Your name: ______________________

Your classmate's name: ______________________

Questions to Ask

Where were you born? ______________________

Where is your favorite place to go? ______________________

Do you have any pets? ______________________

Do you have any collections? ______________________

What is your favorite color? ______________________

What is your favorite food? ______________________

What is your favorite radio station? ______________________

What is your favorite music group or singer? ______________________

____

What is your favorite TV show? ______________________

What is your favorite book? ______________________

What is your favorite sport? ______________________

What is something that bugs you? ______________________

____

If you could be anyone for a day, who would you be, and why? ______________________

____

What is the best advice you've ever received? ______________________

____

ACTIVITY CARD FOR THE FRIENDSHIP CENTER

49. INTELLIGENCE: INTERPERSONAL (SOCIAL)

LET ME TELL YOU ABOUT MY FRIEND

Directions:

1. Choose a friend to write about. It can be someone in this class, outside this class, older or younger.

2. Get a copy of the handout for this activity and ask your friend the questions on the handout. Write the answers in the blanks. When you've written down all the answers, fold the top half of the paper down so all you see is the back of the handout.

3. Now, get an ink pad. Ask your friend to make you a bunch of fingerprints on a separate piece of paper.

4. Using a pencil, turn each fingerprint into a little picture of your friend doing something he or she likes to do.

5. Cut out the fingerprint pictures you like the best and paste them to the front of the folded handout.

6. Give the completed card to your teacher so he or she can put it up for the rest of the class to see.

You'll need: a pencil, the "Let Me Tell You About My Friend" handout, a second piece of paper, scissors, paste or glue, an ink pad, and soap and water for clean up.

ACTIVITY 49 HANDOUT FOR THE FRIENDSHIP CENTER

LET ME TELL YOU ABOUT MY FRIEND

My friend's name is ____
First Middle Last

My friend likes to do the sports I've circled:

play basketball
play soccer
play baseball
jump rope
skateboard
snow ski
waterski
ice skate
roller skate
swim
gymnastics

My friend's favorite sport is ____________________________

My friend's favorite sports star is ____________________________

At recess my friend likes to ____________________________

During P.E. my friend likes to ____________________________

My friend gets mad when ____________________________

My friend's favorite place to go is ____________________________

My friend's favorite animal is ____________________________

My friend's favorite snack is ____________________________

My friend's favorite game is ____________________________

My friend's favorite dessert is ____________________________

My friend's favorite school subject is ____________________________

The thing I like most about my friend is ____________________________

ACTIVITY CARD FOR THE FRIENDSHIP CENTER

50. INTELLIGENCE: INTERPERSONAL (SOCIAL)

HOW WELL DO YOU KNOW YOUR FRIENDS?

Directions:

How well do you know things about your friends? This is a fun way to find out the difference between what you know and what you think you know!

You'll need: a pencil and the "How Well Do You Know Your Friends?" handout.

HOW WELL DO YOU KNOW YOUR FRIENDS?

Directions:

Answer the following questions about your friends, and then find out how well you really know them.

1. What is your friend's middle name?
2. What color are your friend's eyes?
3. What does your friend like to do the most?
4. Where would your friend choose to go on a two-week vacation?
5. What is your friend's favorite animal?
6. Name one thing that your friend does well and feels good about.
7. What is your friend's favorite school subject?
8. What would your friend do with a prize of $20,000?
9. What is your friend's favorite TV show? Song? Movie?
10. Suppose your friend was moving to a desert island. Which three people would be invited along?

Friend #1	Friend #2
Name: ______	Name: ______
1. ______	1. ______
2. ______	2. ______
3. ______	3. ______
4. ______	4. ______
5. ______	5. ______
6. ______	6. ______
7. ______	7. ______
8. ______	8. ______
9. ______	9. ______
10. ______	10. ______

ACTIVITY 50 HANDOUT FOR THE FRIENDSHIP CENTER

HOW WELL DO YOU KNOW YOUR FRIENDS?

Directions:

Answer the following questions about your friends, and then find out how well you really know them.

1. What is your friend's middle name?
2. What color are your friend's eyes?
3. What does your friend like to do the most?
4. Where would your friend choose to go on a two-week vacation?
5. What is your friend's favorite animal?
6. Name one thing that your friend does well and feels good about.
7. What is your friend's favorite school subject?
8. What would your friend do with a prize of $20,000?
9. What is your friend's favorite TV show? Song? Movie?
10. Suppose your friend was moving to a desert island. Which three people would be invited along?

Friend #1

Name: ______

1. ______
2. ______
3. ______
4. ______
5. ______
6. ______
7. ______
8. ______
9. ______
10. ______

Friend #2

Name: ______

1. ______
2. ______
3. ______
4. ______
5. ______
6. ______
7. ______
8. ______
9. ______
10. ______

ACTIVITY CARD FOR THE FRIENDSHIP CENTER

51. INTELLIGENCE: INTERPERSONAL (SOCIAL)

PEN PALS

Directions:

A way to make a friend is to have a pen pal. It can be really fun to have a friend who lives in a different place. If you've studied another part of the world in class, it might be fun to try to make friends with someone who lives there by becoming their pen pal.

People, no matter how different, often find many things they enjoy sharing with each other. Use the handout to find someone to write to.

You'll need: a pencil, writing paper, and the "How to Find a Pen Pal" handout.

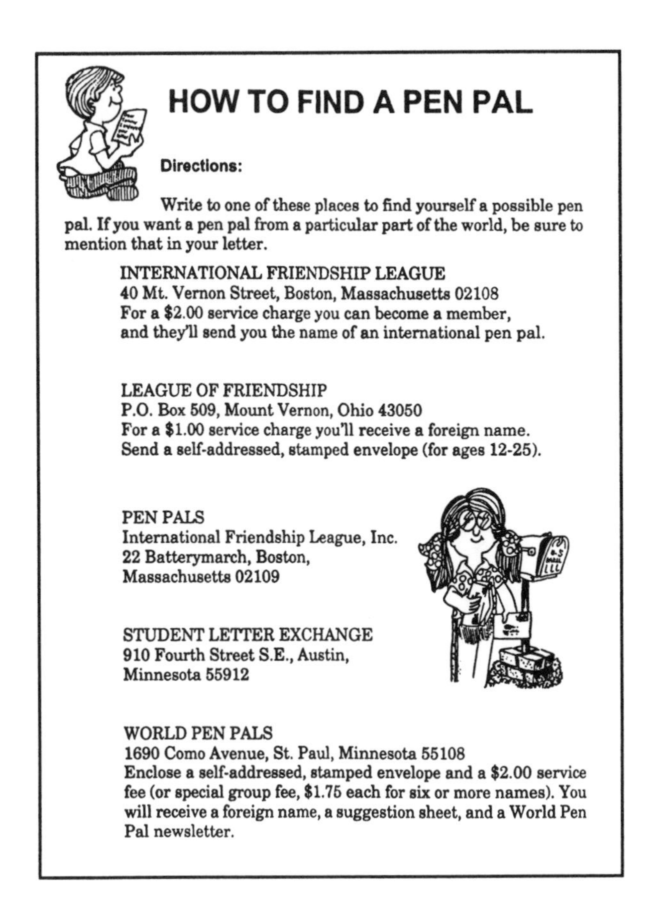

HOW TO FIND A PEN PAL

Directions:

Write to one of these places to find yourself a possible pen pal. If you want a pen pal from a particular part of the world, be sure to mention that in your letter.

INTERNATIONAL FRIENDSHIP LEAGUE
40 Mt. Vernon Street, Boston, Massachusetts 02108
For a $2.00 service charge you can become a member,
and they'll send you the name of an international pen pal.

LEAGUE OF FRIENDSHIP
P.O. Box 509, Mount Vernon, Ohio 43050
For a $1.00 service charge you'll receive a foreign name.
Send a self-addressed, stamped envelope (for ages 12-25).

PEN PALS
International Friendship League, Inc.
22 Batterymarch, Boston,
Massachusetts 02109

STUDENT LETTER EXCHANGE
910 Fourth Street S.E., Austin,
Minnesota 55912

WORLD PEN PALS
1690 Como Avenue, St. Paul, Minnesota 55108
Enclose a self-addressed, stamped envelope and a $2.00 service fee (or special group fee, $1.75 each for six or more names). You will receive a foreign name, a suggestion sheet, and a World Pen Pal newsletter.

ACTIVITY 51 HANDOUT FOR THE FRIENDSHIP CENTER

HOW TO FIND A PEN PAL

Directions:

Write to one of these places to find yourself a possible pen pal. If you want a pen pal from a particular part of the world, be sure to mention that in your letter.

INTERNATIONAL FRIENDSHIP LEAGUE
40 Mt. Vernon Street, Boston, Massachusetts 02108
For a $2.00 service charge you can become a member,
and they'll send you the name of an international pen pal.

LEAGUE OF FRIENDSHIP
P.O. Box 509, Mount Vernon, Ohio 43050
For a $1.00 service charge you'll receive a foreign name.
Send a self-addressed, stamped envelope (for ages 12-25).

PEN PALS
International Friendship League, Inc.
22 Batterymarch, Boston,
Massachusetts 02109

STUDENT LETTER EXCHANGE
910 Fourth Street S.E., Austin,
Minnesota 55912

WORLD PEN PALS
1690 Como Avenue, St. Paul, Minnesota 55108
Enclose a self-addressed, stamped envelope and a $2.00 service fee (or special group fee, $1.75 each for six or more names). You will receive a foreign name, a suggestion sheet, and a World Pen Pal newsletter.

ACTIVITY CARDS FOR THE FRIENDSHIP CENTER

52. INTELLIGENCE: INTRAPERSONAL (SELF)

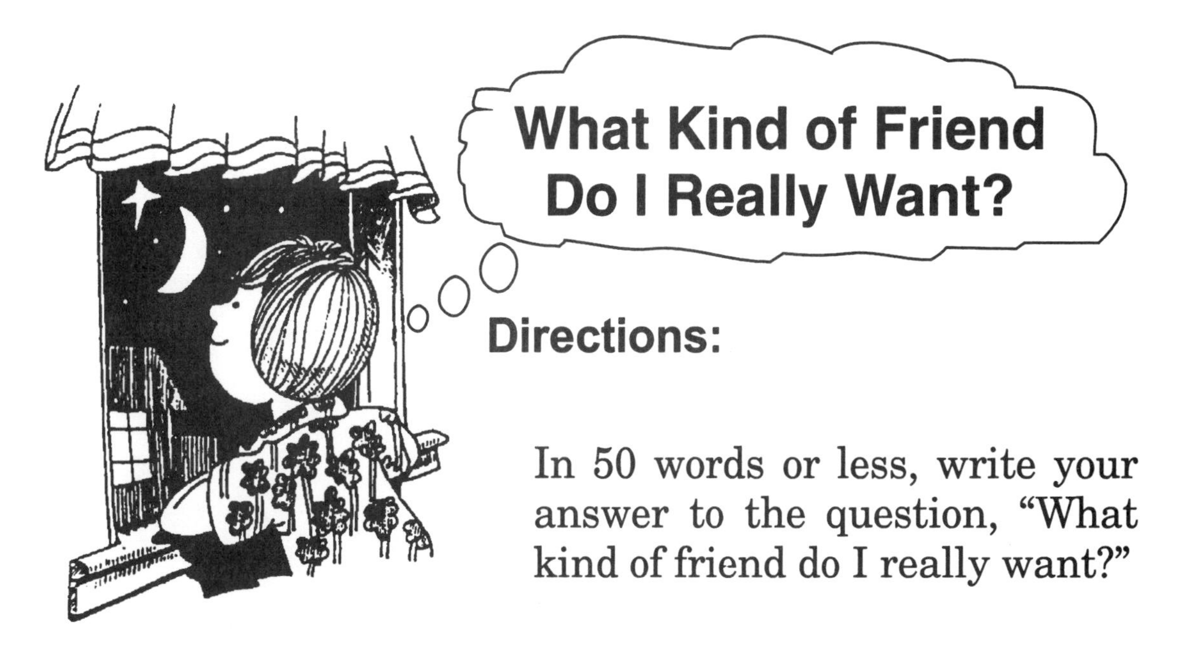

Directions:

In 50 words or less, write your answer to the question, “What kind of friend do I really want?”

53. INTELLIGENCE: INTRAPERSONAL (SELF)

THE REASONS WHY SOMEONE WOULD WANT ME FOR A FRIEND

Directions:

In 50 words or less, write your answer to the question, “Why would someone want me for a friend?”

54. INTELLIGENCE: INTRAPERSONAL (SELF)

A LETTER TO AN IMAGINARY BEST FRIEND

Directions:

Write a letter to an imaginary best friend. Tell about your feelings:

- What you're happy about.
- What you worry about.
- What you're excited about.
- What you're sad about.
- What you're afraid of.

Next, write about what kind of friend it would take for you to actually share these private feelings with.

When you're done, fold your paper in half and staple it together. Show your teacher you've done this activity, then put the letter in your Friendship Folder.

55. INTELLIGENCE: INTRAPERSONAL (SELF)

A TIMELINE OF YOUR FRIENDS

Directions:

Create a timeline of the friends you've had in your life. Draw a long line on a piece of paper. With a ruler, mark the line off into equal sections, enough so there is one section for each year of your life. For each year, draw a picture above the line of the friends you had that year. Write their names below the line.

Did you remember some friends you'd forgotten? Have some friends been there for many years?

You'll need: a pencil, paper, ruler, and colored pencils or markers.

ACTIVITY CARDS FOR THE FRIENDSHIP CENTER

56. INTELLIGENCE INTRAPERSONAL (SELF)

Directions:

In 50 words or less, write your answer to the question, "How good a friend am I to others?"

57. INTELLIGENCE: INTRAPERSONAL (SELF)

KNOW YOURSELF

Directions:

Write a letter to yourself in which you talk about the friends in your life.

Write about what you like about your friendships and what things you wish were different. Write about how you think you help yourself have friends and what things you do that hurt your friendships.

When you're done, fold your paper in half and staple it together. Show your teacher you've done this activity, then put the letter in your Friendship Folder.

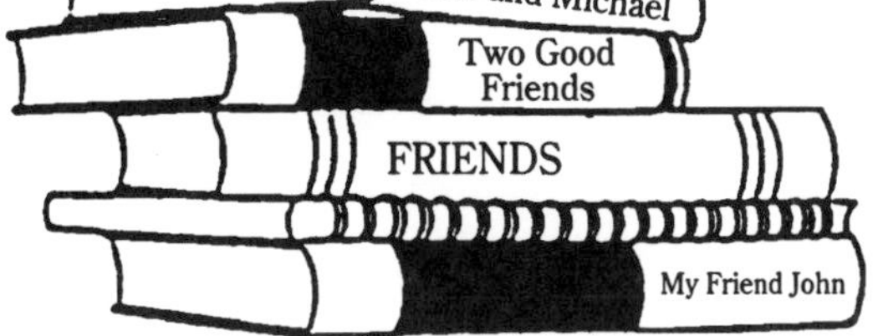

Using Literature to Enhance Students' Understanding of Friendship

The following lists of children's books all relate to friendship themes and were generated in the following manner:

A master list was compiled utilizing the latest edition of *Bookfinder* and the *Anthology of Children's Picture Books*. This list was divided into a compilation appropriate for grades 4-6. (A compilation for grades 1-3 can be found in *Teaching Friendship Skills: Primary Version*.) This list was sent to librarians in public libraries, public schools, and at children's book stores. The librarians were asked to comment on age appropriateness, readability, and popularity of the books with children. They also selected their own favorites. The lists on the following pages are the result. You can readily promote students' understanding of friendship issue's through books either by reading aloud to the class or by encouraging independent reading.

When you read aloud to your class you'll find many opportunities for discussing how a character felt about something or why the character made particular decisions. You can ask a number of questions requiring students to use critical thinking skills. These discussions can strengthen students' friendship skills and increase their understanding of others.

A useful technique is to stop reading a story just short of the conclusion and ask the class to end the story. You can compare their conclusion with the author's.

These books can be used as an introduction to a friendship lesson or to extend a theme a lesson presents. They can be placed in a "Friendship Center" and used for independent reading. They can be given to parents to read to children at home. Students can reconstruct favorite stories through art and drama. They can use them as springboards for writing their own friendship stories.

By reading about the friendships of others, students can become better equipped to understand social relationships of their own.

Using Books About Friendship With Intermediate Age Students

Reading Friendship Books to Your Class

You can read one or more of the suggested books (following) to the class, or you can have students each select a book to read. If you read aloud to the class, use the book as a discussion guide regarding friendship themes. Ask questions like the following:

1. Who is a friendly person in this book?
2. What made this person a friend? What specific things did the person do that made you feel he or she is a good friend?
3. How did the other characters feel about this person?
4. Would you like to have this person as a personal friend? Why or why not?
5. Can you describe a particularly friendly part of the story?
6. Do you know anyone who has done friendly things similar to those described in this book?

You may want to have students create "sequels" to the book by choosing a character in the book whose place he or she would like to take. They can then write stories telling about the further adventures of the character.

Friendship Book Auction

If you intend to have students each read a book on friendship, you might want to conduct a "Friendship Book Auction." Find at least one book on friendship for each student in your class. Use the friendship book list that follows, the computer or card catalog listings under "friendship," and/or the knowledge of your librarian to help you make selections.

Copy the auction money bills from the "Friendship Book Auction Currency" handout and create one set for each student (one 5,000, four 1,000, and ten 100 bills.) At auction time, distribute the packets of auction money to the students. Explain to them that they will be bidding with each other for the friendship book they would like to read and write a report on. You may choose to have the books on a table, and let them look briefly to see which books are available.

Before conducting the auction, explain the rules: (1) students will bid by raising their hands as you, the auctioneer, call out for bids; (2) students can bid up to the amount of auction money they have; and (3) successful bidders are to come up immediately to hand over their money and collect their book.

Hold up each book, call out its title, and briefly describe the plot. Enliven the process by "selling" the book and encouraging competitive bids. Continue until each student has "purchased" a book.

Give each student the "Questions Regarding Your Friendship Book" handout. Explain that they may use these questions as a guide in writing their book report.

Using the "Seven Intelligences" to Share Thoughts and Feelings After Reading Books Dealing With Friendship

You may want to suggest some of the following ways of sharing:

- Choose a scene in the book that particularly interests you. Write an alternate dialogue for the scene and, with a partner, present it to the class.
- Create an emotional collage of words or pictures to reveal one of the character's feelings about his or her problem in the story.
- Make a cartoon (comic strip) of a situation depicting the character solving a friendship problem.
- Write five journal entries in the first person point of view (as if you were a character in the book).
- Write a poem or free verse describing the feelings this particular book evoked for you.
- Choose music that describes the mood of the story. Create a dance to demonstrate your interpretation of that mood.
- Role-play with a friend certain portions of the book in front of the class.
- Write about a problem you have had recently that was similar to one in the story. Tell how you felt, what you thought, how you acted, and how you solved it.

Books for Intermediate Age Students

Avi		*Romeo and Juliet Together at Last*
Beckman, G.		*The Girl Without a Name*
Blume, J.	☆	*Blubber*
		Iggie's House
		Super Fudge
Bulla, C.R.	☆	*Dexter*
		Shoeshine Girl
Brink, C.R.	☆	*The Bad Times of Irma Baumlien*
Burch, R.		*Almost A Hero*
		Queenie Peavy
Burnett, F.H.	☆	*The Secret Garden*
Byars, B.	☆	*The 18th Emergency*
	☆	*The Pinballs*
Cohen, B.		*Thank You, Jackie Robinson*
Cole, S.		*Meaning Well*
Cunningham, J.		*Burnish Me Bright*
Estes, E.	☆	*The Hundred Dresses*

Gaeddert, L.A.		*Your Former Friend, Matthew*
Garrigue, S.		*Between Friends*
Giff, P.R.		*Love, From the Fifth Grade Celebrity*
Graeher, C.		*Grey Cloud*
Greene, C.C.		*A Girl Called Al*
. . . .		*Ask Anybody*
Hassler, J.		*Four Miles to Pinecone*
Hayes, S.		*You've Been away All Summer*
Hermes, P.	☆	*Friends Are Like That*
Howe, J.	☆	*A Night without Stars*
Keatley, Z.	☆	*The Changeling*
Knaff, J.C.		*Manhattan*
LeFarge, P.		*The Gumball Necklace*
Neville, E.C.	☆	*It's Like This, Cat*
Patterson, K.	☆	*Bridge to Terbithia*
Perl, L.		*Hey, Remember Fat Glenda?*
. . . .		*Me and Fat Glenda*
Prelutsky, J.		*Poems of A. Nonny Mouse*
Rock, G.		*The Thanksgiving Day Turkey*
Sachs, M.		*A Secret Friend*
Selden, G.	☆	*The Cricket in Times Square*
Spears, E.G.	☆	*The Sign of the Beaver*
Stolz, M.		*The Noonday Friends*
. . . .		*Cider Days*
Ure, J.		*You Two*

HANDOUT

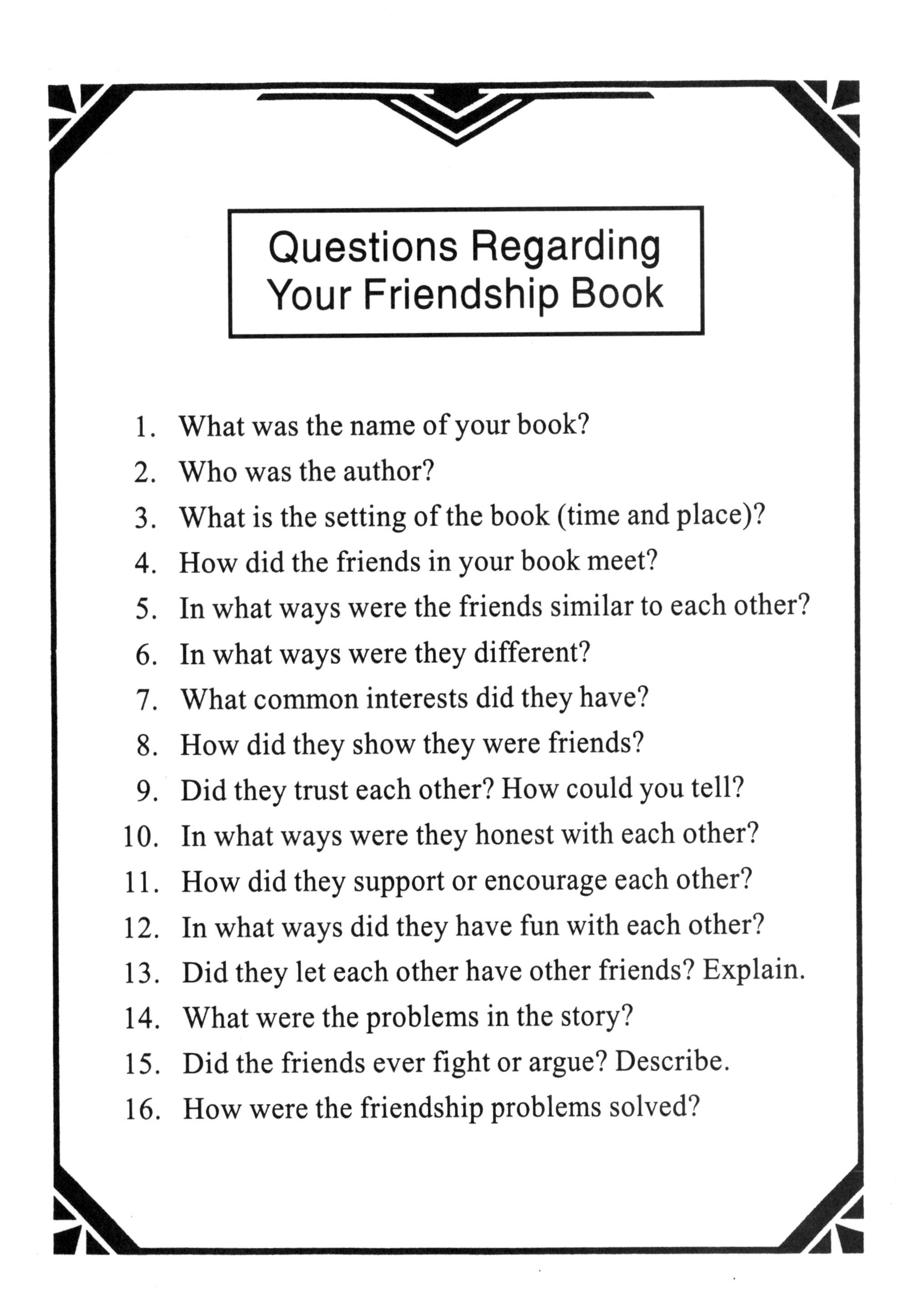

Questions Regarding Your Friendship Book

1. What was the name of your book?
2. Who was the author?
3. What is the setting of the book (time and place)?
4. How did the friends in your book meet?
5. In what ways were the friends similar to each other?
6. In what ways were they different?
7. What common interests did they have?
8. How did they show they were friends?
9. Did they trust each other? How could you tell?
10. In what ways were they honest with each other?
11. How did they support or encourage each other?
12. In what ways did they have fun with each other?
13. Did they let each other have other friends? Explain.
14. What were the problems in the story?
15. Did the friends ever fight or argue? Describe.
16. How were the friendship problems solved?

FRIENDSHIP BOOK AUCTION CURRENCY

Friendship Games

Use the following games to reinforce the concepts and skills taught in the lessons:

The Be a Chum, Not a Chump Game

Objective

Students will discern which behaviors promote friendship and which behaviors impede it by playing a board game together.

Materials

Be a Chum, Not a Chump Game board (Be a Chum, Not a Chump Game, Parts One and Two): one copy per pair of Learning Partners or small group of students

One die (one of the cubes of a set of dice) per game board

One marker or playing piece per student (use any small objects: candy, erasors, etc.)

Paper and pencil (for each player)

Procedure

Make copies of the two game board sheets and tape or paste them together to make game boards. This game can be played by Learning Partners or by small groups of students. Provide students with one die per game board and playing pieces as required by the number of students playing. Students will need paper and pencils so they can keep track of their scores.

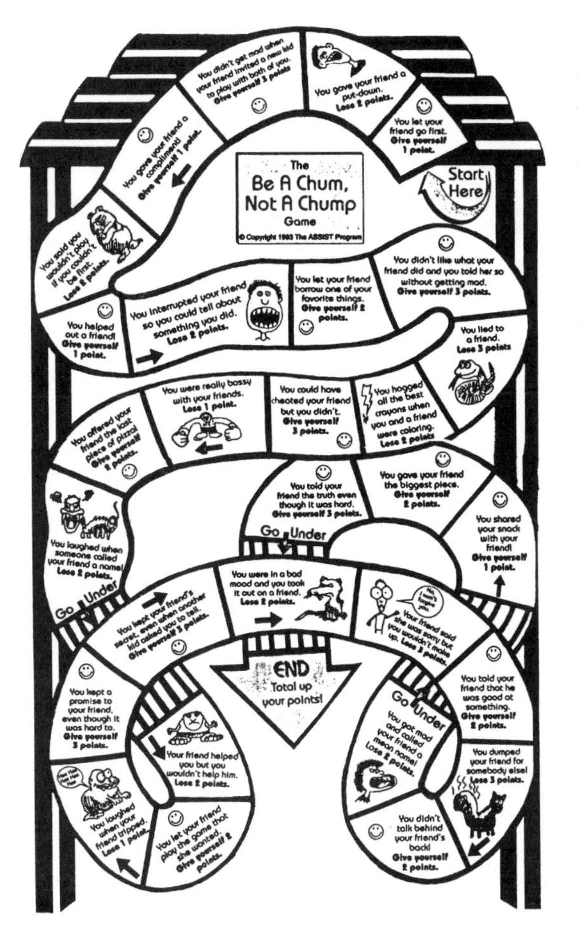

Explain to students that they'll be playing a game about the friendship behaviors they've been learning.

To play, all players will roll the die and the person rolling the highest number will go first. As players move around the board they will land on smiley face "chum" squares and unfriendly behavior "chump" squares. Whichever square a player lands on, he or she should read aloud to the other players in the group the behavior on the square. He or she should then add or subtract points as indicated on the square. Play ends when all players have would to the "END" arrow. Players then total their points and the person with the highest score is the winner.

Because play on this game can proceed quickly, you may wish to have students play the game several times.

BE A CHUM, NOT A CHUMP GAME (PART ONE)

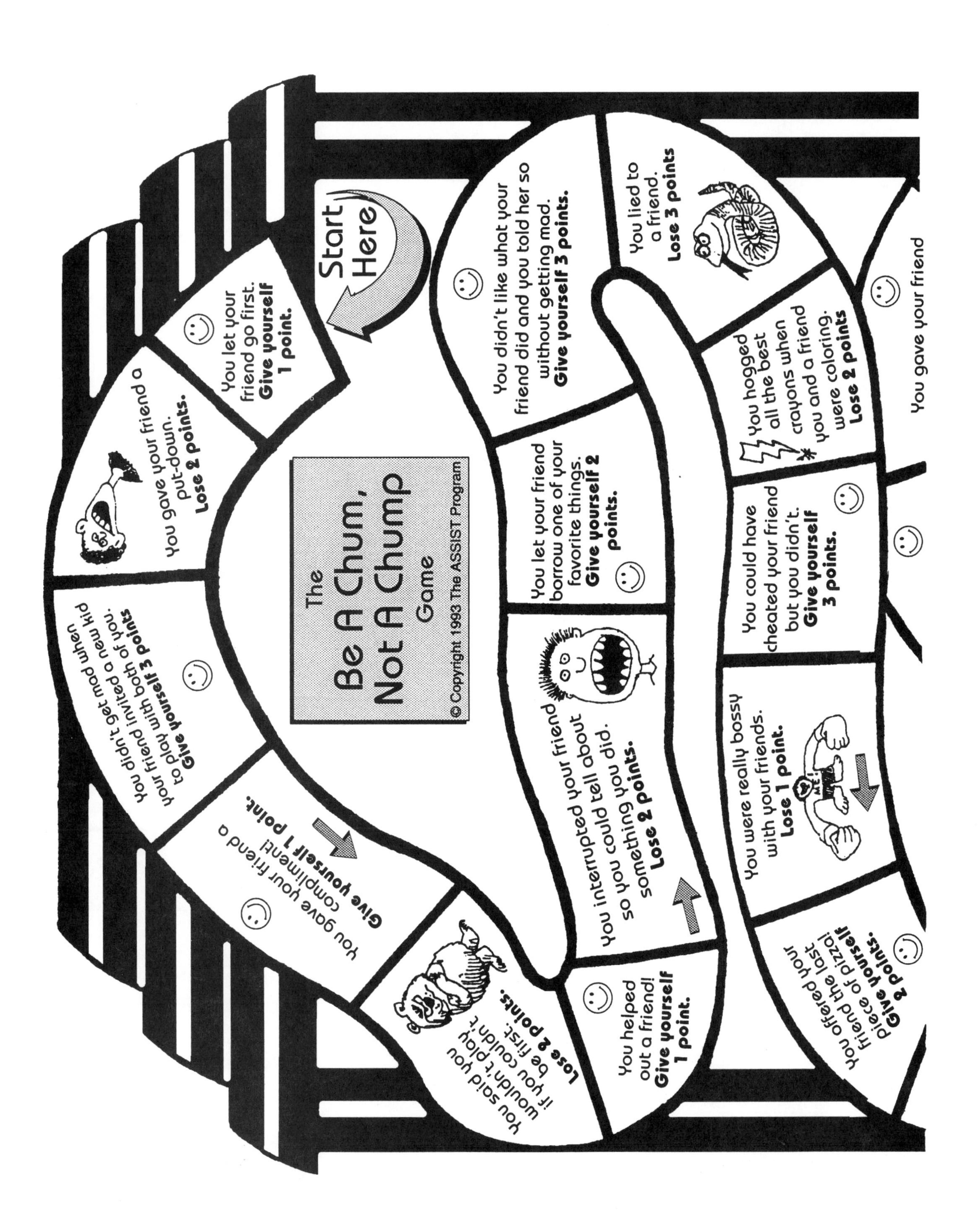

BE A CHUM, NOT A CHUMP GAME (PART TWO)

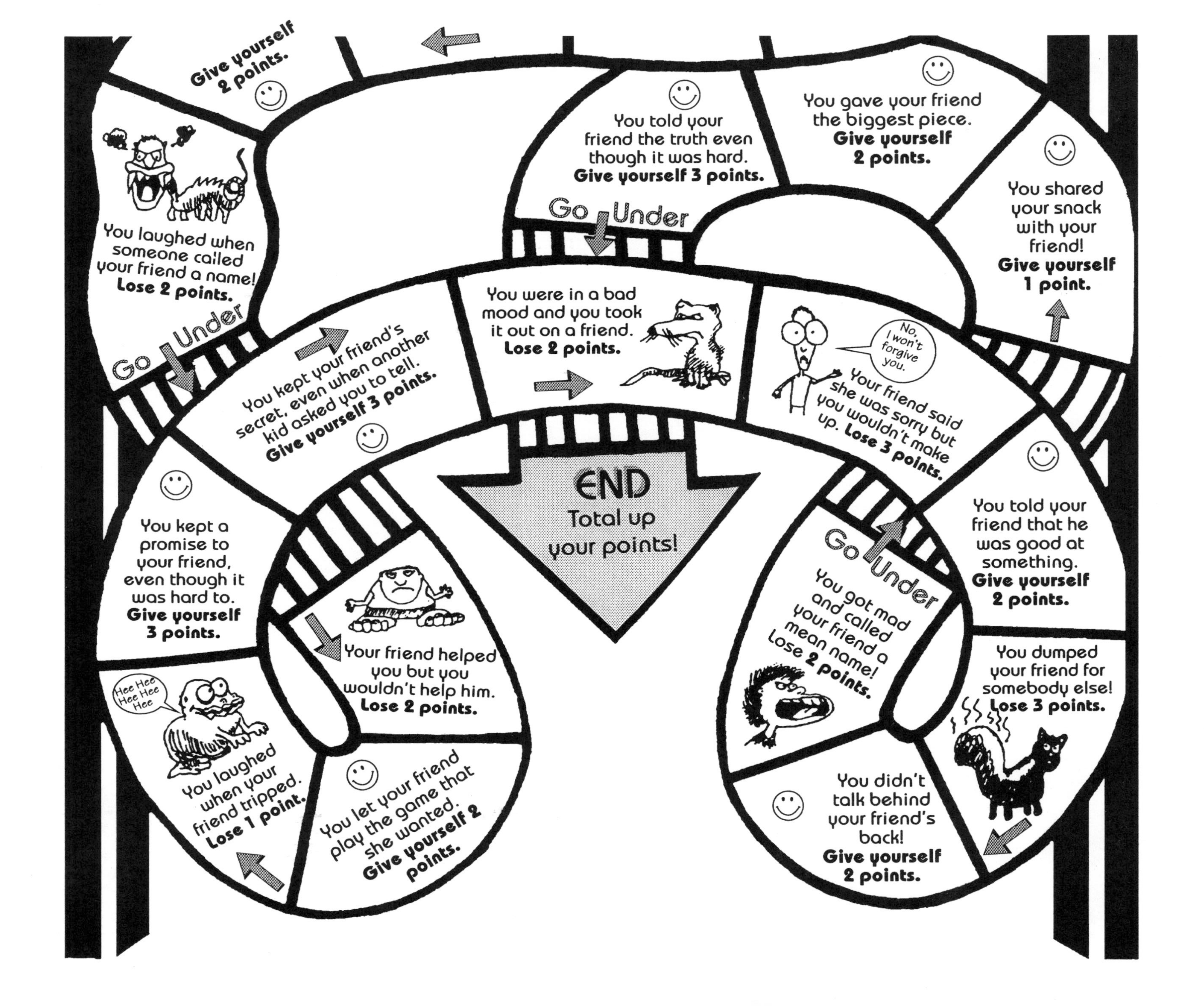

The Friendship Facts Game

Objective

Students will have their learning about friendships reinforced by a fun activity.

Materials

Friendship Facts Game boards (Friendship Facts Game, Parts One and Two): one copy per class or small group of students

One marker or playing piece per student (use erasors, candy, or any small objects)

One die (one of the cubes of a set of dice) per game board

Paper and pencil (for each player)

Procedure

This is a game for two to six players. Create the game board by copying the Friendship Facts Game board sheets and glueing them together onto a piece of cardboard or other stiff paper. You may wish to make up one game board for the "Multiple Intelligences Friendship Center" or enough for the whole class to play simultaneously in small groups. Have some students color each game board, then laminate them or cover them with clear contact paper.

To play the game, have students roll a die to determine who goes first. Highest roll will start, and turns will go clockwise.

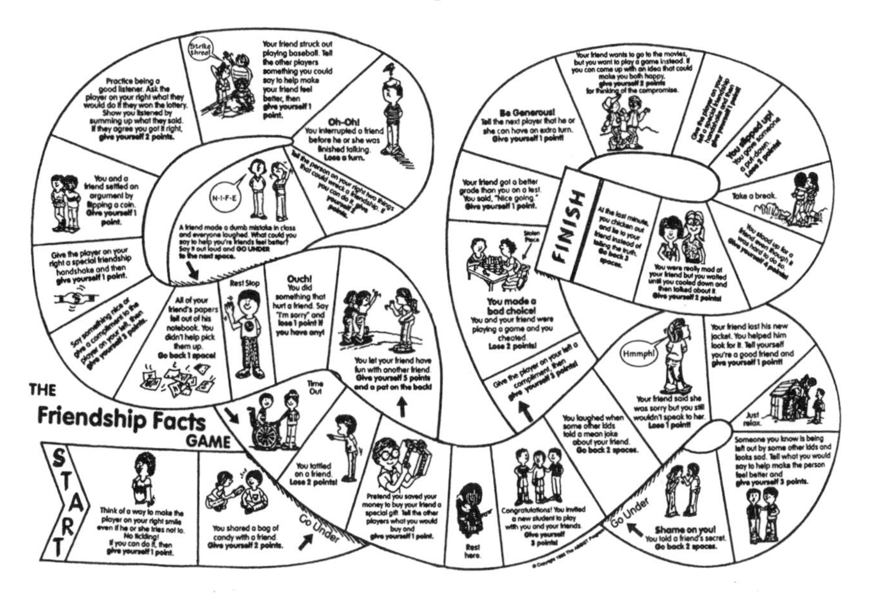

The first player rolls the die to move ahead. Upon landing on a square, the student reads the instructions aloud and does what they tell him or her to do. Players tally their points earned or lost around the complete board. Play ends when all players have moved to the "FINISH" square. The player with the most points at the end of the game is the winner.

FRIENDSHIP FACTS GAME (PART ONE)

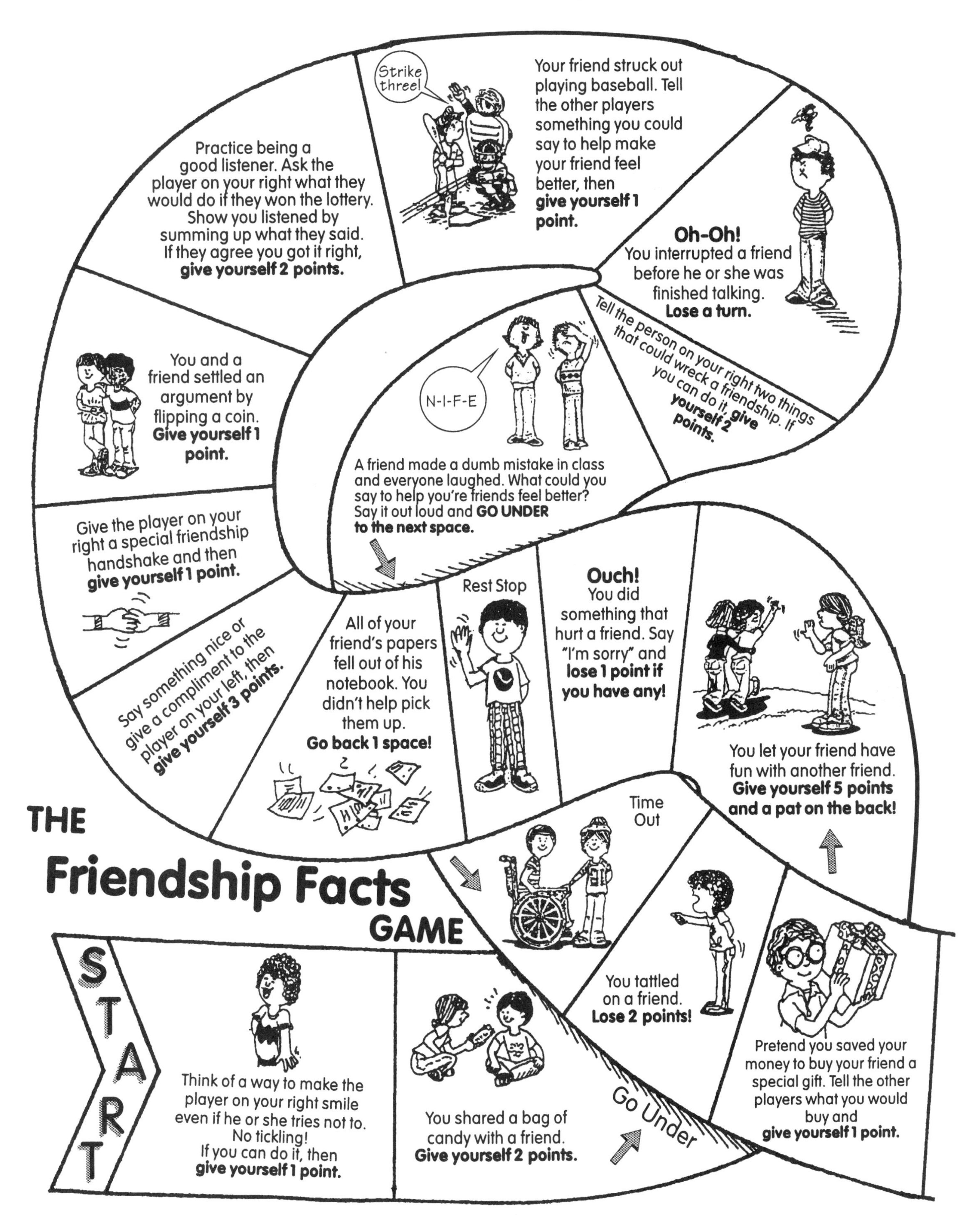

FRIENDSHIP FACTS GAME (PART TWO)

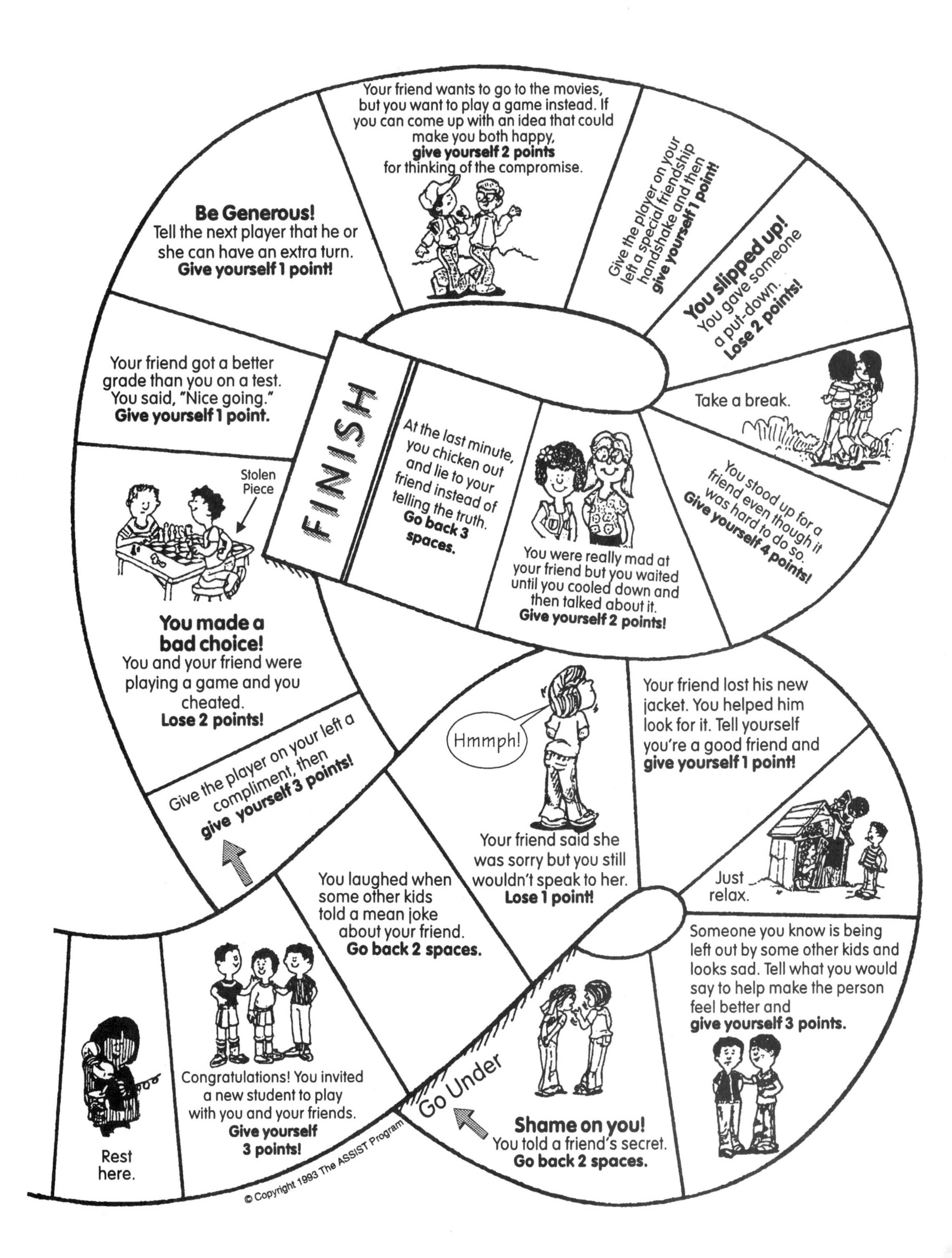

School-Wide Procedures That Promote Friendship

Friendship Weeks

At the beginning of "Friendship Weeks," a set of posters which name the keys to friendship can be put in each teacher's mailbox. The posters are contained in Appendix E. These look best when run off on different colors. Teachers can be asked to display one poster each day in a prominent place in the classroom. The messages on these posters can be read over the intercom by the principal or school counselor. The posters serve as visual reminders throughout the day of the friendship behavior students should focus on.

Friendship Awards Assembly

This activity is a good culmination to the school-wide Friendship Weeks. Each teacher can be given the set of awards that follow (Awards #1-#8) and can designate students who exemplify the quality specified on each award. The teacher can fill out the awards and sign them. School principals or counselors can be asked to sign them as well.

It is best to have separate "Friendship Awards Assemblies" for primary and intermediate students due to the length of the assembly. During the assembly, each teacher can present the awards to his or her students.

During the "Friendship Awards Assembly," different students can present things they have written or produced as a result of doing one of the many activities in this manual.

A rousing skit-like presentation can be made using the handout "Which Response Would You Rather Hear?" A teacher or counselor reads a situation to the audience. Two preselected student volunteers are on stage, one wearing a sign marked "A" and the other a sign marked "B." These volunteers read two different responses to the situation, of which only one is honest but kind. (It helps to have the volunteers speak into a microphone.) Audience members listen carefully to decide which response they would rather have said to them. After the responses are read, students in the audience shout aloud "A!" or "B!" depending on which response they would rather hear.

Another audience-involvement presentation is to read the statements on the sheet "True or False Statements About Friendship." For each statement, have the audience call out "True!" or "False!" Next, have student volunteers on the stage hold up a large sign saying "True" or "False" to indicate the answer. (Cue these students by looking at them or touching the correct sign.) Comment on reasons for the correct answer after each statement.

Friendship Tickets

This activity is a school-wide "Friendship Raffle." It is a fun accompaniment to Friendship Weeks. Make copies of the Friendship Tickets handout (behind the Friendship Awards) and cut these into tickets. Make a Raffle Box for each classroom by decorating a small box or coffee can. Cut a hole in the lid large enough for the tickets to be inserted. Make a larger Raffle Box for the office.

Explain to students over the school intercom that during the next few weeks everyone in the school will be participating in a Friendship Raffle. When anyone does something particularly friendly or helps another person in some way, the recipient of the friendly behavior can fill out a "Friendship Ticket" as a thank you to that person. All school staff members including lunchroom, playground, and custodial staff can also be asked to be on the lookout for friendly behaviors they see students do and can write up tickets for these students as well.

Friendship Tickets can first be put into the Raffle Box in each classroom. At the end of each day, a student can transfer these tickets to the large Raffle Box in the office. At the beginning or end of each day or at the end of the week, three or four tickets should be drawn from the raffle box and winning students should receive a designated prize or privilege. The winners' names and the friendly behavior they did should be read over the intercom.

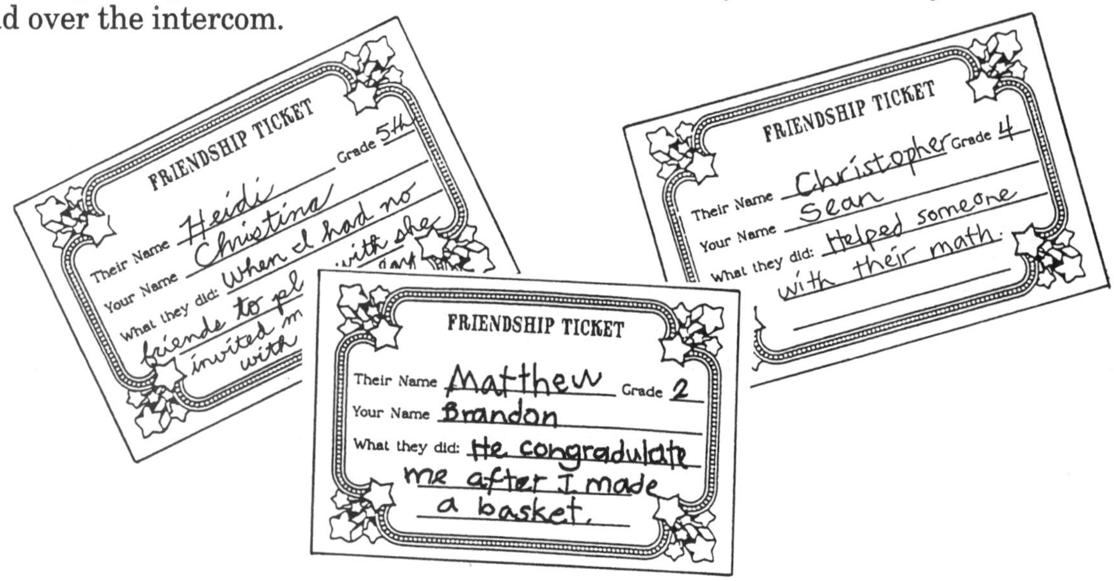

FRIENDSHIP AWARDS ASSEMBLY

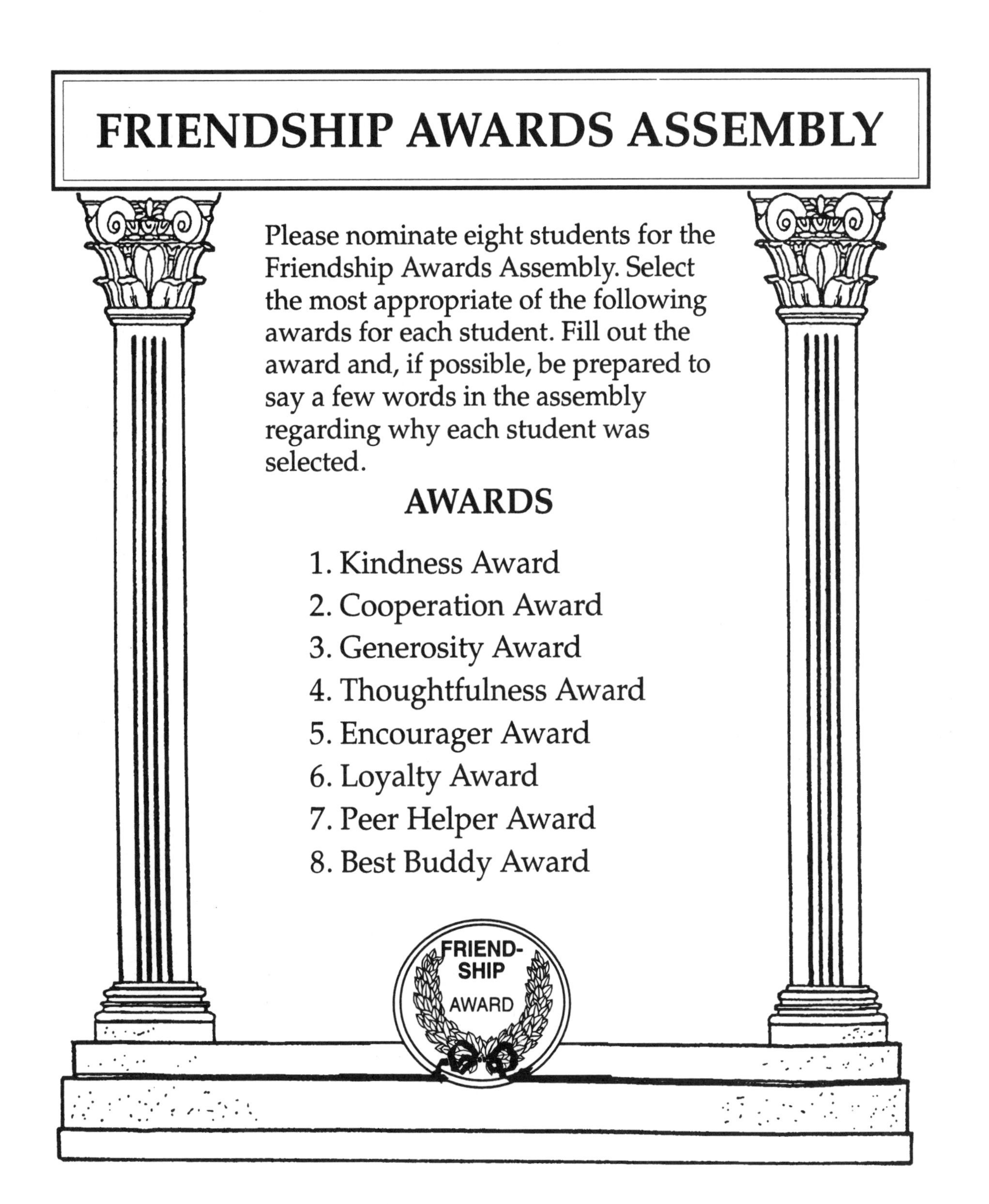

FRIENDSHIP AWARDS ASSEMBLY

Please nominate eight students for the Friendship Awards Assembly. Select the most appropriate of the following awards for each student. Fill out the award and, if possible, be prepared to say a few words in the assembly regarding why each student was selected.

AWARDS

1. Kindness Award
2. Cooperation Award
3. Generosity Award
4. Thoughtfulness Award
5. Encourager Award
6. Loyalty Award
7. Peer Helper Award
8. Best Buddy Award

FRIENDSHIP AWARDS AT-A-GLANCE

7.

8.

—Award for—
Best Buddy

FRIENDSHIP AWARD

To all who may read this document:

is hereby officially honored in recognition
of being a good friend to others.

Teacher
Date

FRIENDSHIP AWARD #1

FRIENDSHIP AWARD #2

FRIENDSHIP AWARD #3

FRIENDSHIP AWARD #4

—Award for—

Thoughtfulness

To all who may read this document:

____

is hereby officially honored
for outstanding thoughtfulness.

_______________________________ _______________
Teacher Date

FRIEND-
SHIP
AWARD

FRIENDSHIP AWARD #5

Encourager Award

FRIEND-SHIP AWARD

To all who may read this document:

____

is hereby officially honored in recognition of the support given to others.

____________________ Teacher

__________ Date

FRIENDSHIP AWARD #6

FRIEND-SHIP AWARD

Loyalty Award

To all who may read this document:

____

is hereby officially honored in recognition of outstanding loyalty to others.

____
Teacher

____
Date

FRIENDSHIP AWARD #7

FRIENDSHIP AWARD #8

Which Response Would You Rather Hear?

Directions:

Read the first situation to the student audience. Tell audience members that volunteers will now say two possible responses. The students should listen carefully to decide which response they would rather have said to them. Have your student volunteer with the "A" sign read aloud one response, and the "B" sign volunteer read the other, as indicated below. When they have finished, ask the students in the audience to shout aloud "A!" or "B!" depending on which response they would rather hear. Then read the other five situations, following the procedures above.

SITUATION 1:

Alan wants to borrow his friend Mack's new bike. Mack just got it yesterday and doesn't want to lend it. Which of these two comments would be the most "honest but kind" thing for Mack to say?

A's RESPONSE *(Honest but UNKIND)*	**B's RESPONSE** *(Honest but KIND)*
No way—you might wreck it! Go ride your own bike.	Sorry, but I just got it. I'm not ready to lend it to anybody yet.

SITUATION 2:

Arthur likes to put down an unpopular kid in his class. Ted doesn't think the unpopular kid is that bad and thinks Arthur is being mean. If you were Arthur, which of these two responses would be easiest to hear?

A's RESPONSE *(Honest but KIND)*	**B's RESPONSE** *(Honest but UNKIND)*
I know that kid isn't popular, but he's really nice. I feel bad when you put him down.	You should talk! You're the one that's a jerk. Nobody likes you!

SITUATION 3:

Shara just got a new jacket and she's wearing it to school for the first time. She says to her friend, "How do you like my new jacket?" Her friend doesn't like the jacket at all. If you were Shara, what would you rather hear?

A's RESPONSE *(Honest but KIND)*	**B's RESPONSE** *(Honest but UNKIND)*
To be honest, it's not my style, but the color looks good on you.	That's the ugliest jacket I ever saw. You look really stupid in it.

Which Response Would You Rather Hear? (continued)

SITUATION 4:

Ivan brags a lot. It really bugs his friend, Jake. Jake wishes that he would stop and has decided to say so. If you were Ivan, which of these comments would be easiest to hear?

A's RESPONSE
(Honest but UNKIND)

You're ALWAYS bragging! You think you're **so** cool! Nobody believes anything YOU say!

B's RESPONSE
(Honest but KIND)

It makes me feel bad when you say you're better than me. Can't we just be equal for a change?

SITUATION 5:

April sees her friend Zelda just after she's found out Zelda has said some mean things about her behind her back. If you were Zelda, which of April's comments would you rather hear?

A's RESPONSE
(Honest but UNKIND)

I'm never speaking to you again, you creep! I hate your guts!

B's RESPONSE
(Honest but KIND)

If you don't like something about me, I wish you'd tell me to my face. I don't like it when you talk behind my back.

SITUATION 6:

Most of the kids in the class don't like Jane because she's so bossy. She isn't bossy very often with her friend Sally, though. Jane tells Sally she's feeling hurt because the other kids don't like her. Sally knows that it's because Jane's so bossy. If you were Jane, which of these responses would be easiest to hear?

A's RESPONSE
(Honest but KIND)

If you'd let the other kids choose what to do more often, they'd like you better. If you were as nice to them as you are to me, I'm sure more kids would like you.

B's RESPONSE
(Honest but UNKIND)

Of course no one likes you! You're too mean and bossy! If you weren't such a brat, maybe you'd have some friends.

True or False Statements About Friendship

Directions:

Read each true or false statement to the student audience. For each statement, ask the students in the audience to shout aloud "True!" or "False!" depending upon which answer they feel is correct. Cue your student volunteer with the sign for the correct answer to indicate the answer by holding up the sign.

1. _____ You can be mad at someone and still be their best friend.
2. _____ You should "forgive and forget" when a friend hurts you in some way.
3. _____ When you apologize it always means you're admitting that you were wrong.
4. _____ If you get a compliment you should give one right back.
5. _____ You should encourage your friends to play with others if they want to.
6. _____ You should say you "hate" the same people your friends do.
7. _____ It's **easy** to treat others the way you want them to treat you.
8. _____ You should let your **best** friends borrow anything of yours they ask to.
9. _____ Once you tell someone's secret, it's impossible to keep it from spreading.
10. _____ It's impossible to be close friends with two people who don't like each other.
11. _____ It's normal to feel left out when your friend plays with someone else.
12. _____ A person can be your friend even if you don't trust him or her.
13. _____ It helps to use your imagination to understand your friend's point of view.
14. _____ Your friends can say mean things to you and still like you.
15. _____ If your friend already knows part of a secret you know and wants you to tell him or her the rest, it's O.K. to tell if your friend promises not to tell anyone else.
16. _____ If you want kids to like you it helps to act tough.
17. _____ Sometimes popular kids can be mean.

Answer Key for True or False Statements About Friendship

1. __T__ You can be mad at someone and still be their best friend.
2. __F__ You should "forgive and forget" when a friend hurts you in some way.
3. __F__ When you apologize it always means you're admitting that you were wrong.
4. __F__ If you get a compliment you should give one right back.
5. __T__ You should encourage your friends to play with others if they want to.
6. __F__ You should say you "hate" the same people your friends do.
7. __F__ It's **easy** to treat others the way you want them to treat you.
8. __F__ You should let your **best** friends borrow anything of yours they ask to.
9. __T__ Once you tell someone's secret, it's impossible to keep it from spreading.
10. __F__ It's impossible to be close friends with two people who don't like each other.
11. __T__ It's normal to feel left out when your friend plays with someone else.
12. __F__ A person can be your friend even if you don't trust him or her.
13. __T__ It helps to use your imagination to understand your friend's point of view.
14. __T__ Your friends can say mean things to you and still like you.
15. __F__ If your friend already knows part of a secret you know and wants you to tell him or her the rest, it's O.K. to tell if your friend promises not to tell anyone else.
16. __F__ If you want kids to like you it helps to act tough.
17. __T__ Sometimes popular kids can be mean.

FRIENDSHIP TICKETS

FRIENDSHIP TICKET

Their Name ____________________ Grade ____

Your Name ____________________________

What they did: ________________________

____

____

FRIENDSHIP TICKET

Their Name ____________________ Grade ____

Your Name ____________________________

What they did: ________________________

____

____

FRIENDSHIP TICKET

Their Name ____________________ Grade ____

Your Name ____________________________

What they did: ________________________

____

____

FRIENDSHIP TICKET

Their Name ____________________ Grade ____

Your Name ____________________________

What they did: ________________________

____

FRIENDSHIP TICKET

Their Name ____________________ Grade ____

Your Name ____________________________

What they did: ________________________

____

____

FRIENDSHIP TICKET

Their Name ____________________ Grade ____

Your Name ____________________________

What they did: ________________________

____

____

FRIENDSHIP TICKET

Their Name ____________________ Grade ____

Your Name ____________________________

What they did: ________________________

____

____

FRIENDSHIP TICKET

Their Name ____________________ Grade ____

Your Name ____________________________

What they did: ________________________

____

____

Posters

1.	Don't give put-downs.
2.	Tell others what you like about them.
3.	Make others feel special.
4.	Be honest with others.
5.	Keep secrets and promises.
6.	Be a good listener.
7.	Put yourself in the other person's place.
8.	Encourage others when they try new things.
9.	Help others feel better if they make mistakes.
10.	Apologize if you hurt another's feelings.
11.	Forgive others if they hurt your feelings.
12.	Let your friends have other friends.

POSTER #1

POSTER #2

Tell others what you like about them.

You're *generous!*

POSTER #3

Make others feel special.

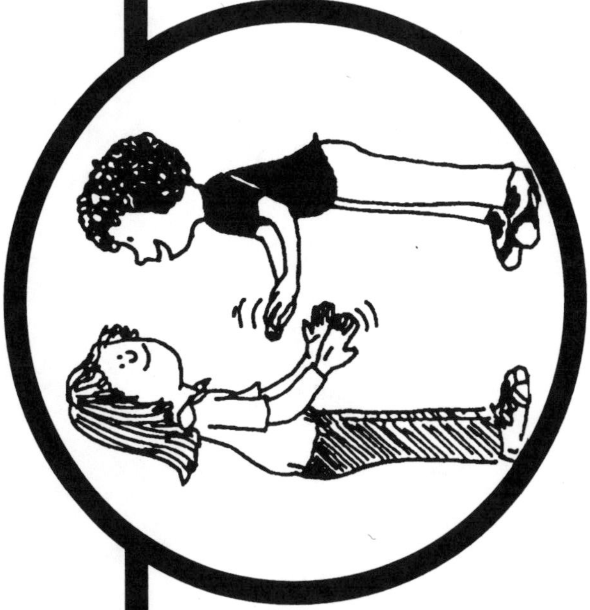

POSTER #4

POSTER #5

Keep secrets and promises.

POSTER #6

POSTER #7

Put yourself in the other person's place.

POSTER #8

Encourage others when they try new things.

POSTER #9

Help others feel better if they make mistakes.

Did I really say N-I-F-E?

POSTER #10

Apologize if you hurt another's feelings.

I'm sorry.

POSTER #11

POSTER #12

Let your friends have other friends.

DATE DUE
Brodart Co.
Cat. # 55 137